HARVARD ECONOMIC STUDIES

VOLUME LXXXII

LONDON : GEOFFREY CUMBERLEGE
OXFORD UNIVERSITY PRESS

PRODUCTION
in
The United States

1860–1914

BY

EDWIN FRICKEY

PROFESSOR OF ECONOMICS
HARVARD UNIVERSITY

CAMBRIDGE · MASSACHUSETTS
HARVARD UNIVERSITY PRESS
1947

To G.

PREFACE

THE AUTHOR is indebted to the Harvard University Committee on Research in the Social Sciences for a grant of funds which made possible the research incorporated in this book, and for assistance in publication. Particular portions of the research were aided also by a grant from the Committee on Research in the Trade Cycle of the Economics Department of Harvard University.

A great variety of material from published sources has been used in the preparation of this volume. Individual acknowledgments are later made at appropriate points in the text. This opportunity is taken to express appreciation for the kindness of the various organizations, publications, and writers concerned.

The author desires to express his sincere gratitude to all those who had a part in the tedious task of carrying out the extended analytical work involved in this study. In particular, thanks are given to Dr. M. J. Fields, Mr. Edgar Eaton, and Dr. F. H. Sanderson, who at successive stages of the program exercised general supervision over the computing staff; to Mr. Frank L. Hall, for the construction of the published charts; to Mr. J. O. Gadd, for the verification, intercomparison, and audit of these charts, and for special computations; to Mrs. Anna H. Thorpe, for the typing of the manuscript; to Mr. Joseph P. McKenna, for aid in verification of the manuscript and the proof sheets, and for preparation of the index. Also gratefully acknowledged is the constant and helpful coöperation of Miss Althea MacDonald of the Harvard University Committee on Research in the Social Sciences, and Miss Lillian Buller of the *Review of Economic Statistics*.

The author is especially indebted to Miss Ruth Crandall, Miss Dorothy Wescott, and Mr. Louis Weiner for invaluable aid in fundamental research and in preparation of manuscript.

As is more fully set forth on succeeding pages, the investigations described in this book were originally carried out as a part of a general study of economic fluctuations in the United States over the interval 1866–1914 developed by this writer and presented in his *Economic Fluctuations in the United States*. The reader is referred to this earlier volume for discussion of the relationship of the variations over time of the production indexes herein shown to those of economic series in general and to the problem of separating secular trends and cyclical movements.

Subsequent to the publication of *Economic Fluctuations in the United States*, certain detailed revisions were made here and there in the basic data and procedure for the various production indexes; these revisions, however, have resulted in only comparatively minor alterations in the indexes.

EDWIN FRICKEY

Cambridge, Massachusetts
September 2, 1947

CONTENTS

CHAPTER I. MANUFACTURE: BASIC DATA   3

The Available Physical-Quantity Data; the Criterion for
Selection   3
Our Compilation and Development of Basic Quantity Data   6

CHAPTER II. MANUFACTURE: WEIGHTS   18

The Derivation of the Weights   19
Critical Consideration of Value-Added Weights   26

CHAPTER III. MANUFACTURE: THE PRELIMINARY CONTINUOUS
ANNUAL INDEX   31

Development of Indexes for Nine Major Groups   31
Transference of Certain Fiscal-Year Data to a Calendar-Year
Basis   34
Tabular and Graphic Presentation of Group Indexes . .   36
Derivation of the Preliminary Continuous Annual Index .   37

CHAPTER IV. MANUFACTURE: THE FINAL INDEX   47

The "Post Method"   47
Derivation of Census-Year Indexes for Three Additional
Major Groups   52
Derivation of the Combined Census-Year Index . . .   53
Derivation of Indexes for Inter-Censal Years   55
The Final Combined Index Adjusted for Secular Trend . .   59
Bias of the Manufacture Index   61
Indexes for Durable and Non-Durable Commodities . . .   63

CHAPTER V. TRANSPORTATION AND COMMUNICATION: THE
STEAM-RAILROAD SERIES—(A) BASIC DATA   68

The General Plan of Procedure   69
Survey of Available Basic Data: 1866–90   70
The "Sample List": 1866–90   72
Survey of Available Basic Data, and "Sample List": 1855–71   90

CHAPTER VI. TRANSPORTATION AND COMMUNICATION: THE
STEAM-RAILROAD SERIES—(B) RECTIFICATION AND TESTS . .   94

The "Cross-Section" Totals for 1871, and Rectified Series for
1866–90   94

The "Cross-Section" Totals for 1855, and Rectified Series for
1855–66   98
Testing Validity of Short-Run Movements: "Sampling by
Size of Road"   99

CHAPTER VII. TRANSPORTATION AND COMMUNICATION: THE
COMBINED INDEX   106
Basic Data for Series Other than Steam-Railroad   106
Weights for the Combined Annual Index   107
Computation of the Combined Annual Index   114
The Calendar-Year Adjustment   114
The "Continuity" of the Index   116
The Final Combined Index Adjusted for Secular Trend . .   118
An Estimated Monthly Index, Adjusted for Secular Trend
and Seasonal Variation   119

CHAPTER VIII. AN INDEX OF INDUSTRIAL AND COMMERCIAL
PRODUCTION   125
The Mode of Attack   125
The New Index Adjusted for Secular Trend   127

APPENDICES   131
Appendix A. Manufacture Index—Constituent Series . .   133
Appendix B. Manufacture Index—Derivation of Weights .   201
Appendix C. Transportation and Communication Index—
Constituent Series (Other than Steam-Railroad) . . .   216
Appendix D. Transportation and Communication Index—
Weights   224
Appendix E. Sundry Technical Details   240

INDEX   259

TABLES

TABLES IN TEXT

1. Annual Series Included in Manufacture Index, 1860–1914 .   7

2. Certain Series Included in Census-Year Manufacture Index, 1859–1914 16

3. Derivation of Weights for Manufacture Index 20

4. Group Indexes of Manufacturing Production: by Years, 1860–1914 38

5. The "Post Method": Illustrative Case 49

6. Index of Production for Manufacture: by Years, 1860–1914 54

7. Index of Production for Manufacture, Adjusted for Secular Trend: by Years, 1860–1914 60

8. Indexes of Production for Manufacture—Durable and Non-Durable Commodities: by Years, 1860–1914 64

9. Data for "Sample List" of Steam Railroads, 1866–90 . . 74

10. "Sample List" of Steam Railroads, 1866–90: Totals for Geographical Groups and Grand Totals, by Fiscal Years . . . 81

11. "Sample List" of Steam Railroads, 1855–71 91

12. "Sample List" of Steam Railroads, 1855–71: Totals by Fiscal Years 91

13. Rectified Series for Steam-Railroad Tons and Passengers: by Fiscal Years, 1855–1914 100

14. Comparison of Trend-Ratios, by Fiscal Years, 1881–90 . . 102

15. Annual Series (Other than Steam-Railroad) Included in Transportation and Communication Index, 1860–1914 . . . 108

16. Derivation of Weights for Transportation and Communication Index 112

17. Index of Production for Transportation and Communication: by Years, 1860–1914 117

18. Index of Production for Transportation and Communication, Adjusted for Secular Trend: by Years, 1860–1914 119

19. Index of Production for Transportation and Communication, Adjusted for Secular Trend and Seasonal Variation: by Months, January 1866 to June 1914 120

20. Index of Industrial and Commercial Production: by Years, 1860–1914 127

21. Index of Industrial and Commercial Production, Adjusted for Secular Trend: by Years, 1860–1914 128

TABLES IN APPENDICES

22. United States Census Data on Consumption of Pig Iron and Scrap, with Ratios Computed Therefrom 164

23. Data for Imputing Value Added by Manufacture in the Hosiery and Knit Goods Industry to Cotton, Wool, and Silk . . 203

24. United States Census Data on "Iron and Steel, Blast Furnaces" 205

25. Value Added by Manufacture, 1899, for Industries of the Metals Sub-Group 211

26. Derivation of Weights for Constituent Series of Group X . 212

CHARTS

1. Group Indexes of Manufacturing Production: by Years, 1860–
   1914 . . . . *facing* 36

2. Indexes of Production: by Years, 1860–1914 57

3. Indexes of Production, Adjusted for Secular Trend: by Years,
   1860–1914 61

4. Indexes of Production for Manufacture—Durable and Non-
   Durable Commodities: by Years, 1860–1914 65

5. "Sample List" of Steam Railroads, 1866–90: Totals for Geographical Groups and Grand Totals, by Fiscal Years . . . 88

6. "Sample List" of Steam Railroads, 1855–71: Totals by Fiscal
   Years 92

7. Index of Production for Transportation and Communication,
   Adjusted for Secular Trend and Seasonal Variation: by Months,
   January 1866 to June 1914 122

8. "End-Products" Experiments: Annual Figures, 1860–1914 . 171

PRODUCTION IN THE UNITED STATES, 1860–1914

CHAPTER I

MANUFACTURE: BASIC DATA

OUR MANUFACTURE index, developed as described in Chapters I–IV of this volume, was originally set up as part of a general study of economic fluctuations over the interval 1866–1914 carried out by this writer and presented in an earlier work.[1] The index was extended back to 1860, though (as is set forth more fully on subsequent pages) the index is less trustworthy over the interval 1860–65 than for later years.

This chapter is mainly devoted to a discussion of the basic data for our manufacture index.

THE AVAILABLE PHYSICAL-QUANTITY DATA; THE CRITERION FOR SELECTION

The first step in the present investigation was the examination of the available physical-quantity data pertinent to the problem of constructing a production index for manufacturing activity in the United States over the period from the Civil War to the first World War. This examination immediately revealed that direct measurements of physical output were obtainable for only a limited number of industries. It was clearly necessary to resort to indirect representation.[2] The possibilities for indirect representation were mainly of two sorts: first, the use of "materials-consumed" data (e.g., the so-called "consumption" series for cotton and wool, and for pig iron and the non-ferrous metals, and the import series for

---

[1] Edwin Frickey, *Economic Fluctuations in the United States* (Cambridge, Mass.: Harvard University Press, 1942). A brief nine-page summary statement of the descriptive material which is set forth at length in Chapters I–IV of the present volume was given in *Economic Fluctuations,* pp. 177–185; this earlier book also presents other material relating to manufacture (*passim;* cf. index).

[2] This situation exists even for indexes pertaining to more recent times—though, of course, in lesser degree.

coffee, cocoa, and rubber) to indicate relative changes in the corresponding volume of production; second, the use of a quantity series for one stage of manufacturing production—usually an early and simple stage—as denotative of the whole manufacturing process for the industry in question.

In the year 1899, the United States Bureau of the Census began the collection and publication, systematically and extensively, of quantity figures on consumption of materials and output for manufacturing industries.[3] Within our period of analysis, the Census presented such figures for quinquennial years—1899, 1904, 1909, and 1914. For census years prior to 1899, however, quantity data are highly fragmentary.

After a survey of the available basic data, we decided to confine the selection of series for the index to those extending over all (or nearly all) of our period of analysis—except in cases, such as that of automobile production, where the new series represented the emergence of a new industry. Data for series which met this test, but still were not continuous on an annual basis, were to be brought into the index by a certain methodological device (later to be explained), with a view to avoiding distortions of long-time movement which might otherwise have been occasioned.

The preceding paragraph calls for some elaboration. First, it may be noted that question arose as to the precise definition of "nearly all." The difficulties in meeting this criterion occurred, as might have been expected, at the beginning of the period. As was explained in an earlier paragraph, the time interval in which we were primarily interested was 1866–1914, from the close of the Civil War to the outbreak of the first World War (to be sure, we planned to extend the index back through 1860–65, but we had no hope, in any case, of obtaining more than rough measurements over the Civil-War period itself, especially as regards year-to-year movements). In defining "nearly all" with refer-

---

[3] For extended discussion of the data of the Census of Manufactures, see Solomon Fabricant, *The Output of Manufacturing Industries, 1899–1937* (New York: National Bureau of Economic Research, Inc., 1940), especially pp. 35–42, 327–356.

ence to the interval 1866–1914, our decision was to allow at the beginning a leeway of five years, inasmuch as a number of important series first became available (or usable) somewhere in the years 1867–71. It seemed wise, for the sake of having these important series included in the index, to accept the disadvantages connected with the necessity for interpolation or extrapolation in a few years at the beginning of the interval (these disadvantages being, of course, much less serious than for a long interval). Accordingly, series which began at 1871 or sooner were accepted.

Next, we may consider the reasons for the general decision to confine our selection of series to those extending over all, or nearly all, of the period of analysis (except for series representing the emergence of a new industry). First, the construction of our manufacture index (as is explained on an earlier page of this chapter) was a part of a larger study of long-time trends and cycles, and their interrelations, involving at an early stage an investigation into the patterns of movement inherent in economic data; for this purpose, the qualities of continuity and comparability over time were crucial. Second, with reference to the interval from our limiting date of 1871 up to the year 1899, very little would have been gained in inclusiveness by bringing in the comparatively few new quantity series which became available: this is certainly true for the index of total manufacture; and even for the various major groups, as defined in the next chapter, the gains in inclusiveness would in general have been slight (or dubious, because of poor quality of the statistical data in earlier years). Third, with reference to the period 1899–1914, it is true that appreciable additions in coverage became possible, largely because of the greatly increased volume of data which the United States Bureau of the Census began to publish in 1899, and continued (within our period of analysis) to publish in the quinquennial years 1904, 1909, and 1914: however, it seemed likely that investigators who were interested in examining the period 1899–1914 intensively would naturally turn to one of the several published studies which utilize these Census data; it seemed best not to attempt to duplicate here the work of these other studies,

but rather to concentrate our energies on the task of making indexes as continuous and comparable as possible over our chosen
period of analysis.

A few available series, though meeting our formal criterion for
inclusion, were nevertheless not used. Such exclusions were for
the purpose of avoiding duplication; endeavor was made, in the
few cases where more than one possibility appeared, to choose
for inclusion the series which would give the best representation
for the industry in question. It may also be remarked that the
series for the liquor and tobacco groups, though capable of extension back into the Civil-War years, were not utilized prior to
1870, for it was felt that the figures prior to 1870 were untrustworthy—cf. the appropriate sections of Appendix A.

Our Compilation and Development of Basic Quantity Data

We carried out an extensive survey of basic quantity series over
our period of analysis; every reasonable effort was made to increase the number of such series and to improve their quality. On
the basis of this extensive survey, several new series were developed, and revised and improved figures were set up for a number
of industries. Quite often research made possible the backward
extension, at least in approximate form, of series formerly available only for a part of the period. Such extensions were, of
course, particularly to be desired, since we wished to have the list
of series as comprehensive as possible, and at the same time to
avoid breaks in continuity which might have seriously interfered
with the homogeneity over time of our measurements.

The statements made in the preceding paragraph are elaborated
in Appendix A, which gives detailed information regarding sources
and methods of derivation for the individual series. These series,
as we finally set them up after research and computation, are
mainly shown in Table 1—though certain supplementary data for
census years are given in Table 2.

If we compare our data with those of the only other published

TABLE 1

ANNUAL SERIES INCLUDED IN MANUFACTURE INDEX, 1860–1914*

As is stated in the text, a great deal of effort has been put forth to secure the most authoritative numerical data and to raise their quality wherever possible; nevertheless, it must be said that the trustworthiness and approach to precision of these figures vary greatly from series to series (some series represent the result of careful enumeration, others are little more than rough estimates) and in certain cases also vary over time for a given series (often the figures for the early part of the period are inferior to those for later years). To turn to a particular point, attempt has been made to bring the intrinsic *time-reference* of the items to conform to a uniform calendar-year basis; nevertheless, the time reference of the figures here presented still shows inconsistency—some pertain to calendar years, some to fiscal or crop years. Research workers who desire to make use of any of these individual series should examine the appropriate sections of Appendix A, and may indeed want to go back to the original sources there listed, in order to get the full background of the statistics.

For all footnotes, see end of table.

[7]

TABLE 1 (*Continued*)

Year	(1) Wheat flour produced (*unit: one million barrels*)	(2) Refined sugar produced (*unit: one million pounds*)	(3) Coffee imported (*unit: one million pounds*)	(4) Cocoa imported (*unit: one million pounds*)	(5) Raw cotton consumed (*unit: one thousand bales*)	(6) Raw cotton consumed, adjusted for foreign trade in cotton goods (*unit: one thousand bales*)	(7) Raw wool consumed (*unit: one million pounds*)	(8) Raw wool consumed, adjusted for foreign trade in wool goods (*unit: one million pounds*)	(9) Raw silk and spun silk imported (*unit: one million pounds*)	(10) Minor fibers imported (*unit: one thousand long tons*)
1860	39.8	788	180	1.54	845	..	..	..	0.30	..
1861	41.6	978	146	2.18	842	..	91.1	..	0.32	7.1
1862	42.4	590	94	1.44	369	..	117.5	..	0.34	12.4
1863	42.5	607	101	1.34	287	..	164.0	..	0.36	15.4
1864	42.4	565	105	1.40	220	228	196.8	..	0.37	20.0
1865	42.5	733	126	1.27	344	352	166.2	..	0.17	16.8
1866	42.8	886	175	2.19	614	669	211.4	..	0.53	28.8
1867	44.3	841	220	2.66	715	739	192.2	257.3	0.56	25.1
1868	44.9	1,149	235	3.57	844	854	182.1	234.0	0.58	22.1
1869	46.8	1,254	235	1.63	860	872	206.5	259.5	0.61	31.0
1870	47.9	1,196	272	3.6	797	814	227.3	278.9	0.74	36.7
1871	49.0	1,413	308	2.8	1,027	1,042	228.8	294.8	1.27	45.2
1872	49.2	1,454	289	1.5	1,147	1,174	284.1	357.6	1.24	49.2
1873	51.3	1,526	292	3.7	1,116	1,140	228.4	304.0	0.84	85.5
1874	53.6	1,638	283	3.7	1,213	1,225	193.8	261.7	0.83	59.2
1875	54.4	1,642	360	4.0	1,098	1,101	221.1	287.8	1.32	62.4
1876	56.1	1,583	267	4.4	1,256	1,225	224.0	275.6	1.22	76.2
1877	56.5	1,698	349	4.1	1,314	1,263	231.0	273.0	1.03	69.4
1878	59.8	1,778	325	4.6	1,459	1,394	242.2	285.7	1.63	53.7
1879	61.9	1,709	438	5.9	1,457	1,389	243.0	287.5	2.33	87.9
1880	64.3	1,988	396	5.9	1,501	1,448	335.3	393.8	2.63	111.9
1881	65.6	1,940	426	8.4	1,866	1,791	282.9	339.6	2.62	101.2
1882	67.8	2,368	484	7.5	1,850	1,781	303.9	370.4	3.13	111.6
1883	70.8	2,466	488	9.0	2,038	1,972	338.5	417.1	3.37	119.9
1884	72.5	2,732	494	9.6	1,814	1,748	366.0	438.0	3.49	116.0
1885	74.0	2,912	534	8.6	1,687	1,617	367.4	428.8	4.03	150.2

Year										
1886	75.7	2,949	521	11.0	2,095	1,998	430.5	504.1	4.98	147.4
1887	79.5	3,014	423	11.9	2,050	1,946	409.0	487.6	4.98	147.1
1888	79.5	3,048	507	15.6	2,205	2,120	394.2	483.7	5.64	158.5
1889	80.8	3,170	534	14.4	2,309	2,255	392.1	484.7	6.14	166.1
1890	83.3	3,233	481	18.7	2,518	2,463	366.9	487.9	5.23	158.2
1891	86.3	4,069	574	18.0	2,604	2,519	402.4	500.2	7.77	223.9
1892	92.1	3,896	601	23.4	2,847	2,757	430.5	519.9	8.42	158.6
1893	92.5	4,050	535	19.3	2,416	2,354	462.1	561.6	5.00	187.4
1894	93.7	4,281	601	19.6	2,300	2,206	418.1†	467.5†	8.44	140.7
1895	93.6	3,961	634	28.9	2,984	2,899	475.0†	597.8†	9.91	192.8
1896	96.5	3,957	621	26.1	2,500	2,390	399.7†	565.2†	5.69	182.4
1897	95.7	4,241	787	25.5	2,841	2,679	434.3†	604.3†	10.88	204.3
1898	100.3	4,107	781	26.9	3,472	3,337	420.0†	452.6†	9.21	230.3
1899	104.0	4,578	852	35.8	3,672	3,461	425.1†	456.0†	13.78	203.1
1900	105.8	4,858	741	42.1	3,687	3,513	420.2	451.3	10.20	209.3
1901	108.4	5,156	1,028	49.2	3,604	3,479	388.4	416.6	14.03	228.7
1902	109.1	5,725	901	53.8	4,080	3,812	465.8	499.8	15.77	286.2
1903	111.8	5,467	940	60.2	4,187	3,929	489.9	528.6	13.58	237.6
1904	104.7	5,963	1,074	70.9	3,981	3,862	458.0	496.0	18.55	249.7
1905	105.4	5,699	859	77.7	4,523	4,146	538.4	577.9	17.70	274.6
1906	109.5	6,433	844	83.7	4,877	4,502	491.5	537.5	19.02	247.4
1907	111.5	6,451	930	82.7	4,974	4,825	499.3	542.7	18.24	258.7
1908	109.8	6,479	926	94.0	4,493	4,411	418.4	458.0	20.39	267.6
1909	107.5	6,986	1,126	117.7	5,199	5,019	574.0	609.4	24.95	316.5
1910	107.2	7,317	797	110.9	4,759	4,611	588.0	634.6	24.88	226.2
1911	110.8	7,350	796	130.0	4,713	4,539	450.8	484.4	24.00	238.1
1912	110.8	7,904	938	146.7	5,400	5,147	510.2	532.4	28.21	341.8
1913	113.6	8,274	845	149.0	5,583	5,347	484.8	515.7	31.03	323.9
1914	115.0	8,617	975	164.0	5,449	5,237	542.3	604.3	28.20	332.2

For all footnotes, see end of table.

TABLE 1 (*Continued*)

Year	(11) Pig iron produced (unit: one thousand long tons)	(12) Steel ingots and castings produced (unit: one thousand long tons)	(13) Rails produced (unit: one thousand long tons)	(14) Structural iron and steel produced (unit: one thousand long tons)	(15) Iron and steel "end products," other than rails and structural iron and steel‡ (unit: one thousand long tons)	(16) Lumber produced (unit: one million M ft. board measure)	(17) Lumber consumed (unit: one million M ft. board measure)	(18) Paper produced (unit: one thousand short tons)	(19) Paper consumed (unit: one thousand short tons)	(20) Fermented liquors produced (unit: one million barrels)
1860	821	11.8	183	…	878	…	…	…	…	…
1861	653	..	170	…	623	…	…	…	…	…
1862	703	..	191	…	608	…	…	…	…	…
1863	846	8.1	246	…	785	…	…	…	…	…
1864	1,014	9.3	299	…	894	…	…	…	…	…
1865	832	13.6	318	…	670	…	…	…	…	…
1866	1,206	16.9	385	…	1,033	…	…	…	…	…
1867	1,305	19.6	413	…	1,141	…	…	…	…	…
1868	1,431	26.8	452	…	1,203	…	…	…	…	…
1869	1,711	31.2	530	…	1,457	…	…	386	391	…
1870	1,665	68.8	554	…	1,396	12.76	12.95	…	…	6.6
1871	1,707	73	693	…	1,399	…	…	…	…	7.7
1872	2,549	143	893	…	2,058	…	…	…	…	8.7
1873	2,561	199	795	…	2,006	…	…	…	…	9.6
1874	2,401	216	651	…	1,906	…	…	…	…	9.6
1875	2,024	390	708	…	1,345	…	…	…	…	9.5
1876	1,869	533	785	…	1,167	…	…	…	…	9.9
1877	2,067	570	683	…	1,524	…	…	…	…	9.8
1878	2,301	732	788	…	1,770	…	…	…	…	10.2
1879	2,742	935	994	87	2,447	18.09	18.17	452	457	11.1
1880	3,835	1,247	1,305	…	2,799	…	…	…	…	13.3
1881	4,144	1,588	1,647	…	3,417	…	…	…	…	14.3
1882	4,623	1,737	1,508	…	3,716	…	…	…	…	17.0
1883	4,596	1,674	1,215	…	3,625	…	…	…	…	17.8
1884	4,098	1,551	1,022	…	3,280	…	…	…	…	19.0
1885	4,045	1,712	977	…	3,415	…	…	…	…	19.2

Year										
1886	5,683	2,563	1,601	…	4,728	…	…	…	…	20.7
1887	6,417	3,339	2,140	…	4,990	…	…	…	…	23.1
1888	6,490	2,899	1,404	…	5,335	…	…	…	…	24.7
1889	7,604	3,386	1,522	276	6,175	27.04	27.12	935	1,121	25.1
1890	9,203	4,277	1,885	…	6,825	…	…	…	…	27.6
1891	8,280	3,904	1,307	454	6,802	…	…	…	…	30.5
1892	9,157	4,928	1,552	387	7,417	…	…	…	…	31.9
1893	7,125	4,020	1,136	360	5,574	…	…	…	…	34.6
1894	6,657	4,412	1,022	518	5,378	…	…	…	…	33.4
1895	9,446	6,115	1,306	496	7,890	…	…	…	…	33.6
1896	8,623	5,282	1,122	584	6,706	…	…	…	…	35.9
1897	9,653	7,157	1,648	702	7,147	…	…	…	…	34.5
1898	11,774	8,933	1,981	850	9,261	…	…	…	…	37.5
1899	13,621	10,040	2,273	815	10,573	35.1	34.5	2,168	2,158	36.7
1900	13,789	10,188	2,386	1,013	9,767	…	…	…	…	39.5
1901	15,878	13,474	2,875	1,300	12,283	…	…	…	…	40.6
1902	17,821	14,947	2,948	1,096	14,459	…	…	…	…	44.6
1903	18,009	14,535	2,992	949	14,211	…	…	…	…	46.7
1904	16,497	13,800	2,285	1,661	13,052	43.0	41.6	3,107	3,050	48.3
1905	22,992	20,024	3,376	2,119	17,820	43.5	42.4	…	…	49.5
1906	25,307	23,398	3,978	1,940	19,193	46.0	44.9	…	…	54.7
1907	25,781	23,363	3,634	1,083	20,384	46.0	44.6	…	…	58.6
1908	15,936	14,023	1,921	2,276	12,743	42.0	40.8	…	…	58.8
1909	25,795	23,955	3,024	2,267	20,207	44.5	43.3	4,217	4,224	56.3
1910	27,304	26,095	3,636	1,912	21,145	44.5	43.0	…	…	59.5
1911	23,650	23,676	2,823	2,846	18,242	43.0	40.9	…	…	63.3
1912	29,727	31,251	3,328	3,005	22,324	45.0	43.0	…	…	62.2
1913	30,966	31,301	3,503	2,031	23,549	44.0	41.7	…	…	65.3
1914	23,332	23,513	1,945	…	18,918	40.5	39.2	5,270	5,496	66.2

For all footnotes, see end of table.

TABLE 1 (*Continued*)

Year	(21) Distilled liquors produced (unit: one million tax gallons)	(22) Petroleum produced (unit: one million barrels)	(23) Coke produced (unit: one million short tons)	(24) Superphosphate produced (unit: one thousand short tons)	(25) White lead produced (unit: one thousand short tons)	(26) Flaxseed consumed (unit: one million bushels)	(27) Cottonseed oil produced (unit: one million pounds)	(28) Cottonseed cake and meal produced (unit: one thousand short tons)	(29) Copper consumed (unit: one million pounds)	(30) Lead consumed (unit: one thousand short tons)
1860		0.50							16.1	41.0
1861		2.1							16.8	33.9
1862		3.1							21.2	30.9
1863		2.6							19.0	48.5
1864		2.1							14.0	41.0
1865		2.5							11.1	28.4
1866		3.6							16.6	47.4
1867		3.3							20.2	47.8
1868		3.6		31					21.7	47.8
1869		4.2		60					23.2	61.4
1870	72.6	5.3		103					25.4	60.8
1871	57.0	5.2		76					21.7	70.7
1872	69.4	6.3		58			16	18	35.0	75.2
1873	71.2	9.9		124			16	18	42.8	88.1
1874	69.6	10.9		136			22	26	35.1	82.5
1875	62.7	8.8		121			25	30	34.2	78.0
1876	58.6	9.1		125			37	43	26.7	74.3
1877	61.4	13.4		135			30	34	35.0	89.2
1878	57.3	15.4		201			45	53	33.5	94.4
1879	72.9	19.9		177		8.7	54	64	39.2	93.4
1880	91.4	26.3	3.3	320		9.9	71	82	65.3	101.2
1881	119.5	27.7	4.1	474		8.1	55	64	66.2	119.2
1882	107.3	30.4	4.8	528		8.1	88	103	87.1	135.9
1883	75.3	23.4	5.5	578		9.3	118	137	84.0	146.0
1884	76.5	24.2	4.9	571	65	11.0	119	138	76.5	141.4
1885	76.4	21.9	5.1	563	60	14.0	150	174	86.6	132.3

Year										
1886	81.8	28.1	6.8	573	60	10.4	174	202	113	144.4
1887	79.4	28.3	7.6	578	70	12.0	208	243	142	149.1
1888	71.7	27.6	8.5	676	84	12.3	247	288	119	153.2
1889	91.1	35.2	10.3	837	80	12.6	238	278	182	158.8
1890	111.1	45.8	11.5	606	78	9.9	262	306	193	151.7
1891	117.8	54.3	10.4	787	78	15.7	307	358	213	180.2
1892	118.4	50.5	12.0	649	74	9.4	321	374	265	181.8
1893	131.0	48.4	9.5	885	72	8.5	315	368	158	166.0
1894	92.2	49.3	9.2	863	76	11.7	429	501	189	192.4
1895	81.9	52.9	13.3	900	91	15.6	503	587	266	241.0
1896	90.0	61.0	11.8	893	89	12.8	430	502	229	213.9
1897	64.3	60.5	13.3	972	96	12.4	488	570	274	219.2
1898	83.7	55.4	16.0	1,511	96	13.7	630	735	274	227.5
1899	100.2	57.1	19.7	1,427	110	17.3	706	823	392	226.3
1900	109.2	63.6	20.5	1,868	98	16.4	700	884	357	269.3
1901	128.6	69.4	21.8	1,720	101	21.9	725	845	383	271.9
1902	132.8	88.8	25.4	1,524	115	25.2	890	1,125	552	332.5
1903	148.2	100.5	25.3	1,717	114	26.6	922	1,165	526	300.2
1904	139.5	117.1	23.7	2,151	123	23.6	914	1,156	482	319.5
1905	153.3	134.7	32.2	1,955	137	22.4	1,004	1,360	581	347.0
1906	150.1	126.5	36.4	2,197	132	19.2	943	1,272	677	376.3
1907	174.7	166.1	40.8	2,330	127	21.5	1,153	1,563	488	360.7
1908	133.9	178.5	26.0	2,222	133	25.4	773	1,043	480	318.6
1909	139.9	183.2	39.3	2,419	148	24.7	1,101	1,492	689	368.7
1910	163.9	209.6	41.7	2,876	144	24.7	982	1,326	732	379.2
1911	183.4	220.4	35.6	3,301	133	26.4	1,260	1,792	682	384.8
1912	187.6	222.9	44.0	3,255	147	32.7	1,512	2,151	776	388.1
1913	193.6	248.4	46.3	3,146	143	26.2	1,393	1,999	812	419.5
1914	181.9	265.8	34.6	3,172	159	24.1	1,450	2,220	702	452.5

For all footnotes, see end of table.

TABLE 1 (*Continued*)

Year	(31) Zinc consumed (unit: one thousand short tons)	(32) Tin imported (unit: one million pounds)	(33) Cigars produced (unit: one million cigars)	(34) Cigarettes produced (unit: one million cigarettes)	(35) Manufactured tobacco and snuff produced (unit: one million pounds)	(36) Railroad freight cars produced (unit: one thousand cars)	(37) Railroad passenger cars produced (unit: one car)	(38) Automobiles produced (unit: one motor vehicle)	(39) Rubber imported (unit: one million pounds)	(40) Vessels produced (unit: one thousand gross tons)
1860	7.5	..	..	..	..	..	..	..	5.6	215
1861	5.8	..	..	..	..	..	..	..	3.2	233
1862	5.9	3.6	..	..	..	..	..	..	3.6	175
1863	8.0	3.8	..	..	..	..	..	..	5.4	311
1864	6.4	..	..	..	..	..	..	..	4.2	416
1865	8.6	2.9	..	..	..	..	..	..	3.5	384
1866	9.8	12.3	..	..	..	..	..	..	6.2	336
1867	8.4	7.3	..	..	..	..	..	..	8.0	304
1868	10.8	10.6	..	..	..	..	..	..	8.8	285
1869	16.3	8.6	..	..	..	..	..	..	9.5	275
1870	14.8	10.2	1,183	16.4	102	..	..	..	7.5	277
1871	16.9	13.6	1,353	19.8	107	1.78	185	..	11.2	273
1872	19.5	12.3	1,578	23.9	112	8.69	387	..	12.5	209
1873	16.3	10.9	1,755	27.9	118	5.69	280	..	13.2	359
1874	14.8	12.6	1,835	35.0	124	4.63	256	..	14.6	433
1875	20.5	10.9	1,828	59.4	124	9.13	185	..	9.7	298
1876	18.7	10.9	1,776	113.2	124	8.10	836	..	10.4	204
1877	18.1	13.5	1,816	157.2	123	7.00	708	..	14.5	177
1878	18.9	13.0	1,923	209.8	125	8.74	211	..	11.8	236
1879	21.2	22.6	2,217	371.4	136	25.6	524	..	16.8	193
1880	28.6	29.0	2,510	533	146	46.2	685	..	18.0	157
1881	32.0	17.6	2,806	595	172	73.8	1,188	..	18.4	280
1882	44.4	23.5	3,118	599	159	67.8	1,711	..	23.7	282
1883	46.6	28.0	3,232	844	194	44.9	2,135	..	21.8	265
1884	41.9	25.1	3,373	920	172	24.5	1,063	..	23.1	226
1885	43.3	23.5	3,294	1,080	207	12.5	813	..	25.1	159

Year									
1886	44.9	29.4	3,462	1,607	210	42.4	953	..	30.8	95
1887	54.9	29.0	3,662	1,865	226	78.0	1,277	..	30.7	150
1888	57.9	34.2	3,668	2,212	209	71.7	1,452	..	33.9	218
1889	60.0	35.0	3,787	2,413	246	70.6	1,580	..	31.8	231
1890	67.1	33.8	4,229	2,505	253	103.8	1,654	..	33.9	294
1891	78.5	41.0	4,422	3,137	271	95.5	1,640	..	35.7	369
1892	78.0	46.8	4,675	3,282	274	98.1	2,195	..	36.5	200
1893	72.8	39.9	4,341	3,661	251	56.9	1,986	..	37.8	212
1894	72.4	39.1	4,164	3,621	269	17.0	516	..	33.7	131
1895	87.7	53.9	4,099	4,238	274	38.1	430	..	39.4	112
1896	70.1	44.3	4,048	4,967	261	51.2	474	..	30.8	227
1897	88.8	54.3	4,136	4,927	297	43.6	494	..	39.1	232
1898	108.2	62.0	4,459	4,843	275	99.8	699	..	41.3	180
1899	124.6	70.2	4,910	4,307	295	119.9	1,305	3,874	51.6	300
1900	99.4	68.9	5,566	3,870	301	115.6	1,636	4,192	45.5	394
1901	141.7	72.5	6,139	3,503	314	137.0	2,055	7,000	51.4	483
1902	152.7	84.0	6,232	3,647	348	162.6	1,948	9,000	47.6	469
1903	154.4	82.0	6,806	3,959	351	152.8	2,007	11,235	52.0	436
1904	180.9	82.0	6,640	4,170	354	60.8	2,144	22,830	58.4	379
1905	200.4	88.0	6,748	4,477	368	163.3	2,500	25,000	60.5	330
1906	220.8	99.2	7,148	5,502	391	233.4	3,084	34,000	64.2	419
1907	227.0	81.3	7,302	6,345	388	275.0	5,353	44,000	64.5	471
1908	214.2	82.0	6,489	6,333	408	68.0	1,637	65,000	72.6	614
1909	270.7	94.4	6,668	7,880	431	86.8	2,749	130,986	89.1	238
1910	245.9	103.7	6,810	9,782	447	170.8	4,288	187,000	84.0	342
1911	280.1	104.7	7,049	11,700	424	62.2	3,466	210,000	77.2	291
1912	340.3	114.7	7,044	14,239	435	126.4	2,818	378,000	112.6	233
1913	295.4	101.8	7,572	16,530	444	185.7	2,779	485,000	111.7	346
1914	300.0	93.3	7,174	17,944	441	98.1	3,366	509,954	137.2	316

* For general statement regarding these data, see Chapter I.
† Note that these figures for 1894–99 are arrived at by a special "substitute method." See the appropriate sections of Appendix A.
‡ This series is probably more reliable with respect to relative movements than with respect to absolute size. See the section of Appendix A devoted to this series.

TABLE 2

Certain Series Included in Census-Year Manufacture Index, 1859–1914*

The comments appearing at the beginning of Table 1 are in general applicable here also.

Year	(1) Lumber produced (unit: one million M ft. board measure)	(2) Lumber consumed (unit: million M ft. board measure)	(3) Paper produced (unit: one thousand short tons)	(4) Paper consumed (unit: one thousand short tons)	(5) Petroleum produced (unit: one million barrels)	(6) Coke produced (unit: one million short tons)	(7) Super phosphate produced (unit: one thousand short tons)	(8) White lead produced (unit: one thousand short tons)	(9) Flaxseed consumed (unit: one million bushels)	(10) Cottonseed oil produced (unit: one million pounds)	(11) Cottonseed cake and meal produced (unit: one thousand short tons)
1859......	8.03	8.03	127	127	0.002	..	..	16†	..	..	..
1869......	12.76	12.95	386	391	4.2	..	60	38†	..	..	..
1879......	18.09	18.17	452	457	19.9	..	177	54†	8.7	54	64
1889......	27.04	27.12	935	1,121	35.2	10.3	837	80	12.6	238	278
1899......	35.1	34.5	2,168	2,158	57.1	19.7	1,427	110	17.3	706	823
1904......	43.0	41.6	3,107	3,050	117.1	23.7	2,151	123	23.6	914	1,156
1909......	44.5	43.3	4,217	4,224	183.2	39.3	2,419	148	24.7	1,101	1,492
1914......	40.5	39.2	5,270	5,496	265.8	34.6	3,172	159	24.1	1,450	2,220

* For general statement regarding these data, see Chapter I.
† As estimates for 1859, 1869, and 1879, certain adjusted figures for 1860, 1870, and 1880, respectively, were employed; see Appendix A.

index covering our period of analysis—the Day-Persons index[4] —and for the time being fix our attention on *quantitative* aspects, we find that up to 1874 our coverage is decidedly greater: we have about twice as many series and have more industries represented. For 1875–98, our coverage is still appreciably better. (And as respects *quality* of data, we may fairly claim definite superiority up to 1899.) For 1899–1914, the count of annual series is more or less the same in the two cases, but the Day-Persons index has some advantage in intrinsic coverage through the utilization of census-year material, most of which is not available over our period of analysis.

In various ways there was endeavor to raise the quality of the fundamental data to be used in the computation of our new manufacture index. (In particular, effort was exerted so far as feasible to make the intrinsic *time-reference* of the items conform to a uniform calendar-year basis.) All of this the reader may confirm by perusal in detail of Appendix A.

[4] For a discussion of the Day-Persons index, see the present writer's *Economic Fluctuations*, pp. 179–181.

CHAPTER II

MANUFACTURE: WEIGHTS

IN THE DERIVATION of our indexes of manufacturing production, we in general followed conventional procedure. More specifically, we employed the weighted arithmetic mean of quantity relatives (which, as is well known, is under certain simple conditions equivalent to the aggregative); and with respect to weighting, we took the value-added principle as our standard, and conformed to this standard as nearly as was possible with existing data.[1]

Attention was given to the problem of avoiding technical (type and weight) bias. Simple logical considerations, as well as more complex mathematical analysis, suggested that the base period and the weighting period ought to be identical. Theoretically, the employment of "compromise base" and "compromise weighting-period" seemed to be indicated.[2] The use of "compromise weights" was, however, impracticable, because of lack of adequate pertinent data in the earlier years of the period of analysis. The best available substitute was a set of weights pertaining to some period in-

[1] For a discussion of the rationale of the conventional procedure for computing production indexes, see an article by the present writer: Edwin Frickey, "Some Aspects of the Problem of Measuring Historical Changes in the Physical Volume of Production," in the volume entitled *Explorations in Economics: Notes and Essays Contributed in Honor of F. W. Taussig* (New York and London: McGraw-Hill Book Co., Inc., 1936), pp. 477–486. It will be noted that this article also presents criticisms of the conventional procedure. See also the article by Professor Arthur F. Burns, "The Measurement of the Physical Volume of Production," *Quarterly Journal of Economics*, XLIV (February 1930), 242–262; and his *Production Trends in the United States since 1870* (New York: National Bureau of Economic Research, Inc., 1934), pp. 253–281.

[2] Cf. an article by the present writer: Edwin Frickey, "The Theory of Index-Number Bias," *Review of Economic Statistics*, XIX (November 1937), 161–173. The theory is there explicitly developed for price index numbers, but can very readily be adapted to quantity indexes by a simple interchange of symbols. Cf. also Warren M. Persons, *The Construction of Index Numbers* (Cambridge, Mass.: Houghton Mifflin Company, 1928), pp. 36–44.

termediate between the terminal dates of the computation interval, chosen with a view to obtaining relative weights approximating reasonably well those of the desired "compromise-weight" system. The practical choice lay between the two census years 1889 and 1899. On purely theoretical grounds the year 1889 should probably have been given the preference, as it was situated nearer the center of the computation interval and it seemed likely that many of the long-run economic tendencies pertinent to our weighting problem were at least roughly continuous over this interval. Since, however, the 1899 Census was the first to furnish weighting data in the detail required for our purposes, this year was selected. The final decision, then, was to compute the index with 1899 as base and 1899 weights.

THE DERIVATION OF THE WEIGHTS

Table 3 presents, in summary form, the derivation of the weights used in the computation of our manufacture index. Supplementary Notes, setting forth numerous details, are presented in Appendix B. The classification system of Table 3 follows that of the United States Census of Manufactures for 1914, and has been taken from the convenient *1914 Abstract*.[3]

The main subdivision of Table 3 is according to the major groups of the United States Census, as set forth on page 29 of the *1914 Abstract*.

I. Food and Kindred Products.
II. Textiles and Their Products.
III. Iron and Steel and Their Products.
IV. Lumber and Its Remanufactures.
V. Leather and Its Finished Products.
VI. Paper and Printing.
VII. Liquors and Beverages.
VIII. Chemicals and Allied Products.
IX. Stone, Clay, and Glass Products.

---

[3] Complete designation of this publication: United States Department of Commerce, Bureau of the Census, *Abstract of the Census of Manufactures,* 1914 (Washington: Government Printing Office, 1917).

TABLE 3

DERIVATION OF WEIGHTS FOR MANUFACTURE INDEX

(For general explanation, see accompanying text; for additional details, see Supplementary Notes, Appendix B)

Group, sub-group, and individual production series (1)	Basic data for weighting; value added by manufacture, 1899 (Unit: one million dollars)			Weights (percentage basis)		
	Group (2)	Sub-group (3)	Page references, 1914 Abstract* (4)	Group (5)	Sub-group (6)	Individual production series (7)
All Groups Included..........	3,881.1	..	..	100.00	..	..
Group I—Food and Kindred Products..........	416.3	..	..	10.73	..	..
Flour-mill and gristmill products..........	..	73.3	29	..	7.55	..
Wheat flour produced..........	..	..	621	..	..	7.55
Cane sugar, cane-sugar refining, and beet sugar..........	..	20.8	53, 697	..	2.15	..
Refined sugar produced..........	..	..	‡	..	..	2.15
Coffee and spice, roasting and grinding..........	..	7.2†	‡	..	0.74	..
Coffee imported..........	..	..	..	..	..	0.74
Chocolate and cocoa products..........	..	2.8	597	..	0.29	..
Cocoa imported..........	..	..	..	..	..	0.29
Group II—Textiles and Their Products..........	733.8	..	29	18.91	..	..
Textile fabrics and materials..........	..	383.4	58	..	9.88	..
Raw cotton consumed..........	..	..	..	..	..	4.99
Raw wool consumed..........	..	..	..	..	..	3.34
Raw silk and spun silk imported..........	..	..	..	..	..	1.19
Minor fibers imported..........	..	..	..	..	..	0.36
Articles from textile fabrics..........	..	350.4¶	¶	..	9.03	..
Raw cotton consumed, adjusted for foreign trade in cotton goods..........	..	..	..	..	..	5.41
Raw wool consumed, adjusted for foreign trade in wool goods..........	..	..	..	..	..	3.62

Group III—Iron and Steel and Their Products	818.5	29	21.09		
Pig iron produced					1.34
Steel ingots and castings produced					0.88
Rails produced					0.29
Structural iron and steel produced					0.20
Iron and steel "end products," other than rails and structural iron and steel					18.38
Group IV—Lumber and Its Remanufactures	526.6	29	13.57		
Lumber and timber products and pulpwood	312.4	134		8.05	8.05
Other products	214.2¶	¶		5.52	5.52
Group VI—Paper and Printing	393.3	29	10.13		
Paper and wood pulp	56.8	666		1.46	1.46
Paper produced					
Other products	336.5¶	¶		8.67	8.67
Paper consumed					
Group VII—Liquors and Beverages	160.0§	§§	4.12		
Liquors, malt	129.0§	§		3.85	3.85
Fermented liquors produced					
Liquors, distilled	9.0§	§		0.27	0.27
Distilled liquors produced					
Group VIII—Chemicals and Allied Products	310.2	29	7.99		
Petroleum, refining	21.1	671		1.85	1.85
Petroleum produced					
Coke	15.9	602		1.39	1.39
Coke produced					
Fertilizers	15.7	618		1.38	1.38
Superphosphate produced					

For all footnotes, see end of table.

TABLE 3 (Continued)

(1) Group, sub-group, and individual production series	Basic data for weighting; value added by manufacture, 1890 (Unit: one million dollars)			Weights (percentage basis)		
	Group (2)	Sub-group (3)	Page references, 1914 Abstract* (4)	Group (5)	Sub-group (6)	Individual production series (7)
Paint and varnish................		24.8	665, 704		2.18	
White lead produced.............						1.16
Flaxseed consumed..............						1.02
Oils, cottonseed, and cake........		13.6	663		1.19	
Cottonseed oil produced..........						0.68
Cottonseed cake and meal produced...						0.51
Group X—Metals and Metal Products, Other than Iron and Steel....	218.5		29	5.63		
Copper consumed................						3.45
Lead consumed.................						1.01
Zinc consumed.................						0.74
Tin imported..................	119.6§		§,§	3.08		0.43
Group XI—Tobacco Manufactures....		81.1§			2.09	
Tobacco, cigars and cigarettes.....						
Cigars produced................						1.81
Cigarettes produced.............						0.28
Tobacco, chewing and smoking, and snuff...		38.5§	§		0.90	
Manufactured tobacco and snuff produced......						0.99
Group XII—Vehicles for Land Transportation.....	124.2		29	3.20		
Cars, steam railroad, not including operations of railroad companies.....		28.8	594		3.04	
Railroad freight cars produced..........						2.72
Railroad passenger cars produced.....						0.32
Automobiles, including bodies and parts.....		1.5	†		0.16	
Automobiles produced.............						0.16

Group XIV—Miscellaneous Industries	60.1‡	..	..	..	..
Rubber industries	..	39.6†‡	‡	1.55	..	1.02	..
Rubber imported	..	..	‡	..	..	..	1.02
Shipbuilding, including boat building (new construction)	..	20.5‡	‡	..	0.53	..
Vessels produced	..	..	..	..	0.53

* Complete designation: United States Department of Commerce, Bureau of the Census, *Abstract of the Census of Manufactures, 1914* (Washington: Government Printing Office, 1917).
† Special computation; see Supplementary Notes, Appendix B.
‡ See Supplementary Notes, Appendix B.
¶ Obtained by subtraction; see Supplementary Notes, Appendix B.
§ Estimated value added, after deduction of federal tax; for details, see Supplementary Notes, Appendix B.

X. Metals and Metal Products, Other than Iron and Steel.

XI. Tobacco Manufactures.

XII. Vehicles for Land Transportation.

XIII. Railroad Repair Shops.

XIV. Miscellaneous Industries.

These subdivisions by major groups are indicated by bold-faced entries in Table 3. Of the fourteen Census groups, three—Group V, Leather and Its Finished Products; Group IX, Stone, Clay, and Glass Products; Group XIII, Railroad Repair Shops—were not represented in our physical-quantity series, and consequently do not appear in the tabulation of weights.

For each of the remaining eleven Census groups, a figure for value added by manufacture, 1899, was derived and is shown in Column 2 of Table 3. In eight cases (Groups I, II, III, IV, VI, VIII, X, XII), the value-added total for the group was simply copied from the *1914 Abstract*, page 29. In the other three cases (Groups VII, XI, XIV), modification was required. For Group VII, Liquors and Beverages, and Group XI, Tobacco Manufactures, estimated value-added figures, excluding federal taxes, were computed—as explained in the Supplementary Notes of Appendix B—and entered in Column 2 of the table. For Group XIV, Miscellaneous Industries, it seemed best—having in mind the heterogeneity of the constituent industries—to confine our value-added total to the sum of the value-added figures for the two industries represented in the physical-quantity statistics: rubber industries; and shipbuilding, including boat building (new construction).

The value-added total in Column 2 for All Groups Included was computed by taking the sum of the value-added figures for the eleven constituent groups, obtained as just described.

The weights for the several major Census groups (set down in bold-faced type in Column 5 of the table) were derived upon a percentage basis; that is, they were obtained by distributing the total weight, or 100.00 per cent, among the eleven constituent groups in proportion to the value-added amounts respectively assigned these groups (as shown in Column 2).

When the process of obtaining weights for the major Census groups had thus been completed, the next step for most of these groups (all except Groups III and X, where the available statistical material was not well adapted for such an arrangement) was to develop weights for sub-groups. The entries for these have been made in italics in Table 3. The sub-group weights were derived on the "imputed-weighting" principle, employing value-added data; that is, in each case the weight for the major group was apportioned among the sub-groups in proportion to the respective value-added totals (Column 3) for those constituent sub-groups which were represented in our list of physical-volume series. The resulting weights for sub-groups are entered in Column 6, in italics. For example, the total weight for Group I, Food and Kindred Products (10.73, Column 5) was divided among the four represented industries—flour-mill and gristmill products; cane sugar, cane-sugar refining, and beet sugar; coffee and spice, roasting and grinding; chocolate and cocoa products—in proportion to the value-added totals assigned (73.3 million dollars, 20.8 million dollars, 7.2 million dollars, and 2.8 million dollars, respectively, in Column 3), to obtain the weights for these several industries (7.55, 2.15, 0.74, and 0.29, respectively, in Column 6). Various technical details regarding the derivation of the sub-group weights are given in the Supplementary Notes of Appendix B.

The final step in the calculation was the assignment of weights to the individual production series within the respective sub-groups (in Groups III and X, where no sub-groups had been set up, such assignment was made within the major group itself). The entries relating to the individual production series have been made in roman type in Table 3, the weights being shown in Column 7. If in a particular case only one production series was involved in the assignment of weight—as, for example, in each of the four sub-groups of Group I—the entire weight was allocated to that production series (compare Columns 6 and 7 for Group I). If, on the other hand, two or more production series were involved —as, for example, in each of the two sub-groups of Group II— the apportionment of the sub-group weight among the production series was made on whatever appeared to be the best statistical basis possible in the particular case at hand. Wherever feasible, the value-added basis was employed. In instances where this could not be used—whether because of lack of statistical data, or for other reason—resort was had to some other criterion. The Census "standard list"—appearing in the set-up of the general summary table by industries (cf. pages 568–714 of the *1914 Abstract*)—was in each case examined. This list comprised, in addition to value added by manufacture, the following: value of products, cost of materials, wages, capital, primary horsepower, average number of wage earners, number of establishments. Not all of these were obtainable, in the weighting year 1899, for every industry. But, as has been said, the endeavor was in each case to make the allocation of weight on the best statistical basis possible, choosing among the available data in the criteria of the Census "standard list" or other suitable data. The fact that—as will be seen from a reading of the Supplementary Notes of Appendix B —varying criteria have been used in the several cases is not, then, the result of capricious selection, but of attempt to reach the most appropriate decision in each individual problem.

Critical Consideration of Value-Added Weights

As is well known, the Census value-added figures differ from those which would be established according to the ordinary "net-value" principle. Dr. Solomon Fabricant, in his comprehensive study of the output of manufacturing industries from 1899 to 1937, presented a thoroughgoing discussion of the Census value-added data.[4] He pointed out that such value added "includes many items which should be deducted if a truly net value added is to be obtained. These are mainly overhead items, such as depreciation, taxes, rent, interest on short-run debt, maintenance and repairs, and other purchased supplies and services (advertising, light, office supplies, professional services)." He presented, for

---

[4] Cf. Solomon Fabricant, *The Output of Manufacturing Industries, 1899–1937* (New York: National Bureau of Economic Research, Inc., 1940), pp. 340–350 (see also pp. 35–42, 327–340, 605–639). The quotations in the accompanying text are taken from pp. 347–349.

the census year 1929, a tabulation of sundry adjustment items and arrived at the conclusion that for that year the ratio of the net value added to the Census value added was 0.63.[5]

Dr. Fabricant indicated that "not all the overhead items included in value added are inflexible in the short run, but a comparison of the Census value added and estimates of net value added by major manufacturing divisions in the Census years 1919–37, and by manufacturing combined in 1909–37, shows that the total of these overhead items is relatively inflexible [reference is made to a supporting table on page 349 of Dr. Fabricant's book] As a consequence net value added falls more rapidly during business recessions than does the Census value added, and rises more sharply during advances in business. Further, the amplitude of cyclical changes in the ratio of net value added to the Census value added varies from major group to major group: the greater the cyclical amplitude of changes in value added, the greater seems to be the cyclical amplitude of the ratio." He went on to point out that "the two values are somewhat closer in respect of movements from peak to peak."

In view of the above analysis, it became a matter of importance to consider the cyclical position of business in the census year 1899. Some doubt exists as to the exact time reference of this census year. The schedules of the Census asked that "information returned should cover the business year of the establishment most nearly conforming to and preceding the Census year which ends June 1, 1900." On the other hand, the Census indicated that "a very large proportion of the reports made in the Twelfth Census actually relate to the business of the calendar year 1899" (cf. Fabricant, *The Output of Manufacturing Industries, 1899–1937*, page 342, footnote 21). However—whether we regarded the census year 1899 as virtually coincident with the calendar year 1899, or as "lagging" somewhat into the early part of the calendar year 1900—examination of available "indexes of business conditions" suggested that the *average* cyclical position

---

[5] If taxes, interest, and rent are regarded as income originating in manufacture, this ratio becomes 0.70.

of business over this census year was relatively close to the "100-line," or "base line," separating areas of prosperity from areas of depression.[6]

This evidence as to the average cyclical position of business in the census year 1899 was, of course, highly favorable to the view that our selection of such year was opportune, from the point of view of avoiding aberrations in weights due to cyclical fluctuations in the ratio of net value added to Census value added. Another consideration, however, was involved: while, as just indicated, the census year 1899 was close to the "100-line," or "base line," in its *average* cyclical position, the year was one of rather rapid *change* in business activity. Now for such a year of rapid change, value-added figures are subject to possible distortion, owing to the operation of dynamic forces which may materially affect various price margins. With this possibility in mind, we took care to scrutinize the value-added weights, as indicated by the Census data for 1899, in the light of available information for preceding and following census years, and to investigate apparent anomalies. In only one case did modification of the 1899 weight seem called for because of this cyclical factor: the value-added weight for pig-iron production in 1899 was markedly out of line with that for preceding and following census years and was, accordingly, reduced (cf. the section on "Group III—Iron and Steel and Their Products" in the Supplementary Notes of Appendix B).

Still another point remained. Even if we should in some way make a rough correction for the element of cyclical change in the ratio of net value added to Census value added, it might still develop that, as respects the size of this ratio, some groups stand above total manufacture and other groups stand below total manufacture. We turned again to the tabulation in Dr. Fabricant's *Output of Manufacturing Industries* (page 349), referred to above. This tabulation showed, for six groups and for total manufacture, the ratio of net value added to Census value added in each of the ten census years contained within the interval 1919–37. We computed averages over the ten census years for each of his

---

[6] Cf., for example, the first curve—labeled "Standard pattern"—on Chart 34, opposite p. 338, in Frickey, *Economic Fluctuations*.

groups and for total manufacture, obtaining the values shown in the accompanying tabulation.[7]

Group	Average ratio (per cent)
Foods, beverages and tobacco products	50
Textile and leather products	64
Forest, stone, clay, and glass products	66
Paper products and printing and publishing	62
Metal products	61
Chemical and petroleum products	52
Total	62

Now, of course, it is *variation,* among the constituents of a production index, in the ratio of net value added to Census value added which may cause indexes computed by the two weighting systems to differ. If the ratio is the same for all the elements entering the index, then the *relative* weights under the two systems will be identical. With this consideration in mind, we examined the average ratios, tabulated above. In only two cases—foods, beverages and tobacco products; chemical and petroleum products —did any appreciable deviation appear of the average ratio for the group from that for total manufacture; and even in these two cases the discrepancy was by no means pronounced. The evidence afforded by these computations suggested (though, of course, it did not fully demonstrate) that—setting aside the cyclical element, already discussed—the failure of Census value added to conform to net value added was not likely to have any serious effect on our production index for total manufacture.

To be sure, if we were to extend this type of computation to more finely divided segments of manufacturing production we might expect to find greater dispersion among the ratios. However, as the individual weights thus become smaller, departure

[7] In a few cases, Dr. Fabricant gave *two* ratios for a given year—these two ratios pertaining to two different classification systems. Since, in each instance, the two ratios differed only slightly, we simply entered their mean on our computation sheet.

from precision in any individual weight would be less significant with reference to the index of total manufacture.[8]

All in all, taking into account the various possible defects of the
1899 Census value-added data: (1) the application of corrections
to the Census figures did not for the most part seem feasible, and
(2) these defects did not seem capable of producing any significant
error in our index for total manufacture. Accordingly, we in
general accepted the Census value-added weights. (Appendix B
gives the details regarding application of the value-added principle, indicating certain exceptions made because of paucity of
data or of individual peculiarities in particular series.)

A question of a somewhat different sort required consideration.
For the present study we made the decision—following procedure
which has on the whole become usual—to employ the "imputed-
weighting" system. Objection might be made that materially different results would perhaps have been obtained if the so-called
"earned-weighting" system had been used.[9] To determine the
practical force of this objection in the present case, test computations were made at a later stage of our work. Anticipating the
results, we may say that these test computations indicated that
the substitution of the "earned-weighting" system for the "imputed-weighting" system would have left the cyclical fluctuations
of our index of total manufacture practically unchanged; and so
far as the secular movements were concerned, the only effect
would have been a relatively slight alteration in the average annual rate of growth over the period of analysis.

[8] The effect on *group* indexes might be more serious.

[9] For contrast of the two systems, see E. E. Day, *An Index of the Physical Volume of Production* (Cambridge, Mass.: Harvard University Committee on Economic Research, 1921), p. 51, and W. Floyd Maxwell, "The Revised Index of the
Volume of Manufacture," *Review of Economic Statistics*, XI (May 1929), 108–109,
respectively.

CHAPTER III

As WAS SET FORTH in the preceding chapter, the general method of computation decided upon for our new manufacture index involved the use of the weighted arithmetic mean of quantity relatives on 1899 base, combined with 1899 value-added weights. Since the base period and the weighting period were identical, we could (following a simple and well-known theorem) equally well regard the index as an aggregative—actual quantities for the several series being multiplied by 1899 "value-added *per unit*" weights.

The development of our manufacture index comprised two stages: first, derivation of a preliminary continuous annual index (the force of the adjectives "preliminary" and "continuous" will appear presently); and, second, the broadening of the coverage of the index by bringing in certain important production series which were available only discontinuously. These two stages are discussed in Chapters III and IV, respectively.

As was indicated at the beginning of Chapter I, our new manufacture index was derived with a view to use in connection with a study of general economic fluctuations over the interval from the end of the Civil War to the outbreak of the first World War. Accordingly, when we came to undertake the actual construction of our manufacture index, we devoted major attention to the period 1866–1914, though certain supplementary computations were carried out for the years 1860–65.

DEVELOPMENT OF INDEXES FOR NINE MAJOR GROUPS

We began the work of deriving the preliminary continuous annual index of manufacturing activity by computing annual indexes for those major groups of the United States Census for which such computation seemed feasible. The groups included in this operation were as follows:[1]

    I. Food and Kindred Products, 1860–1914.
    II. Textiles and Their Products, 1860–1914.
    III. Iron and Steel and Their Products, 1860–1914.
    VII. Liquors and Beverages, 1870–1914.
    X. Metals and Metal Products, Other than Iron and Steel, 1860–1914.
    XI. Tobacco Manufactures, 1870–1914.
    XIIA. Steam-Railroad Cars, 1871–1914.
    XIIB. Automobiles, 1899–1914.
    XIV. Miscellaneous Industries, 1860–1914.

This listing calls for certain comments. In the first place, since the constituents of Group XII, Vehicles for Land Transportation, had such diverse movements, we did not compute a combined index for the group, but instead computed two indexes, which we designated as applying to Group XIIA for Steam-Railroad Cars, and Group XIIB for Automobiles, respectively. Further, it will be observed that for some of the groups just listed, the index does not extend over the entire interval 1860–1914; the bearing of this fact upon the computation of the preliminary annual index for manufacture, and upon the "continuity" of this index, will be considered presently.

The plan for computation of the nine group indexes, listed just above, involved what we may call the "hierarchy principle," developed at length in Chapter II. More specifically, the general procedure was to progress by successive steps, starting with relatives for the individual production series, next going on to subgroup indexes, and then arriving at indexes for the major groups themselves.[2] This general procedure leading to the derivation of

---

[1] For the complete list of the Census groups, as set forth in the *1914 Abstract*, see Chapter II.

[2] The final step in this application of the "hierarchy principle"—the joining of these group indexes to form a combined index—will be considered on later pages.

the several group indexes (cf. the schematic arrangement of series and weights in Table 3)[3] may be illustrated by reference to Group II, Textiles and Their Products. For this group, the successive steps in the computation of the annual index, 1860–1914, were as follows. First, for each of the six *individual production series* assigned to the group (cf. again Table 3) annual quantity relatives to the base 1899 were calculated.[4] Next annual production indexes were computed for each of the two constituent *sub-groups* (textile fabrics and materials, and articles made from textile fabrics, respectively—cf. Column 1 of Table 3); these sub-group indexes were in each case calculated as annual arithmetic means of the relatives to base 1899 for the constituent individual production series, employing the weights shown in Column 7 of Table 3. Then the sub-group indexes were combined, year by year, to form a production index for the *major group* Textiles and Their Products; here again the weighted arithmetic mean was employed (the weights now being those shown in Column 6 of Table 3).

For the other eight groups included in our present operations— Groups I, III, VII, X, XI, XIIA, XIIB, XIV—the general computation scheme was similar to that just described. Occasionally, however, the set-up of the available data was such as to simplify the process somewhat. In cases where a sub-group was represented by only one individual production series, the relatives for that series were taken as the sub-group index (as, for example, in each of the sub-groups of Group I—cf. Table 3). In cases where no sub-groups were set up, because the available statistical material was not well adapted to such an arrangement, the group index was computed directly from the relatives for the individual production series (in Groups III and X—cf. again Table 3).[5]

---

[3] The method of derivation of the weights shown in Table 3 is explained in broad outline in Chapter II; details are given in the Supplementary Notes of Appendix B.

[4] For the original items of the various individual series, see Table 1.

[5] Reference to the tabulation of basic data of individual production series reveals that for some of the group indexes involved in the present calculation certain short gaps (mainly affecting the earlier years of our period of analysis) appear in the array of original items for constituent series (cf. Table 1). These gaps were filled in by interpolation or extrapolation (details are given in Appendix E, Part One). We postpone to a later page in this chapter consideration of the prob-

TRANSFERENCE OF CERTAIN FISCAL-YEAR DATA
TO A CALENDAR-YEAR BASIS

One important feature of the computation of the group indexes may now be described. In two instances—(1) for Group VII, the Liquors and Beverages group, and (2) for the series "vessels produced," one of the components of Group XIV, Miscellaneous Industries—it was possible to effect a decided improvement in the *time reference* of the figures. In both cases, the problem involved was that of making, from an available fiscal-year series (years ending June 30), as reliable an estimate as possible of the corresponding calendar-year series.

We discuss the two cases in turn.

The Liquors and Beverages Group. For Group VII, Liquors and Beverages, the production index was first computed on a fiscal-year basis, by methods which have already been described. It was then noted that this fiscal-year index presented a particularly favorable case for estimation of calendar-year figures, inasmuch as its short-run fluctuations corresponded rather closely with the movements of those monthly or quarterly indexes of general economic activity which are capable of being transferred to a fiscal-year basis. The cyclical movements of the production index for Group VII were found to correlate quite well, for example, with those of fiscal-year averages for the quarterly *standard pattern* of short-run fluctuation in economic series derived by the present writer and described in an earlier volume.[6] The existence of this high correlation suggested that the fiscal-year index for Group VII might readily be redistributed on a calendar-year basis, employing the short-time movements of the standard pattern as a guide. However—inasmuch as the secular influence had been eliminated from the standard pattern, but was still distinctly present in the Group VII index—it seemed desirable to correct the latter series for

able effects of these interpolations and extrapolations upon the continuity of our computed indexes.

[6] Edwin Frickey, *Economic Fluctuations in the United States* (Cambridge, Mass.: Harvard University Press, 1942), pp. 327–329. The present reference is to the quarterly series labeled "standard pattern, second revision."

secular trend (at least approximately) as a preliminary operation to such redistribution. Graphic inspection indicated that over the period 1870–1914 the secular trend of the Group VII index could be represented, with accuracy amply adequate for the purpose at hand, by a logarithmic parabola.[7]

The procedure, then, was—after fitting a logarithmic-parabola secular trend to the Group VII fiscal-year index—(1) to obtain fiscal-year ratios to trend for the series; (2) to redistribute these fiscal-year trend-ratios between calendar years on the basis of the short-time movements of the quarterly standard pattern, above mentioned;[8] (3) to restore the secular element through multiplication of (a) the calendar-year trend-ratios (estimated by redistribution, as just described) by (b) calendar-year ordinates of secular trend;[9] and, finally, (4) to reduce the series just obtained to the base 1899 (i.e., to the base, *calendar year* 1899 = 100), by dividing this series through by its 1899 item.

Vessels produced. Here the correlation of short-run movement with indicators of general economic activity (and, specifically, with the standard pattern above referred to), while not so clear-cut as in the case of the Group VII index, was nevertheless on the whole quite high. The procedure previously applied to the index for

---

[7] No close approach to precision in secular correction was required at this point. Indeed, the redistribution process could have been applied directly to the *original items* without any large alteration of the results. (For discussion of the properties of the logarithmic parabola, see Frickey, *Economic Fluctuations,* pp. 144 ff.)

[8] The procedure for this redistribution may be indicated more specifically in symbols. For purposes of illustration, let us refer to the calendar year 1900.

Let F_{00} and F_{01} be the trend-ratios for the Group VII index in the *fiscal years* 1900 and 1901, respectively. Let s^i_{99}, s^{ii}_{99}, s^{iii}_{99}, s^{iv}_{99}; and s^i_{00}, s^{ii}_{00}, s^{iii}_{00}, s^{iv}_{00}; and s^i_{01}, s^{ii}_{01}, s^{iii}_{01}, s^{iv}_{01} be the successive quarterly items of the standard pattern for the three calendar years 1899, 1900, and 1901, respectively. Then C_{00}, the estimated trend-ratio for the Group VII index in the *calendar year* 1900, is:

$$C_{00} = \left(\frac{s^i_{00} + s^{ii}_{00}}{s^{iii}_{99} + s^{iv}_{99} + s^i_{00} + s^{ii}_{00}} \times F_{00} \right) + \left(\frac{s^{iii}_{00} + s^{iv}_{00}}{s^{iii}_{00} + s^{iv}_{00} + s^i_{01} + s^{ii}_{01}} \times F_{01} \right)$$

The redistribution for the year 1914 was made on the basis of the cyclical fluctuations of bank clearings outside New York City (since the standard pattern ended with June 1914)—cf. *Review of Economic Statistics,* 1 (January 1919), 69.

[9] These calendar-year ordinates of secular trend were, of course, readily obtainable by interpolation between successive pairs of fiscal-year ordinates, or directly from the mathematical equation.

Group VII, Liquors and Beverages, was here modified only slightly. A simplification was, in fact, possible: since from one year to the next the secular movement of vessels produced clearly was quite minor as compared with the cyclical and other short-run variations, no adjustment for secular trend was required for the purpose at hand, and the reallocation process was applied directly to the *original items* of the series for vessels produced. That is to say, the successive steps were simply: (1) to redistribute the fiscal-year original items of the vessels-produced series between calendar years on the basis of the short-time movements of the quarterly standard pattern;[10] and (2) to reduce the series just derived to the base 1899, by dividing this series through by its 1899 item. We thus secured the relatives for the vessels series, transferred to a calendar-year basis, 1860–1914. This calendar-year series of relatives was used in the computation of the index for Group XIV.

For a series whose short-run fluctuations correlate at least reasonably well with those of general business activity—as was true for the two cases just considered—the procedure above described is clearly far superior to the method of simple straight-line interpolation between fiscal-year figures, to which we are so often compelled to resort, *faute de mieux*. We have, therefore, been able to bring about a significant betterment in the short-run measurements for the two cases at hand.

TABULAR AND GRAPHIC PRESENTATION OF GROUP INDEXES

By the methods which have been described on preceding pages, we arrived at annual production indexes for the nine Census

---

[10] The redistribution method was analogous to that described just above for Group VII—original items of the vessels-produced series being involved, however, rather than trend-ratios.

The standard pattern was not available prior to 1866. The redistribution for the years 1860–66 was made on the basis of the fluctuations of Philadelphia bank clearings, corrected for seasonal variation. As to this series, and its relation to "outside bank clearings" as a whole and to measures of general business conditions, see articles by the present writer: Edwin Frickey, "Bank Clearings Outside New York City, 1875–1914," *Review of Economic Statistics*, VII (October 1925), 252–262; and "A Statistical Study of Bank Clearings, 1875–1914," *Review of Economic Statistics*, XII (May 1930), 90–99. See also Frickey, *Economic Fluctuations*, p. 360.

groups involved in our present operations—Groups I, II, III, VII, X, XI, XIIA, XIIB, XIV. The indexes are presented in Table 4—except for Group XIV, which has been omitted from the array, inasmuch as the nonhomogeneity of its composition makes it of very little significance (the index for Group XIV was, however, retained upon the computation sheets, as one of the components in the calculation of the combined index, described in the next section). For Group II there are shown—in addition to the group index itself—sub-group indexes for textile fabrics and materials, and articles from textile fabrics, respectively.

The corresponding graphic presentation occurs in Chart 1. (Here again, Group XIV is omitted.) The index for Group XIIB, Automobiles, is not shown, since its high percentage rate of growth over the years 1899–1914 makes very difficult its presentation on the same scale as the other curves.

Chart 1 inaugurates a device of presentation which is followed for the first five charts of this book: in each chart, the several curves are drawn with uniform logarithmic vertical scale, but this scale is shifted vertically from curve to curve, in order to separate the lines and thus facilitate graphical comparison of their form of fluctuation. Readers who are interested in the *numerical values* of the series shown in these charts should consult the corresponding tables.

It will be observed that Table 4 and Chart 1 also present indexes for certain groups not yet considered—IV, VI, VIII. The derivation of these indexes and that of the final index for total manufacture—top curve of the chart—will be described in the next chapter.

Derivation of the Preliminary Continuous Annual Index

We come next to describe the final step in the series of computations now under consideration. This final step consisted in taking annual weighted arithmetic averages of the indexes—which, it will be remembered, were on the base 1899—for the nine major groups previously listed (I, II, III, VII, X, XI, XIIA, XIIB, XIV), the weights being those earlier derived on the value-added basis and shown in Column 5 of Table 3 (cf. the preceding chapter). We

TABLE 4

GROUP INDEXES OF MANUFACTURING PRODUCTION: BY YEARS, 1860-1914*

(*Base: 1899*)

Research workers making use of the group indexes here presented should bear in mind that for the most part these indexes are based upon sample data and indirect representation. Such workers are urged, before drawing conclusions from the indexes or employing them in further computations, to examine carefully into the origin of the basic material (cf. Chapter I and Appendix A) and the methods of construction (Chapters II and III).

Year	I Food and kindred products	II Textiles and their products			III Iron and steel and their products	IV Lumber and its remanufactures	VI Paper and printing
		Group index	Textile fabrics and materials	Articles from textile fabrics			
1860	32	22	19	26	8	..	..
1861	34	22	19	26	6	..	..
1862	32	18	15	20	5	..	..
1863	32	21	18	24	7	..	..
1864	32	23	20	27	8	..	..
1865	33	22	18	26	6	..	..
1866	34	31	26	36	9	..	..
1867	36	31	26	35	10	..	..
1868	38	31	27	35	11	37	18
1869	39	33	29	38	13	..	..
1870	40	34	30	39	13	..	..
1871	42	39	34	44	13	..	..
1872	42	46	40	52	19	..	..
1873	44	41	36	46	18	..	..
1874	46	39	34	44	17	..	..
1875	47	40	35	44	13	..	..

1876............	47	41	38	45	11	:	:
1877............	49	42	39	46	14	:	:
1878............	51	45	42	49	16	:	:
1879............	53	46	43	49	22	52	21
1880............	56	56	52	60	26	:	:
1881............	57	56	52	61	32	:	:
1882............	61	59	54	64	34	:	:
1883............	63	65	60	71	34	:	:
1884............	66	64	59	69	30	:	:
1885............	68	62	59	66	32	:	:
1886............	69	74	70	79	44	:	:
1887............	71	72	68	76	47	:	:
1888............	72	74	70	79	49	:	:
1889............	74	76	72	82	57	78	51
1890............	76	78	71	86	64	:	:
1891............	82	83	79	88	63	:	:
1892............	86	88	84	94	69	:	:
1893............	86	84	78	90	52	:	:
1894............	88	77	75	79	50	:	:
1895............	88	97	91	103	73	:	:
1896............	90	82	74	91	63	:	:
1897............	92	93	87	100	68	:	:
1898............	94	95	94	98	87	:	:
1899............	100	100	100	100	100	100	100
1900............	102	99	97	100	93	:	:

For footnote, see end of table.

TABLE 4 (*Continued*)

Year	I Food and kindred products	II Textiles and their products Group index	II Textile fabrics and materials	II Articles from textile fabrics	III Iron and steel and their products	IV Lumber and its remanufactures	VI Paper and printing
1901.	108	97	97	97	117	. .	. .
1902.	110	111	112	110	137	. .	. .
1903.	112	114	113	114	134	. .	. .
1904.	111	111	112	110	123	122	142
1905.	109	124	126	122	169	124	. .
1906.	116	126	127	125	184	131	. .
1907.	118	130	129	131	194	130	. .
1908.	117	117	118	117	120	119	. .
1909.	121	142	144	141	193	126	196
1910.	119	137	138	136	202	126	. .
1911.	123	123	126	121	174	121	. .
1912.	128	141	145	136	215	127	. .
1913.	131	143	148	138	226	124	. .
1914.	136	146	149	144	179	115	254

Year	VII Liquors and beverages	VIII Chemicals and allied products	X Metals and metal products, other than iron and steel	XI Tobacco Manufactures	XII Vehicles for land transportation	
					Steam railroad cars	Automobiles
1860.	..	..	7	..	..	..
1861.	..	..	6	..	..	..
1862.	..	..	7	..	..	..
1863.	..	..	8	..	..	..
1864.	..	..	7	..	..	..
1865.	..	..	5	..	..	..
1866.	..	..	9	..	..	..
1867.	..	..	9	..	..	..
1868.	..	..	10	..	..	..
1869.	..	12	11	..	..	..
1870.	21	..	12	25	..	..
1871.	23	..	12	28	3	..
1872.	26	..	15	31	10	..
1873.	28	..	17	34	6	..
1874.	26	..	15	35	6	..
1875.	27	..	15	35	8	..
1876.	27	..	13	35	13	..
1877.	28	..	16	35	11	..
1878.	29	..	16	37	8	..
1879.	33	27	19	42	23	..
1880.	40	34	25	47	40	..

For footnote, see end of table.

TABLE 4 (*Continued*)

Year	VII Liquors and beverages	VIII Chemicals and allied products	X Metals and metal products, other than iron and steel	XI Tobacco manufactures	XII Vehicles for land transportation	
					Steam railroad cars	Automobiles
1881	45	34	25	54	65	..
1882	47	37	32	56	64	..
1883	48	38	33	61	51	..
1884	50	40	31	61	27	..
1885	50	42	31	64	16	..
1886	57	44	37	68	39	..
1887	63	48	43	72	68	..
1888	63	52	41	71	65	..
1889	68	58	52	77	65	..
1890	77	59	53	83	91	..
1891	80	69	60	89	84	..
1892	86	62	69	93	91	..
1893	90	61	50	87	58	..
1894	83	66	57	87	17	..
1895	89	78	76	88	32	..
1896	87	76	65	87	42	..
1897	89	80	76	92	36	..
1898	92	91	79	94	80	..
1899	100	100	100	100	100	100
1900	100	106	96	108	99	126

1901............	110	113	104	115	119	177
1902............	117	130	138	120	137	228
1903............	124	139	131	128	130	284
1904............	120	148	129	127	62	577
1905............	134	164	149	130	142	632
1906............	144	163	169	140	199	860
1907............	158	190	138	143	248	1,112
1908............	134	175	132	136	64	1,642
1909............	148	200	175	143	87	3,220
1910............	159	215	182	151	162	4,726
1911............	156	226	178	155	74	5,310
1912............	165	247	200	162	117	9,556
1913............	169	250	202	174	161	12,260
1914............	156	249	187	172	100	14,500

* The *1859* indexes for Groups IV, VI, and VIII are 23, 6, and 4, respectively (with reference to the interpolations or extrapolations involved in the estimation of the 1859 index for Group VIII, see Appendix E, Part One).

thus obtained our preliminary continuous index of manufacturing production, by years, 1860–1914.

The index for Group XIIB, Automobiles, was computed for the period 1899–1914 only; for years prior to 1899 this index, therefore, did not appear in the weighted-average computation of the combined index. This is *not* regarded as a "discontinuity," however, since the entrance of the automobile series into the index represented the emergence of a new industry.[11]

Data were not available for extending the index for Group XIIA, Steam-Railroad Cars, back of 1871; consequently, in the calculation of the combined index for 1870 and previous years, this group did not appear in the weighted-average computation. It seems improbable, however, that the absence of this group in the computation prior to 1871 could have had any important influence on the results, in view of the facts that the weight for the group was relatively low (cf. Table 3, Column 6), and that the industry composed only a comparatively small part of the nation's manufacturing effort in 1871.

We may say, then, that the absence of Group XIIB, Automobiles, from the computation sheets for the combined index prior to 1899 does not even theoretically constitute a "discontinuity"; and the absence of Group XIIA, Steam-Railroad Cars, prior to 1871 cannot have given rise to any perceptible break in the combined index. The two groups, XIIB and XIIA, then, we may safely dismiss from further consideration in the present connection.

We turn now to a somewhat different point. As is set forth in a previous footnote of this chapter, in the computation of the preliminary combined index we were obliged to make some interpola-

---

[11] The selection of 1899 as the initial year for inclusion of Automobiles in the computation of the combined index was largely a matter of statistical convenience. The year 1899 is the base period for our index: estimated annual totals for automobile production could be obtained for four previous years, 1895–98, but the production of automobiles during this interval was so unimportant a part of the national product that the inclusion of the series would have had no perceptible effect on the combined index for manufacture; in fact, it was not until some years after the turn of the century that automobile production began to have any significant influence upon the combined index.

tions and extrapolations (mainly in the earlier years of our time period of analysis) to fill certain gaps which appeared in the array of original items for constituent series (cf. again Table 1). Attention is expressly directed to the consideration that these interpolations and extrapolations were developed solely for the purposes of index-number calculation; they were not, in any given case, put forth as necessarily being approximations to the unknown missing items of the series itself. This distinction is worth stressing: as is well known, very often an interpolated or extrapolated figure—even when decidedly untrustworthy as an estimate of the missing value itself—may be quite adequate for the purposes of the general computation process of which the interpolation or extrapolation is a part.

What can we say as to the probable effects of our interpolations and extrapolations upon the indexes whose computation has been described in the present chapter? This question is considered at length in Appendix E, Part One, to which the reader is referred for details.

So far as the preliminary combined annual index is concerned, the conclusions of Appendix E, reached after an extended analysis, may be summarized as follows. For the period in which our major interest lies, *1866–1914,* we may feel confident that our interpolations and extrapolations could not have produced any appreciable alteration in the contour of short-run movement for the preliminary combined annual index; and we may further feel confident that any error of long-run drift which may have accumulated through the gap-filling operations could hardly have had any appreciable effect upon this index. For the period *1860–65,* in which our interest is definitely secondary and incidental, it is quite possible that through the various interpolations and extrapolations some errors in year-to-year movement may have been introduced, but it does not seem likely that such errors could have produced any very noteworthy alteration in the picture of short-run fluctuation presented by the preliminary combined annual index; it is further quite possible that this index has through the gap-filling operations suffered some deflection in long-run drift, but it does not seem likely that such deflection can be very significant.

All in all, we conclude that, so far as continuity of constituent series is concerned, we may properly apply the adjective "continuous" to our preliminary combined annual index—with only very slight reservations, certainly, for the period of our major interest, 1866–1914; and with somewhat greater, but still only moderate, reservations for the period of our secondary and incidental interest, 1860–65.[12]

In this chapter we have described the development of a preliminary continuous annual index of manufacturing production over the years 1860–1914. We shall next turn, in Chapter IV, to consideration of a further step: the broadening of the coverage of the index by bringing in certain important production series which are available only discontinuously.

[12] As no doubt the attentive reader has already noted, the present discussion of "continuity" is definitely limited in scope: the only issue here considered is that relating to the error of interpolation and extrapolation, which we define as the difference between (i) the index as we have actually computed it with interpolations and extrapolations for missing items, and (ii) the index as it would have been if the missing statistical items *were known* and *had been used* in the computation. Now, this writer fully recognizes that numerous elements exist which affect the significance and trustworthiness of indexes of manufacturing production, over and above the matter of completeness of the basic statistical items for constituent individual series; and, indeed, a discussion of some of these other elements is presented in the next chapter.

CHAPTER IV

MANUFACTURE: THE FINAL INDEX

As is indicated in the concluding paragraph of Chapter III, we turn in Chapter IV to the description of the operations involved in the task of broadening the basic data for the combined manufacture index by bringing in certain supplementary series which were available only discontinuously—mainly census-year series.

The "Post Method"

In utilizing these census-year series, we had resort to a procedure which we have designated as the "post method"—a procedure often quite helpful in instances where the more frequent data (say, annual) lack something in comprehensiveness and a more satisfactory coverage can be attained by bringing in, as supplementary, certain less frequent data (say, census-year).

If we fix our attention upon the case where there are available annual data with limited coverage and additional data on a census-year basis—the case pertinent to our present discussion—we may outline the procedure as follows: (1) we construct the census-year index, utilizing all available data (including, quite possibly, the census-year items of the *annual* series) to obtain as broad a coverage as possible; (2) we construct the annual index with its more limited coverage; (3) we consider the several items of the more comprehensive census-year index as constituting a series of stronger and more substantial "posts," so to speak, to which the frailer series of less comprehensive annual indexes is attached by a process of adjustment. This last step involves estimation between each pair of successive census-year indexes. Such estimation is based essentially upon the year-to-year movements shown, over the inter-censal interval, by the annual index—the movements being measured statistically by the link relatives of the annual index. However, it is almost always necessary to make an adjustment in these link relatives before using them for purposes of the estimation, such adjustment being occasioned by difference in the average annual rate of growth over the inter-censal interval as between the census-year index and the annual index. The detailed procedure is illustrated by Table 5.[1]

This method is quite often advantageous, in that the final index is more broadly representative of the entity under measurement. In view of the limitations of coverage in our fundamental data, the employment of the "post method" seemed clearly desirable for the task at hand—the development of the final combined index for manufacture.[2]

The method is not without its defects, particularly if the average cyclical amplitude of the industries represented in the census-year index differs essentially from that of the industries represented in the annual index. Suggestion has sometimes been made that a supplementary correction be applied to the index, as compensation for the difference in amplitude. This, in general, raises the question as to what principle should be followed in making such supplementary correction. So far as our index of manufacturing production for the years 1860–1914 is concerned, the available evidence —including the behavior of the several group indexes in later years —suggests that in fact there were not, over our period of analysis, any great differences between the average cyclical amplitudes of the industries embraced by our census-year and annual indexes, respectively.

In the work on page 49, the census-year index and annual index (Columns 2 and 3, respectively) are assumed figures, and are taken as given data for the purpose of illustrating the method. The link relatives of annual index (Column 4) are year-to-year ratios of change, expressed

---

[1] The "post method"—as will be obvious to the mathematical reader—can be explained in a variety of ways, all algebraically equivalent; e.g., we may use the link relatives of the annual index as they stand (thus letting the discrepancy accumulate, over the inter-censal interval, in the chain index developed by successive multiplication of the link relatives), and then apply a gradual "sliding-scale" adjustment to the chain index itself (cf. this variation with the procedure of Table 5).

So far as this writer is aware, the method was first used in connection with production indexes by Dr. Edmund E. Day in 1920.

[2] This is not to be taken to imply a universal rule that the "post method" would be the better *in all cases*. In particular instances, it might turn out that—all things considered—the census data were inferior to the annual data.

TABLE 5

THE "POST METHOD": ILLUSTRATIVE CASE

Assumed Data

Year (1)	Census-year index (2)	Annual index (3)	Link relative of annual index (4)	Adjustment for link relative of annual index (5)	Adjusted link relative of annual index (6)	Final index (7)
I..........	100.0	100.0	..	..	..	100.0
II..........	..	95.9	95.9	Divide by 1.005	95.4	95.4
III..........	..	117.4	122.4	Divide by 1.005	121.8	116.2
IV..........	..	128.8	109.7	Divide by 1.005	109.2	126.9
V..........	..	120.7	93.7	Divide by 1.005	93.2	118.3
VI..........	127.1	130.3	108.0	Divide by 1.005	107.4	127.1
VII..........	..	118.3	90.8	Divide by 0.993	91.4	116.2
VIII..........	..	156.2	132.0	Divide by 0.993	133.0	154.5
IX..........	..	142.5	91.2	Divide by 0.993	91.9	141.9
X..........	..	134.8	94.6	Divide by 0.993	95.3	135.2
XI..........	150.2	148.7	110.3	Divide by 0.993	111.1	150.2

This table is continued on p. 51

as percentages, for that index—given in each case (according to the usual convention) the date of the second of the two years involved.

Explanation of the adjustment over the years I-VI. The average annual ratio of change over the five-year interval from Year I to Year VI for the census-year index is $\sqrt[5]{\dfrac{127.1}{100.0}} = \sqrt[5]{1.271} = 1.0491$; the corresponding ratio for the annual index is $\sqrt[5]{\dfrac{130.3}{100.0}} = \sqrt[5]{1.303} = 1.0544$.

Comparison of these two ratios indicates that, over the inter-censal interval from Year I to Year VI, the average annual ratio of change for the annual index is somewhat higher than that for the census-year index —the proportion is $\dfrac{1.0544}{1.0491} = 1.005$. We accordingly set up, in each of the years from II to VI, an adjustment statement (Column 5) reading "divide by 1.005." We next adjust each link relative of annual index (Column 4), dividing by 1.005, to obtain the corresponding adjusted link relative (Column 6). Then we secure the final index by taking the census-year index for Year I—100.0—as starting point, and multiplying successively by the adjusted link relatives shown in Column 6 to obtain the continuous chain index shown in Column 7. This final index "matches up," in the terminal year VI, with the census-year index in Column 2—as of course it must, as a matter of mathematical necessity. We have thus in our final index obtained interpolated figures for inter-censal years which present the general form of short-run fluctuation exhibited by the annual index, and at the same time preserve the census-year movement between the terminal years I and VI.

Explanation of the adjustment over the years VI–XI. The average annual ratio of change over the five-year interval from Year VI to Year XI for the census-year index is $\sqrt[5]{\dfrac{150.2}{127.1}} = \sqrt[5]{1.182} = 1.0339$; the corresponding ratio for the annual index is $\sqrt[5]{\dfrac{148.7}{130.3}} = \sqrt[5]{1.141} = 1.0268$. Comparison of these two ratios indicates that over the inter-censal interval from Year VI to Year XI, the average annual ratio of change for the annual index is somewhat *lower* than that for the census-year index—the proportion is $\dfrac{1.0268}{1.0339} = 0.993$. We accordingly set up, in each of the years from VII to XI, an adjustment statement (Column 5) reading "divide by 0.993." The remainder of the procedure is analogous to that for the earlier interval, described just above.

(Cf. also the logarithmic computation on the next page.)

TABLE 5 (*Continued*)

Logarithmic Work

Year (1a)	Logarithm of census-year index (2a)	Logarithm of annual index (3a)	Logarithm of link relative of annual index (= first difference of Column 2a) (4a)	Adjustment for link relative of annual index (5a)	Logarithm of adjusted link relative of annual index (6a)	Logarithm of final index (= cumulation of Column 6a) (7a)
I..........	0.00000	0.00000	..	..	..	0.00000
II..........	..	9.98182–10	9.98182–10	Subt. 0.00216	9.97966–10	9.97966–10
III..........	..	0.06967	0.08785	Subt. 0.00216	0.08569	0.06535
IV..........	..	0.10992	0.04025	Subt. 0.00216	0.03809	0.10344
V..........	..	0.08171	9.97179–10	Subt. 0.00216	9.96963–10	0.07307
VI..........	0.10415	0.11494	0.03323	Subt. 0.00215	0.03108	0.10415
VII..........	..	0.07298	9.95804–10	Subt. 9.99697–10	9.96107–10	0.06522
VIII..........	..	0.19368	0.12070	Subt. 9.99697–10	0.12373	0.18895
IX..........	..	0.15381	9.96013–10	Subt. 9.99697–10	9.96316–10	0.15211
X..........	..	0.12969	9.97588–10	Subt. 9.99697–10	9.97891–10	0.13102
XI..........	0.17667	0.17231	0.04262	Subt. 9.99697–10	0.04565	0.17667

DERIVATION OF CENSUS-YEAR INDEXES FOR THREE ADDITIONAL
MAJOR GROUPS

The first step in the computations to be described in the present
chapter was the derivation of a census-year index of manufacturing production for those census years which were pertinent to our
general period of analysis. These years occurred at decennial
intervals up to 1899, quinquennially thereafter: 1859, 1869, 1879,
1889, 1899, 1904, 1909, 1914.

A word of comment may be inserted regarding the year 1859.
This year was included in the computation scheme not, so to speak,
for its own sake (we make no attempt to present a combined manufacture index for 1859), but merely as a means to an end: we
planned to use 1859 data only for the purposes of setting up a
"post" to be employed in adjusting the 1860–68 annual indexes to
the census-year basis.

We began by constructing census-year indexes for the following
three major groups of the Census classification:

    IV. Lumber and Its Remanufactures.
    VI. Paper and Printing.
  VIII. Chemicals and Allied Products.

With the variation that these three indexes were derived for
census years only, the methods closely paralleled those for the nine
Census groups, discussed at length in the preceding chapter. Only
a brief statement of procedure, therefore, is required here. As
before, the general method of computation involved the weighted
arithmetic mean of relatives to the base 1899, combined with 1899
weights developed so far as possible on the value-added basis.
And, as before, the "hierarchy principle" was followed: that is, the
progress was by successive stages, starting with relatives for the
individual production series, next going on to sub-group indexes,
and then arriving at production indexes for each of the major
groups. (In lieu of a detailed outline of procedure here, reference

may be made to the extended statement of the preceding chapter and to the schematic arrangement of Table 3.)[3]

The production indexes for the three groups now under consideration—Group IV, Lumber and Its Remanufactures; Group VI, Paper and Printing; and Group VIII, Chemicals and Allied Products—are presented in Table 4. They are also shown graphically on Chart 1.[4]

DERIVATION OF THE COMBINED CENSUS-YEAR INDEX

Our next step was the derivation of a combined census-year index with the broadest coverage which seemed feasible for our period of analysis, taken as a whole: that is, this combined index embraced twelve groups in all—the nine groups which had been included in the preliminary combined annual index, as described in the preceding chapter (Groups I, II, III, VII, X, XI, XIIA, XIIB, XIV) together with the three groups considered just above (Groups IV, VI, VIII).

The combined census-year index was computed for the years previously listed—1859, 1869, 1879, 1889, 1899, 1904, 1909, 1914. The general procedure was consistent with that earlier employed in obtaining the preliminary annual index based on nine groups, as described in the preceding chapter. The combined census-year index was calculated, for each census year, as a weighted arithmetic mean of its constituent indexes (such constituent indexes being on the base 1899). On the formal computation sheets, the preliminary index for nine groups was taken as one constituent —that is to say, the *census-year items* of this index were thus taken—and the census-year indexes for Groups IV, VI, and

---

[3] Here, as before, some interpolations and extrapolations had to be made to fill certain gaps in the tabulation of original items for constituent series. These gap-filling operations (all appearing in Group VIII and affecting only the earlier years of our period of analysis) are described in detail in Appendix E, Part One. We postpone to a later page of this chapter consideration of the probable effects of these interpolations and extrapolations upon the continuity of our computed indexes.

[4] It will be noted that, in addition to the census-year indexes, *annual* intercensal indexes are shown for Groups IV and VIII over part of the period. The derivation of these annual indexes will be described in a later section of this chapter.

VIII, respectively (derived as set forth just above) were taken as the remaining constituents.

TABLE 6

INDEX OF PRODUCTION FOR MANUFACTURE:
BY YEARS, 1860–1914

(*Base: 1899*)

Year	Index	Year	Index	Year	Index
1860............	16	1879............	36	1897............	80
		1880............	42	1898............	91
1861............	16			1899............	100
1862............	15	1881............	46	1900............	100
1863............	17	1882............	49		
1864............	18	1883............	50	1901............	111
1865............	17	1884............	47	1902............	127
		1885............	47	1903............	126
1866............	21			1904............	121
1867............	22	1886............	57	1905............	140
1868............	23	1887............	60		
1869............	25	1888............	62	1906............	152
1870............	25	1889............	66	1907............	156
		1890............	71	1908............	127
1871............	26			1909............	166
1872............	31	1891............	73	1910............	172
1873............	30	1892............	79		
1874............	29	1893............	70	1911............	162
1875............	28	1894............	68	1912............	194
		1895............	81	1913............	203
1876............	28			1914............	192
1877............	30	1896............	74		
1878............	32				

The weights for the calculation of the combined census-year index were those earlier derived on the value-added basis and shown in Table 3 of Chapter II: the preliminary index for the nine groups was given the aggregate weight of the groups included in its calculation; Groups IV, VI, and VIII were given the weights respectively assigned them (cf. Column 5 of Table 3).[5]

[5] In the computation of the census-year index for 1859, it was necessary to extrapolate an 1859 item for the preliminary combined annual index, which was available only beginning with 1860. This 1859 extrapolation and its probable effects are discussed at length in Appendix E, Part One.

As is indicated in the text on an earlier page of this chapter, we must emphasize that this extrapolation was made *only for the purpose of deriving the 1859 "post"* *for the computation of the final combined annual index;* we do not, at any stage of our procedure, put forward an 1859 manufacturing production index, as such.

The items of the combined census-year index may be read off from Table 6. The derivation of the *annual* inter-censal items shown in Table 6 will be explained in the next section of this chapter.

DERIVATION OF INDEXES FOR INTER-CENSAL YEARS

When the computation of the combined census-year index—as described in the preceding section—had been concluded, we turned next to the derivation of an index for inter-censal years. The inter-censal items for the combined index were obtained by the "post method," outlined and illustrated in the earlier pages of this chapter. The items of the census-year index were taken as the "posts" for 1859, 1869, 1879, 1889, 1899, 1904, 1909, and 1914. Annual inter-censal items were estimated on the basis of the movements of annual indexes (for detailed explication of the technique, see Table 5 and the discussion accompanying it).

Within the intervals 1859–69 and 1869–79, the inter-censal estimates were in each case based upon the preliminary annual index for nine groups, described in the preceding chapter. After 1879, however, the coverage of the inter-censal estimates was broadened somewhat. The index for Group VIII, Chemicals and Allied Products, could be developed on an annual basis over the period 1879–1914; and the index for Group IV, Lumber and Its Remanufactures, over the period 1904–14. Accordingly, within the intervals 1879–89, 1889–99, and 1899–1904 the inter-censal estimates were in each case based upon an annual index for *ten* groups—the nine groups of the preliminary annual index, joined with Group VIII; and within the intervals 1904–09 and 1909–14 the inter-censal estimates were in each case based upon an annual index for *eleven* groups—the nine groups of the preliminary annual index, joined with Groups VIII and IV.

(The annual indexes for Group VIII, 1879–1914, and Group IV, 1904–14, were computed by the methods previously employed for the other group indexes, as described in the preceding chapter;[6]

---

[6] Certain technical details regarding Group VIII are presented in Appendix E, Part One.

these annual indexes are shown in Table 4 and on Chart 1. The annual indexes for ten groups, 1879–1904, and for eleven groups, 1904–14—referred to just above—were developed by procedures precisely analogous to the methods used in connection with the annual index for nine groups, as earlier set forth—cf. the pertinent parts of the preceding chapter, and also Table 3.)

Our final combined index of manufacturing production, by years, 1860–1914—the ultimate product of the chain of operations which has been described in Chapters I–III and up to this present point in Chapter IV—is given in Table 6. This index is shown graphically as the top curve of Chart 1 (cf. the preceding chapter), in conjunction with the group indexes, and is also shown as the second curve on Chart 2.[7]

At this point, we resume the discussions of pages 44–46, in Chapter III. In the course of the computations leading to the emergence of the final combined annual index we were obliged to make some interpolations and extrapolations (mainly in the earlier years of our time period of analysis) to fill certain gaps in the array of original items for constituent series. (Here, as before, it is stressed that these interpolations and extrapolations were developed solely for the purposes of index-number calculation; they were not, in any given case, put forth as necessarily being approximations to the values of the unknown missing items of the series itself.) And now we ask, in connection with the final combined annual index—as we previously asked in connection with the preliminary combined annual index—what are the probable effects of these interpolations and extrapolations? Here again, reference may be made to Appendix E, Part One, where this question is considered in detail.

The statement of the conclusions reached in Appendix E, with reference to the final combined annual index, can closely follow the pattern of the summary previously presented (on page 45, in Chapter III) with reference to the preliminary combined annual

---

[7] The thin dotted line, drawn through the manufacture index on Chart 2, will be discussed in the next section.

CHART 2

INDEXES OF PRODUCTION: BY YEARS, 1860–1914*

(*Base: 1899*)

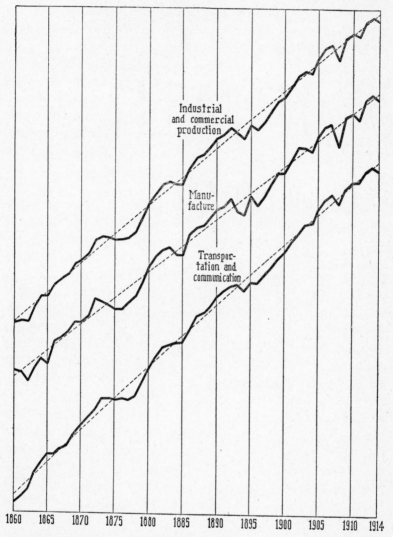

Industrial and commercial production

Manu-facture

Transportation and communication

1860 1865 1870 1875 1880 1885 1890 1895 1900 1905 1910 1914

* Logarithmic vertical scales. The secular trends of the series are indicated by dotted lines. The derivation of the indexes is described in Chapters I–IV (manufacture), Chapters V–VII (transportation and communication), and Chapter VIII (industrial and commercial production).

index. It is, however, necessary to be slightly more conservative in our language as respects the conclusions regarding "long-run drift."

With this necessity for modification of language in mind, we may summarize regarding the final combined annual index as follows. For the period in which our major interest lies, *1866–1914*, we may feel confident that our interpolations and extrapolations could not have produced any appreciable alteration in the contour of short-run movement for the final combined annual index; and we may further feel confident that any error of long-run drift which may have accumulated through the gap-filling operations could hardly have had any important effect upon this index. For the period *1860–65*, in which our interest is definitely secondary and incidental, it is quite possible that through the various interpolations and extrapolations, some errors in year-to-year movement may have been introduced, but it does not seem likely that such errors could have produced any very noteworthy alteration in the picture of short-run fluctuations presented by the final combined annual index; it is further quite possible that this index has through the gap-filling operations suffered some deflection in long-run drift, but it does not seem likely that such deflection can be anything more than moderate.

Bearing in mind all of the evidence which is presented in Appendix E, we may take the succinct conclusion stated in Chapter III regarding the preliminary combined annual index and, with appropriate variation of language, bring it forward here: so far as continuity of constituent series is concerned, we may properly think of our final combined annual index as essentially continuous —with only minor reservations for the period of our major interest, 1866–1914; and with somewhat greater, but still little more than moderate, reservations for the period of our secondary and incidental interest, 1860–65.[8]

[8] With respect to other elements affecting the significance and trustworthiness of indexes of manufacturing production, see again fn. 12, in Chapter III, and also the later section of this chapter entitled "Bias of the Production Index."

The Final Combined Index Adjusted for Secular Trend

In a previous study by the present writer, an extended investigation was made into the nature of the secular movements of certain production indexes over the interval extending from the Civil War to the outbreak of the first World War.[9] The production indexes included in this investigation were: a new index of manufacture, a new index of transportation and communication, a new index of industrial and commercial production, and a "check production index" based upon constituents which had been developed independently by other investigators. The general conclusion reached was that, in each case, the secular trend over our pre-war period (i.e., up to 1914) could be represented with reasonably close approach to precision by a logarithmic parabola.

The logarithmic parabola ($log\ y = a + bt + ct^2$) is a curve exhibiting constancy in rate of relative acceleration, or of retardation, as the case may be. Over our period of analysis, most production indexes exhibit retardation in ratio of growth.[10] (For a nontechnical discussion of the logarithmic parabola, accompanied by a numerical example, see the writer's *Economic Fluctuations*, pages 144–146.)

For the particular case at hand—the index of manufacturing production—the situation was simplified by the fact that the retardation constant in the mathematical equation came out almost precisely zero, and therefore could be neglected. The logarithmic

---

[9] See Edwin Frickey, *Economic Fluctuations in the United States* (Cambridge, Mass.: Harvard University Press, 1942), especially chaps. XIII and XIV. The conclusions regarding these secular movements were reached through an elaborate analysis; in the final steps of this analysis, two independent methods were used, which confirmed one another.

[10] In this connection, however, the reader should carefully bear in mind the distinction between statistical properties of an *index number* and those of the *corresponding economic entity*. Because of the deficiencies of available data, as well as unavoidable logical limitations of methodology, these two sets of properties may diverge. Cf. an article by the present writer, previously referred to: Edwin Frickey, "Some Aspects of the Problem of Measuring Historical Changes in the Physical Volume of Production," in the volume entitled *Exploration in Economics: Notes and Essays Contributed in Honor of F. W. Taussig* (New York and London: McGraw-Hill Book Co., Inc., 1936), pp. 477–486; also see the next section of this chapter.

parabola, then, here degenerated into a compound-interest curve
—a curve which exhibits a constant relative rate of growth, and
appears as a straight line when plotted with logarithmic vertical
scale.

TABLE 7

INDEX OF PRODUCTION FOR MANUFACTURE, ADJUSTED FOR SECULAR TREND:
BY YEARS, 1860–1914

(Unit: one per cent)

Year	Adjusted Index	Year	Adjusted Index	Year	Adjusted Index
1860	106	1879	95	1897	88
		1880	106	1898	95
1861	99			1899	99
1862	87	1881	110	1900	95
1863	94	1882	111		
1864	98	1883	109	1901	100
1865	88	1884	97	1902	109
		1885	92	1903	103
1866	104			1904	94
1867	102	1886	106	1905	104
1868	102	1887	107		
1869	107	1888	104	1906	108
1870	101	1889	106	1907	106
		1890	110	1908	82
1871	102			1909	102
1872	114	1891	107	1910	101
1873	106	1892	110		
1874	98	1893	93	1911	90
1875	90	1894	86	1912	103
		1895	98	1913	102
1876	86			1914	93
1877	87	1896	85		
1878	88				

The compound-interest curve fitted to our final combined index
of manufacturing production is represented by the dotted line
drawn through the graph of the index number itself (cf. Chart 2);
this trend line indicates an average annual rate of increase of 4.95
per cent. The "index of production for manufacture, adjusted for
secular trend"—obtained by dividing the successive annual items
of the actual index-number series through by the corresponding
trend values ("ordinates of trend")—is presented in Table 7 and
shown as the second curve on Chart 3.

CHART 3

INDEXES OF PRODUCTION, ADJUSTED FOR SECULAR TREND:
BY YEARS, 1860–1914*

(*Unit: one per cent*)

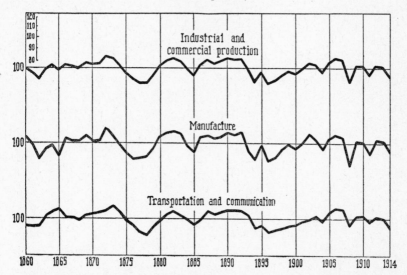

* Logarithmic vertical scales. The derivation of these indexes adjusted for secular trend is described in Chapter IV (manufacture), Chapter VII (transportation and communication), and Chapter VIII (industrial and commercial production).

BIAS OF THE MANUFACTURE INDEX

We may now consider the possible bias of our new manufacture index.

So far as *technical* (type and weight) bias is concerned, we have (as is set forth in Chapter II) made every effort to avoid such bias —both in the selection of formula, weighting period, and base period and in the derivation of the actual weighting data. And, as earlier indicated, the writer is confident that a high degree of success has been attained in this effort.

There are, however, other sources of bias which must be given consideration. We must take into account the influence of the *defects and limitations of actual production data*. It is generally agreed among research workers in this field that the preponderant

influence of these defects and limitations upon indexes of manufacturing production is clearly in the direction of understatement
of average rate of growth—i.e., a downward growth bias.[11]

Still another possible source of growth bias requires mention.
We here allude to the considerations earlier developed by the
present writer in a volume of notes and essays dedicated to F. W.
Taussig.[12] This paper was written with reference to the concept
the index of total production. The principal point of the paper was
that, even if technical (type and weight) bias is avoided, and the
component statistical series represent complete and perfect measurements, the ordinary procedure for computing an index of total
production (i.e., by averaging constituent sub-indexes) is nevertheless open to a secular growth bias. It was argued that, for a
closed economy and an indefinitely long period, it is pertinent to
think in terms only of the size of the stream of final consumable
goods and services.[13] It was further indicated that in the application of this principle to concrete cases, there are important qualifications relating to (a) the fact that the actual computation interval
for an index—even if as long as forty or fifty years—cannot be
regarded as an "indefinitely long period," and (b) the fact that
exports and imports of commodities (in all stages of production—
raw materials, partly finished goods, finished goods) are in actual
life constantly taking place.

For the case at hand in this chapter, it becomes pertinent to ask
how we shall adapt the above argument, relating to *an index of*
total production, to the evaluation of *an index of manufacturing*

[11] At this point, reference may be made to the convenient summary by Professor
Arthur F. Burns in his *Production Trends in the United States since 1870* (New
York: National Bureau of Economic Research, Inc., 1934), pp. 258–259. Professor
Burns' summary is, to be sure, presented with respect to the index of total pro-
duction, but all of the points listed—except the first on p. 258—are applicable also
to the index of manufacture.

[12] Edwin Frickey, "Some Aspects of the Problem of Measuring Historical
Changes in the Physical Volume of Production," in the volume entitled *Explora-*
tions in Economics: Notes and Essays Contributed in Honor of F. W. Taussig (New
York and London: McGraw-Hill Book Co., Inc., 1936), pp. 477–486.

[13] For any actual historical period, of course, we must (as is set forth in the
above-named Taussig-volume paper, p. 484) take account of the lag between the
formation of capital and its exhaustion in the course of operation—that is, we must
take account of net capital formation.

production. Briefly, instead of saying "the size of the stream of final consumable goods and services," we should have to say "the size of the stream of final end-products of the manufacturing industry"; and we should have to construe "exports and imports," not in the usual literal sense, but as embracing, in addition to dealings with foreign countries, transactions with all other domestic industries than manufacture.

However, it is clear that even as a rough approximation the application of the "Taussig-volume principle," adapted as above suggested to the case at hand, would represent a task of tremendous difficulty, if not indeed an impossibility. The major obstacle, of course, would lie in the great paucity of data on inputs. It hardly seems feasible, then, to make any concrete assessment of growth bias related to the "Taussig-volume principle."

The writer would hazard the guess that on balance our new index of manufacturing production has a downward growth bias, and that the true average annual rate of growth over our period of analysis was appreciably in excess of our computed figure of 4.95 per cent, set forth above.[14]

INDEXES FOR DURABLE AND NON-DURABLE COMMODITIES

Investigators in the field of economic fluctuations—business cycles and secular trends—may find of some interest the pair of indexes presented in Table 8 and Chart 4—the annual indexes of manufacturing production for durable and non-durable commodities, respectively, 1860–1914.

These indexes were obtained by methods altogether analogous to those employed for the combined index of manufacture, as de-

---

[14] With respect to *short-run* bias, a number of considerations can be listed. The most important of these are the use of "consumption-of-materials" series, which create a time lag and sometimes fail to take proper account of foreign trade and year-end stocks; and the necessarily inadequate representation of highly fabricated goods, which have a much smaller amplitude of cyclical fluctuation than the basic materials. In addition, the index cannot accurately represent short-run fluctuations in the large segment of manufacturing activity for which no data are available. Also, the adjustment of the various series to a uniform calendar-year basis can be accomplished only imperfectly. However, a quantitative evaluation of such short-run bias is hardly feasible.

TABLE 8

INDEXES OF PRODUCTION FOR MANUFACTURE—DURABLE AND NON-DURABLE COMMODITIES: BY YEARS, 1860–1914

(Base: 1899)

Year	Durable	Non-durable	Year	Durable	Non-durable
1860............	13	18			
1861............	10	19	1891............	70	77
1862............	10	17	1892............	77	80
1863............	12	18	1893............	56	78
1864............	13	19	1894............	51	77
1865............	10	19	1895............	73	88
1866............	15	24	1896............	63	82
1867............	16	24	1897............	68	89
1868............	17	25	1898............	86	93
1869............	21	27	1899............	100	100
1870............	20	28	1900............	94	102
1871............	19	31	1901............	115	106
1872............	27	34	1902............	138	118
1873............	26	33	1903............	135	123
1874............	24	33	1904............	121	123
1875............	19	33	1905............	152	134
1876............	18	34	1906............	169	138
1877............	21	35	1907............	174	148
1878............	23	37	1908............	123	137
1879............	31	39	1909............	174	157
1880............	38	46	1910............	190	160
1881............	46	47	1911............	171	158
1882............	49	50	1912............	214	174
1883............	46	54	1913............	232	179
1884............	38	54	1914............	208	181
1885............	37	55			
1886............	51	61			
1887............	57	62			
1888............	56	65			
1889............	63	68			
1890............	71	71			

CHART 4

INDEXES OF PRODUCTION FOR MANUFACTURE—DURABLE AND NON-DURABLE
COMMODITIES: BY YEARS, 1860–1914*

(*Base: 1899*)

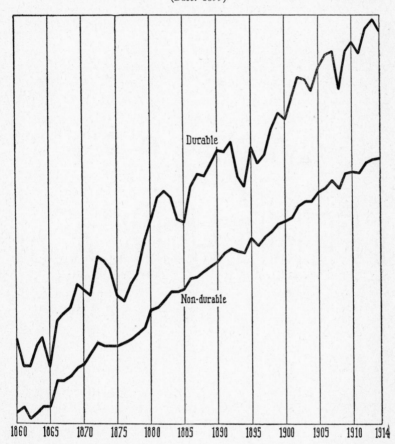

Durable

Non-durable

1860 1865 1870 1875 1880 1885 1890 1895 1900 1905 1910 1914

* Logarithmic vertical scales. The derivation of these indexes is described in the
latter part of Chapter IV.

scribed on preceding pages—including, in each case, the formation of a preliminary continuous annual index, and the application of the "post method" to bring into the computation the census-year data. The index for durable commodities is based upon Groups III, IV, VI, X, XIIA, and XIIB; the index for non-durable commodities, upon Groups I, II, VII, VIII, and XI.[15]

In studying the movements of the two new indexes, proper allowance must be made, of course, for the elements of bias discussed in the preceding section, and undue imputation of precision to the measurements must be avoided. However, the outstanding contrasts are unmistakable.

The first contrast to attract attention upon examination of Chart 4—which, it will be noted, is drawn with logarithmic vertical scale—is that between the *average annual rates of growth* of the indexes, as indicated by the general slopes of the two lines. The annual average rate of growth in the index for durable commodities is appreciably higher, being 5.9 per cent as opposed to 4.5 per cent in the index for non-durable.[16]

The second contrast notable in Chart 4 is that relating to the *amplitude of cyclical fluctuation* for the two curves. In general, the indexes (especially after the very early years, where the measurements are less trustworthy) concur in the main cyclical movements; but the intensity of cyclical variation is decidedly greater

[15] Some small anomalies of behavior appear here and there between (a) the two indexes of Table 8 considered jointly, and (b) the index of total manufacturing production shown in Table 6. These anomalies are probably in the main accounted for by details of computation—e.g., the fact that the implications of the application of the "post method" are not precisely the same in the two cases. The discrepancies are in no way important as regards the main conclusions; and to give too much attention to these small discrepancies would indeed impute to the various measurements an approach to precision which they do not possess, and—taking into account the characteristics of the available data—could not be expected to possess.

[16] The index for durables would be well fitted by a compound-interest curve, but some curvature (upon logarithmic vertical scale) would be required to obtain a proper fit for the non-durables—possibly a logarithmic parabola. [Cf. the present writer's *Economic Fluctuations in the United States* (Cambridge, Mass.: Harvard University Press, 1942), *passim*, especially chaps. VII, XIII–XV.] (Such a pair of trends as those just suggested could quite well be consistent mathematically with the compound-interest trend previously fitted to the index for total manufacture, inasmuch as the combined index may be thought of as essentially an *arithmetic*—not geometric—average of the durable and non-durable indexes.)

in the index for durable commodities. Even after making all reasonable allowance for imperfections of short-run measurements in the indexes, the contrast is striking.

In bringing to a close the discussion of our new indexes for manufacturing activity, certain general statements may perhaps properly be made. As was set forth in Chapter I, a great deal of care and effort was devoted to the derivation of the fundamental data for the individual production series. In spite of this, however, many defects and limitations still remain. Furthermore, difficult questions of theory appear (cf. the earlier references to the author's Taussig-volume article). In presenting our indexes for manufacture, there is, of course, no thought of suggesting that all problems have been solved, or that we have here arrived at statistical measurements which are from all points of view unimpeachable. As has been indicated, there are some theoretical difficulties which are logically unsurmountable, and there are some limitations of basic statistical material which are irremediable, even by the utmost ingenuity and effort. Nevertheless, it would appear that we may properly claim for our new indexes of manufacture some degree of merit, relative to that which lies within the realm of practically achievable possibility—especially as regards the qualities of continuity and comparability over time which were crucial with reference to the purposes of the investigation into the patterns of movement inherent in economic data, described in this writer's *Economic Fluctuations*.

CHAPTER V

TRANSPORTATION AND COMMUNICATION: THE STEAM-RAILROAD SERIES—(A) BASIC DATA

OUR INDEX of transportation and communication, like our index of manufacture, was originally set up as a part of a general study of economic fluctuations over the interval 1866–1914 carried out by the present writer and presented in a previous volume.[1] The transportation and communication index was extended back to 1860, though the index is less trustworthy for 1860–65 than for later years.

So far as is known to the present writer, no attempt has ever previously been made to construct an index of production over our period of study, 1860–1914, for this important group transportation and communication.[2] The advantages in having at hand, for the purposes of the earlier study of economic fluctuations just referred to, a production index pertaining to this highly significant branch of economic activity were so great that it seemed urgently desirable to undertake the task of constructing such an index even though this task could be foreseen to be most intricate and toilsome.

Because of the predominant position of steam railroads, we gave first attention to the development of series pertaining to steam-railroad transportation. Chapters V and VI are devoted to a discussion of the procedures by which these series were developed; in Chapter VII, we turn to consideration of the series other than steam-railroad, and the derivation of the final combined index of transportation and communication.

---

[1] Edwin Frickey, *Economic Fluctuations in the United States* (Cambridge, Mass.: Harvard University Press, 1942).

[2] Professor Walter W. Stewart, in his article, "An Index Number of Production," *American Economic Review*, XI (March 1921), 57–69, published an index for transportation, but this index began with 1890 and embraced railroad traffic only.

Before beginning specific discussion of the steam-railroad data, one technical detail may be noted. The figures which we obtained from our various basic sources pertained in general to *fiscal years*, and the dating of these fiscal years varied not only as among sources, but also among railroads and over time. This point is further discussed on later pages (cf., in Chapter VII, the section on "The Calendar-Year Adjustment").

THE GENERAL PLAN OF PROCEDURE

For the period beginning with 1890, we were able readily to secure basic data—on tonnage, ton-miles, passengers, passenger-miles—substantially complete as to coverage. For these years we made use of the series of *Poor's Manual of Railroads*[3] and of the United States Interstate Commerce Commission.[4] Beginning with 1890, the Poor's data are virtually complete as to coverage of all railroads of the United States; the Interstate Commerce Commission data, which start with 1890, are not fully inclusive in the earlier years.[5] Since the Interstate Commerce Commission's totals had become practically all-inclusive by the turn of the century, and 1899 was to be the base period of our index, it appeared that 1900 would constitute a convenient point for making a transition in our series. Accordingly, we based our annual series upon the Poor's totals, 1890–99, joined to the Interstate Commerce Commission

[3] Before 1895 the title is Henry V. Poor, *Manual of the Railroads of the United States* (New York: H. V. & H. W. Poor). After 1895, Henry V. Poor's name is omitted and the title is *Poor's Manual of the Railroads of the United States.* Throughout this book, we have followed the practice of the Library of Congress in using *Poor's Manual of Railroads* as a short title. Data for 1890–91 were taken from the *Manual* for 1895, pp. xiv, xvi; for 1892–1903 from the *Manual* for 1905, pp. ix, xi; for 1904–11, from the *Manual* for 1912, pp. cxli, cxliii.

The present writer wishes to express his appreciation of the very great kindness and courtesy shown by the Poor's Publishing Company in responding to inquiries—especially with regard to availability of basic data and source and nature of data.

[4] United States Interstate Commerce Commission, *Fortieth Annual Report on the Statistics of Railways in the United States,* Year Ended December 31, 1926 (Washington: Government Printing Office, 1928), p. ci. (Note, however, that the data over our period of analysis pertain to years ended June 30.)

[5] See *Poor's Manual of Railroads* for 1891, p. vii. Also see the Interstate Commerce Commission's *Statistics of Railways* for 1890, p. 14; for 1891, pp. 11–12; and for 1900, pp. 12–13: further, cf. the tabulations of "official" and "unofficial" mileage, as given in the successive issues of *Statistics of Railways,* 1890–1900.

totals, beginning with 1900.[6] However, we made certain experimental computations, carrying along the Poor's totals over the years 1900–11 (the Poor's series end with 1911), for purposes of comparison. For the overlapping interval, 1900–11, some discrepancies in detail of movement were discernible for the various series. It was found, however, that these discrepancies were in the main ascribable to differences in fiscal-year dating, as between the two sets of data (cf. the discussion of this latter point in Chapter VII).

For the period beginning with 1890, totals which were substantially all-inclusive were thus readily obtainable. The situation with respect to fundamental data before 1890, however, was decidedly difficult. We found that as one goes backward from that year, the proportionate coverage of the available statistical material becomes progressively less. Quite clearly, the only satisfactory solution lay in the construction of new basic series of totals, over the three decades prior to 1890, developed with special attention to homogeneity and representativeness of sampling.

Survey of Available Basic Data: 1866–90

In surveying the available basic data prior to 1890 we gave first attention to the period 1866–90. A definitive decision as to the list of railroads to be included in our "sample list," 1866–90, necessarily had to be postponed until after our examination of the available data for individual roads had been completed. A "working list" was, however, evolved from reports on transportation contained in the United States Censuses of 1880 and 1890, and from Dr. Arthur H. Cole's study of railroad earnings.[7] From the

[6] The 1913 tonnage figure given in the Interstate Commerce Commission's *Statistics of Railways* for 1926, p. ci, carries a notation "Class I and II railways," whereas the tonnage figures for the other years pertain to Class I, II, and III railways (*ibid.*, p. xcviii). Study of certain other figures for the various classes, in 1913 and adjacent years, suggests that Class I and II roads accounted for about 99 per cent of the traffic. Presumably, then, any error introduced by the lack of homogeneity in the tonnage figures is slight.

[7] United States Department of the Interior, Census Office, *Tenth Census of the United States,* 1880, vol. IV, *Transportation* (Washington: Government Printing Office, 1883); and United States Department of the Interior, Census Office, *Eleventh*

record of gross earnings for railroads in the United States as given in the 1880 Census, a list was set up comprising the names of all those roads whose gross earnings for *1880* constituted as much as 1 per cent of the 1880 total for the United States. To this list was added the names of all roads, not already included, whose gross earnings for *1890* as tabulated in the 1890 Census constituted as much as 1 per cent of the 1890 total for the United States. Finally, there were added the names of any roads, not already included, which had been used in Dr. Cole's study. The "working list" assembled in the manner just described furnished a starting point for transcription of basic data over the interval 1866–90.

The figures for the individual roads were mainly taken from the convenient summary tables of *Poor's Manual of Railroads*.[8] In general, six annual series were collected for each road: the four series relating to traffic volume, previously mentioned—tonnage, ton-miles, passengers, passenger-miles—together with gross earnings and mileage operated.

We next undertook the tedious task of searching through the various volumes of *Poor's Manual of Railroads*—supplemented by the Census records and the annual reports of the individual roads themselves. The work was rendered extremely intricate as well as laborious by the necessity for aiming at *actual,* as opposed to mere *formal,* homogeneity. The history of the roads—especially as to consolidations, acquisitions, extensions—had to be studied with care. Constant vigilance had to be exercised to avoid being led astray by the "surface appearance of things" in tabulations of figures. Methods of adjustment had to be worked out for application to cases of perplexing breaks of material. The task was thus not merely to assemble arrays of items pertaining to corporations of particular name, but rather to assure real continuity with respect to certain *economic entities.*[9]

Census of the United States, 1890, vol. XIV, *Transportation,* part 1, *Transportation by Land* (Washington: Government Printing Office, 1895).

Arthur H. Cole, "A Monthly Index of Railroad Earnings, 1866–1914," *Review of Economic Statistics,* XVIII (February 1936), 31–41.

[8] See fn. 3, just above.

[9] In the carrying out of this work, the author was extremely fortunate in having the assistance of Miss Ruth Crandall. Without her initiative, resourcefulness, and thoroughness, this study could never have been made.

Beginning with 1890 and working backward to 1866, data for a given road were compiled, note being taken of the inclusion of any roads previously having a separate history. In such cases, data for the subsidiary roads were transcribed for the years of their independent existence and added to those of the parent road. In many instances, resort was required to detailed examination of the annual reports of the road—either to fill in missing items or to unravel the figures of the various subordinate lines of a system.

In the course of the compilation of basic data, certain roads were dropped from the "working list." For some of the roads no pertinent figures could be found either in *Poor's Manual of Railroads* or in the available annual reports. Other roads had such a complex history that it seemed wise to avoid an extremely time-consuming effort which would at best attain only a very doubtful set of results.

In certain instances, it was necessary to employ interpolation or extrapolation, to fill gaps in the figures for a particular road, or for one of its subsidiaries. It is believed, however, that any errors which may have been introduced through such interpolations and extrapolations were not in any case serious enough to produce significant error in the annual totals (later derived) for geographical sections and for the United States.

Finally, as a result of this extended investigation, annual statistics for some twenty-two roads were assembled, and these roads were taken as constituting our "revised working list."

THE "SAMPLE LIST": 1866–90

We came next to the development of a final, definitive list of railroads to be included in our computation of annual totals, 1866–90. The best method appeared to be to divide the country into suitable geographical areas, to set up a group of roads to represent each of these areas, and to combine these groups into a composite which could be related to the whole United States.

In the United States Census of 1880, the statistics for individual roads were presented in six geographical groups; and in the Census of 1890, in ten geographical groups.[10] We first inspected these

[10] See *Tenth Census of the United States*, 1880, IV, *Transportation*, 132–225 for

groups in graphical form. On an outline map of the United States the six groups of the 1880 Census were marked off and in each area the names of the roads, pertaining to that area, for which data had been compiled were written. A similar map was drawn for the groups of the 1890 Census.

After careful examination of the maps, decision was reached to adopt the 1880 system of grouping as being simpler to handle than the 1890 system, and also lying nearer the center of the immediate period of analysis, 1866–90. One modification was, however, made in the 1880 system: the Census Group V (comprising Louisiana, Arkansas, and Indian Territory) was omitted from our further investigations, inasmuch as its transportation activities constituted a relatively small part of those for the country as a whole (in 1880, for example, this group showed railroad earnings of 4.2 million dollars as compared to the Census grand total of 580.5 million dollars).

We next considered the question, to what extent had we attained fair proportionate representation as among the five remaining groups. As a first step in answering this question, five tables were drawn up, one for each of the five geographical areas; each table, in turn, was divided into five parts, pertaining respectively to the categories gross earnings, tons, ton-miles, passengers, and passenger-miles. Then for each category in each area we computed the percentage which (a) the 1880 total for the roads included in the "revised working list" bore to (b) the 1880 total for that geographical group as given by the 1880 Census.

Examination of the tables suggested that, while these percentages varied from category to category and from area to area, a good possibility existed of our being ultimately able to set up a list of roads which would come somewhere near attaining the goal, for each of the five categories, of equal proportionate representation (on the basis of the 1880 figures) for our several geographical areas. Further, it seemed reasonable to hope that, without occasioning undue labor, a standard of 50 per cent representation

---

earnings, 226–245 for operating statistics; and *Eleventh Census of the United States,* 1890, XIV, *Transportation,* part 1, *Transportation by Land,* 202–321 for earnings, 592–613 for operating statistics.

TABLE 9

DATA FOR "SAMPLE LIST" OF STEAM RAILROADS, 1866–90

(Figures apply to the census year 1880)*

Railroad	Gross earnings *(unit: one million dollars)*	Tons *(unit: one million tons)*	Ton-miles *(unit: one million ton-miles)*	Passengers *(unit: one thousand passengers)*	Passenger-miles *(unit: one million passenger-miles)*
Group I					
(Maine, New Hampshire, Vermont, Massachusetts, Rhode Island, Connecticut)					
Census total..........................	46.9	24.98	1,391	52,157	875
Individual roads:					
Boston and Albany Railroad..........	7.2	3.31	375	5,993	113
Boston and Maine Railroad...........	8.0	3.66	172	13,396	194
New York, New Haven and Hartford Railroad............	5.7	2.02	105	5,521	142
Total for individual roads............	20.9	8.99	652	24,910	449
Percentage which total for individual roads bears to Census total....	45	36	47	48	51

Group II

(New York, Pennsylvania, Ohio, Michigan, Indiana, Maryland, Delaware, New Jersey, District of Columbia)

Census total	283.2	192.45	20,416	175,276	3,051
Individual roads:					
Cleveland, Cincinnati, Chicago and St. Louis Railway	8.1	4.19	645	1,850	79
Michigan Central Railroad	12.7	5.85	1,190	2,169	151
New York Central and Hudson River Railroad	33.2	10.53	2,525	8,271	331
New York, Lake Erie and Western Railroad	24.0	11.85	2,195	6,814	236
Pennsylvania Railroad	40.8	26.05	3,239	16,576	383
Philadelphia and Reading Railroad	26.0	18.44	1,290	16,217	243
Total for individual roads	144.8	76.91	11,084	51,897	1,423
Percentage which total for individual roads bears to Census total	51	40	54	30	47

For footnote, see end of table.

TABLE 9 (Continued)

Group III

(Virginia, West Virginia, Kentucky, Tennessee, Mississippi, Alabama, Georgia, Florida, North Carolina, South Carolina)

Railroad	Gross earnings (unit: one million dollars)	Tons (unit: one million tons)	Ton-miles (unit: one million ton-miles)	Passengers (unit: one thousand passengers)	Passenger-miles (unit: one million passenger-miles)
Census total.........................	49.2	15.87	1,646	7,464	329
Individual roads:					
Chicago, St. Louis and New Orleans Railroad....	3.7	.50	120	300	20
Louisville and Nashville Railroad..........	8.6	2.54	354	1,294	63
Mobile and Ohio Railroad..............	2.7	.59	96	330	12
Norfolk and Western Railroad...........	1.9	.43	99	145	9
Richmond and Danville Railroad..........	1.2	.37	41	142	9
Richmond and Petersburg Railroad........	.2	.12	2	121	2
Virginia Midland Railroad..............	1.3	.26	27	197	12
Total for individual roads.............	19.6	4.81	739	2,529	127
Percentage which total for individual roads bears to Census total...	40	30	45	34	39

Group IV
(Illinois, Iowa, Wisconsin, Missouri, Minnesota)

Census total.............................	126.4	45.41	6,960	22,860	956
Individual roads:					
Chicago and Alton Railroad...............	7.7	3.07	481	1,204	78
Chicago and Northwestern Railway.........	17.4	5.58	866	3,965	140
Chicago, Burlington and Quincy Railroad...	20.4	6.64	1,175	2,800	140
Chicago, Milwaukee and St. Paul Railway...	13.1	3.26	505	2,128	112
Illinois Central Railroad.................	8.3	2.70	381	2,753	63
Total for individual roads...............	66.9	21.25	3,408	12,850	533
Percentage which total for individual roads bears to Census total...	53	47	49	56	56

For footnote, see end of table.

TABLE 9 (Continued)

Group VI

(Dakota, Nebraska, Kansas, Texas, New Mexico, Colorado, Wyoming, Montana, Idaho, Utah, Arizona, California, Nevada, Oregon, Washington)

Railroad	Gross earnings (unit: one million dollars)	Tons (unit: one million tons)	Ton-miles (unit: one million ton-miles)	Passengers (unit: one thousand passengers)	Passenger-miles (unit: one million passenger-miles)
Census total............................	70.6	11.45	1,910	11,433	512
Individual roads:					
Atchison, Topeka and Santa Fe Railroad....	8.6	.95	267	381	53
Northern Pacific Railroad............	2.2	.37	81	190	14
Texas and Pacific Railway............	2.6	.53	66	195	11
Union Pacific Railway...............	22.4	1.80	660	600	140
Total for individual roads............	35.8	3.65	1,074	1,366	218
Percentage which total for individual roads bears to Census total...	51	32	56	12	43

* For further explanation, see accompanying text.

(as compared with the Census totals) could be approached fairly closely in most instances. (To have set the hoped-for standard much higher than 50 per cent would in general have very greatly increased the burden, not only of transcription but also of research and adjustment, without materially improving the reliability of the final results—as the sequel will show.)

As the "revised working list" actually stood, however, certain anomalies were plainly present. Group III (southern) clearly suffered from under-representation.[11] Accordingly, effort was made to bring in more roads; and in fact data for four additional roads were obtained, increasing the size of the sample, but still leaving the proportions for the several categories somewhat below the desired 50 per cent. For Group II (eastern central) and Group IV (mid-western), deletions rather than additions were required. The individual roads comprising the sample for each of these two groups were examined carefully; and an effort was made to find for each group a sample of the desired size which would be representative of railroad activity in the given area.

The list of railroads to be included in our subsequent computations, arrived at as a result of these additions and deletions, is shown in the first column of Table 9. This we designate as our final "sample list" of railroads for 1866–90.

Table 9 indicates the degree of success which was attained in our efforts. For three important categories (gross earnings, ton-miles, and passenger-miles), we could fairly hold that both criteria —equal proportional representation as among geographical areas, and 50 per cent sample—were reasonably well approached; to be sure, the proportion for Group III was in each case on a slightly lower level than the others (compare the percentages in the table), but in view of the comparatively small volume of traffic for this group, as related to the grand total, it did not seem that these discrepancies for Group III could be of any great importance from the point of view of our general sampling problem. It was noted that the percentages for the larger groups were quite close together, in each instance—cf. Groups II and IV for gross earnings; Groups

[11] For exact list of states included in each group, see Table 9.

II and IV for ton-miles; and Groups I, II, and IV for passenger-miles.

For a fourth category—tons—the situation was also quite satisfactory. To be sure, the representation percentages were on the whole somewhat below 50 per cent, but this was less important than the fact that these percentages fell fairly closely together for the larger groups—Groups I, II, and IV; the fact that the percentages for Groups III and VI were on a somewhat lower level was not particularly disturbing, in view of the comparatively small size of their tonnage totals (15.87 millions and 11.45 millions, respectively, as related to the Census grand total of 290.90 millions).

For the remaining category—passengers—the variations among the groups with respect to the representation percentages were somewhat larger (for two groups such variation was not particularly significant).[12] But it is believed that even for passengers a reasonably satisfactory sampling has been attained.[13]

The final step in the present set of operations was the computation of certain aggregates. First, for each of our original six categories (gross earnings, tons, ton-miles, passengers, passenger-miles, mileage operated) we calculated a series of annual totals, 1866–90, for each geographical area—thirty series in all. These totals, in each instance, embraced the roads of our final "sample list" (cf., again, Column 1 of Table 9). Second, for each of the six categories we calculated a series of grand totals, by years, 1866–90, through summation of the appropriate geographical-group aggregates. These grand totals we designated as our "sample series" for the United States as a whole.

The various series of totals for geographical groups are presented in Table 10, Part A, and the corresponding grand totals

---

[12] The very low percentage for Group VI can be set aside as not particularly disturbing, in view of the fact that Group VI was at this epoch not highly important, as regards number of passengers carried, compared with the national aggregate. The comparative importance of Group III also was small.

[13] In connection with the tons and passengers series, discussed above, cf. the conclusions of the tests later applied to these series as discussed in the next chapter, especially those discussed in the concluding pages of that chapter.

TABLE 10

"SAMPLE LIST" OF STEAM RAILROADS, 1866–90: TOTALS FOR GEOGRAPHICAL GROUPS
AND GRAND TOTALS, BY FISCAL YEARS

Part A: Totals for Geographical Groups

Gross earnings

(Unit: one million dollars)

Year	Group I	Group II	Group III	Group IV	Group VI
1866	15.06	90.25	9.88	29.22	..
1867	15.69	87.11	9.59	32.97	1.82
1868	15.97	90.96	9.46	38.75	1.91
1869	17.41	99.49	10.84	42.16	2.23
1870	18.11	99.18	13.48	41.26	6.36
1871	19.94	108.53	14.11	40.58	10.83
1872	21.80	119.51	14.77	40.50	12.71
1873	23.21	134.34	18.89	50.41	15.40
1874	22.30	128.30	17.44	51.27	16.44
1875	20.91	116.20	15.91	48.24	18.55
1876	19.44	116.56	16.27	48.20	20.54
1877	18.56	106.78	16.78	47.36	21.17
1878	17.94	111.81	16.72	51.80	23.58
1879	18.19	119.09	16.45	54.66	27.57
1880	20.93	144.83	19.57	66.88	35.84
1881	22.76	152.59	24.98	73.69	43.03
1882	24.84	157.94	26.06	82.75	49.29
1883	26.83	159.41	28.41	91.56	50.03
1884	25.68	151.28	29.35	90.75	52.65
1885	26.29	139.36	28.92	90.90	50.09
1886	29.50	154.13	28.18	92.44	51.56
1887	31.51	172.22	31.78	97.66	56.98
1888	31.33	176.39	34.45	92.53	57.73
1889	32.75	178.54	36.67	97.18	62.41
1890	35.20	190.10	40.90	100.06	67.38

TABLE 10 (*Continued*)

Tons
(*Unit: one thousand tons*)

Year	Group I	Group II	Group III	Group IV	Group VI
1866	3,394	19,734	793	4,982	..
1867	3,491	21,140	1,121	5,958	100
1868	3,562	24,291	1,268	7,078	124
1869	4,174	28,279	1,570	7,495	176
1870	4,568	32,887	2,090	8,231	333
1871	5,239	38,360	2,394	9,123	527
1872	6,200	43,156	2,580	9,956	689
1873	6,539	48,495	3,579	11,052	951
1874	6,272	48,074	3,700	11,845	1,050
1875	6,040	45,695	3,683	11,581	1,165
1876	6,229	48,691	4,055	12,579	1,537
1877	6,543	51,614	5,134	12,668	1,830
1878	6,458	53,453	5,233	14,910	2,617
1879	7,583	68,195	4,863	17,385	2,926
1880	8,986	76,911	4,811	21,248	3,645
1881	10,111	92,247	6,652	23,800	4,395
1882	10,440	96,174	9,980	26,097	5,413
1883	10,884	92,987	11,193	27,941	6,322
1884	10,165	92,609	11,988	28,445	7,887
1885	10,761	96,649	12,787	29,793	7,995
1886	12,079	106,342	13,514	31,208	9,147
1887	13,075	123,602	17,346	35,380	11,015
1888	12,469	132,647	19,843	35,964	10,844
1889	13,111	133,165	23,599	37,261	11,795
1890	14,337	150,822	27,473	41,183	13,549

TABLE 10 (*Continued*)

Passengers
(*Unit: one thousand passengers*)

Year	Group I	Group II	Group III	Group IV	Group VI
1866	13,822	25,811	1,195	4,603	..
1867	14,554	26,711	1,231	4,759	50
1868	15,195	29,047	1,326	6,089	109
1869	17,031	32,380	1,525	6,529	147
1870	18,007	36,343	2,218	6,735	323
1871	19,965	38,354	2,187	6,756	333
1872	21,510	39,855	2,257	6,993	355
1873	23,828	42,477	2,568	7,704	469
1874	24,013	44,299	2,431	8,486	513
1875	24,001	43,998	2,441	9,280	560
1876	22,569	52,374	2,479	10,129	639
1877	21,331	41,843	2,360	9,675	745
1878	20,488	41,518	2,378	9,971	886
1879	21,466	43,941	2,274	10,354	1,067
1880	24,910	51,897	2,529	12,850	1,366
1881	28,307	58,246	4,576	16,181	1,768
1882	31,043	67,212	4,982	20,087	2,437
1883	34,628	68,527	5,829	22,374	3,273
1884	37,714	73,333	6,788	24,289	4,157
1885	39,516	77,629	6,958	24,832	4,289
1886	43,147	84,040	6,237	27,181	4,914
1887	47,411	92,293	6,816	29,751	6,319
1888	49,468	99,814	7,414	32,753	6,839
1889	52,003	105,306	7,811	34,112	6,963
1890	54,227	113,454	9,154	35,372	6,930

TABLE 10 (*Continued*)

Ton-miles
(*Unit: one million ton-miles*)

Year	Group I	Group II	Group III	Group IV	Group VI
1866	161	2,269	65	528	..
1867	176	2,481	87	644	20
1868	202	2,831	123	799	25
1869	251	3,430	146	884	35
1870	285	4,078	215	1,014	122
1871	347	4,751	269	1,093	184
1872	429	5,322	332	1,252	252
1873	464	6,289	413	1,539	316
1874	452	6,365	429	1,655	369
1875	435	6,297	430	1,677	409
1876	464	7,008	460	1,789	462
1877	496	7,199	517	2,091	546
1878	513	8,182	580	2,476	710
1879	553	10,073	588	3,044	828
1880	652	11,084	739	3,408	1,074
1881	754	12,500	993	3,711	1,377
1882	743	12,522	1,118	4,253	1,595
1883	760	11,824	1,237	4,917	1,770
1884	719	12,273	1,273	5,131	2,029
1885	795	13,203	1,490	5,312	1,974
1886	847	13,749	1,694	5,655	2,392
1887	910	15,241	2,049	6,349	2,841
1888	923	15,971	2,355	6,487	3,055
1889	983	16,347	2,677	6,465	3,150
1890	1,089	18,113	3,122	7,236	3,644

TABLE 10 (*Continued*)

Passenger-miles
(*Unit: one million passenger-miles*)

Year	Group I	Group II	Group III	Group IV	Group VI
1866	297	918	58	211	..
1867	303	886	65	202	5
1868	309	925	69	235	10
1869	341	990	77	260	15
1870	377	1,056	103	280	95
1871	378	1,074	112	292	94
1872	421	1,139	119	300	103
1873	444	1,185	128	341	130
1874	475	1,187	118	354	142
1875	438	1,148	114	366	169
1876	426	1,512	120	383	176
1877	398	1,110	117	367	167
1878	382	1,062	119	380	169
1879	390	1,146	108	427	188
1880	449	1,423	127	533	218
1881	526	1,585	185	632	269
1882	593	1,785	224	771	337
1883	618	1,699	244	918	363
1884	658	1,770	296	894	442
1885	684	1,900	332	860	406
1886	743	1,885	265	897	515
1887	808	2,028	299	934	590
1888	820	2,144	327	996	616
1889	880	2,236	332	1,032	668
1890	924	2,365	375	1,078	689

TABLE 10 (*Continued*)

Mileage operated

(*Unit: one mile*)

Year	Group I	Group II	Group III	Group IV	Group VI
1866..........	1,012	4,532	2,078	3,109	..
1867..........	1,012	4,532	2,326	3,256	228
1868..........	1,012	4,857	2,528	3,801	403
1869..........	1,030	4,910	2,602	4,097	439
1870..........	1,058	5,302	2,842	4,355	552
1871..........	1,069	5,326	2,910	4,884	600
1872..........	1,145	5,535	2,964	5,513	866
1873..........	1,414	5,833	3,789	6,548	1,829
1874..........	1,479	6,156	3,843	6,694	2,230
1875..........	1,501	6,250	3,849	6,863	2,660
1876..........	1,505	6,833	3,996	7,048	3,036
1877..........	1,511	7,076	4,002	7,645	3,154
1878..........	1,513	7,309	3,995	7,893	3,252
1879..........	1,516	7,398	3,862	8,755	3,484
1880..........	1,521	7,455	3,975	10,663	4,359
1881..........	1,659	7,773	4,576	11,462	4,786
1882..........	1,734	8,057	4,748	12,597	5,971
1883..........	1,796	8,156	4,828	13,439	6,625
1884..........	1,814	8,745	4,942	14,140	7,974
1885..........	2,042	8,740	4,964	14,662	8,199
1886..........	2,207	8,874	5,069	15,261	8,457
1887..........	2,381	9,148	5,175	16,481	8,809
1888..........	2,106	9,250	5,314	17,552	9,550
1889..........	2,107	9,374	5,488	17,937	9,776
1890..........	2,107	9,741	5,534	18,117	9,928

TABLE 10 (*Continued*)

Part B: Grand Totals (All Groups Combined)

Year	Gross earnings (*unit: one million dollars*)	Tons (*unit: one thousand tons*)	Passengers (*unit: one thousand passengers*)	Ton-miles (*unit: one million ton-miles*)	Passenger-miles (*unit: one million passenger-miles*)	Mileage operated (*unit: one mile*)
1866	144.41	28,903	45,431	3,023	1,484	10,731
1867	147.18	31,810	47,305	3,408	1,461	11,354
1868	157.05	36,323	51,766	3,980	1,548	12,601
1869	172.13	41,694	57,612	4,746	1,683	13,078
1870	178.39	48,109	63,626	5,714	1,911	14,109
1871	193.99	55,643	67,595	6,644	1,950	14,789
1872	209.29	62,581	70,970	7,587	2,082	16,023
1873	242.25	70,616	77,046	9,021	2,228	19,413
1874	235.75	70,941	79,742	9,270	2,276	20,402
1875	219.81	68,164	80,280	9,248	2,235	21,123
1876	221.01	73,091	88,190	10,183	2,617	22,418
1877	210.65	77,789	75,954	10,849	2,159	23,388
1878	221.85	82,671	75,241	12,461	2,112	23,962
1879	235.96	100,952	79,102	15,086	2,259	25,015
1880	288.05	115,601	93,552	16,957	2,750	27,973
1881	317.05	137,205	109,078	19,335	3,197	30,256
1882	340.88	148,104	125,761	20,231	3,710	33,107
1883	356.24	149,327	134,631	20,508	3,842	34,844
1884	349.71	151,094	146,281	21,425	4,060	37,615
1885	335.56	157,985	153,224	22,774	4,182	38,607
1886	355.81	172,290	165,519	24,337	4,305	39,868
1887	390.15	200,418	182,590	27,390	4,659	41,994
1888	392.43	211,767	196,288	28,791	4,903	43,772
1889	407.55	218,931	206,195	29,622	5,148	44,682
1890	433.64	247,364	219,137	33,204	5,431	45,427

CHART 5

"Sample List" of Steam Railroads, 1866–90: Totals for Geographical Groups and Grand Totals, by Fiscal Years*

Tons

Ton-Miles

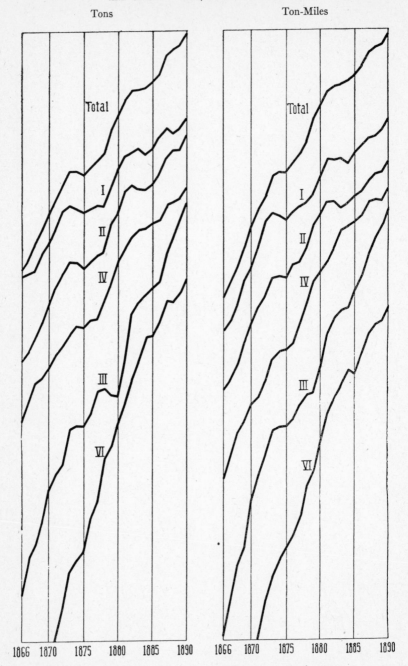

1866 1870 1875 1880 1885 1890   1866 1870 1875 1880 1885 1890

* Logarithmic vertical scales. For explanation, see accompanying text.

[88]

CHART 5 (*Continued*)

"SAMPLE LIST" OF STEAM RAILROADS, 1866–90: TOTALS FOR GEOGRAPHICAL GROUPS
AND GRAND TOTALS, BY FISCAL YEARS

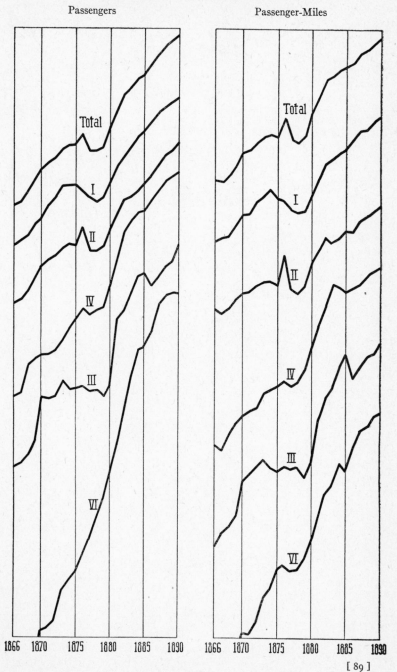

Passengers

Passenger-Miles

in Table 10, Part B. The series for the four traffic categories—tons, ton-miles, passengers, passenger-miles—are shown graphically in Chart 5. [14]

Survey of Available Basic Data, and "Sample List": 1855–71

As has previously been indicated on these pages, our time interval of primary interest was 1866–1914—from the close of the Civil War to the outbreak of the first World War—but we wished incidentally to extend our indexes back to 1860. The investigations to be described in this section were undertaken with a view to fulfilling this incidental purpose.

Though our immediate attention thus was directed to the interval 1860–65, the investigation was extended to cover a somewhat longer period—1855–71. The reasons for this extension lay in the desire to take advantage of an over-all "cross-section" estimate which was obtainable for 1855 (as is later set forth), and to provide an overlapping time period for comparison with our 1866–90 "sample list."

The task of developing a "sample list" of railroads for the period 1855–71 was in one way simplified by the fact that we were not in the position (which we had occupied in the 1866–90 study) of being able to pick and choose among a variety of possibilities. For 1855–71, one could hardly do other than to make the best practicable utilization of the scant volume of data available.

Proceeding along the same general lines as were followed in developing the annual series for individual roads in the 1866–90 investigation, we were able to set up, over the years 1855–71, a list of eight roads for which annual series possessing at least a reasonable degree of homogeneity could be developed, pertaining to five categories—gross earnings, tons, ton-miles, passengers, and passenger-miles.[15] These eight roads are listed in Table 11.

Finally, for each of the five categories we calculated a series of annual totals, 1855–71, for the eight roads combined. (A few

---

[14] This chart is, as indicated, drawn with logarithmic vertical scale. In Group VI (the far-western states), the items for some of the earlier years ran off the chart and had to be omitted in order to keep the drawing within reasonable size.

[15] The basic data for individual roads were taken from various issues of *Poor's Manual of Railroads* and the annual reports of the roads.

TABLE 11

"Sample List" of Steam Railroads, 1855–71

Boston and Albany Railroad
Central Railroad of New Jersey
Chicago, Burlington and Quincy Railroad
Michigan Central Railroad
New York Central and Hudson River Railroad
New York, Lake Erie and Western Railroad
Pennsylvania Railroad
Pittsburgh, Fort Wayne, and Chicago Railroad

interpolations and extrapolations were required for certain individual roads, mainly in the earlier years of the period, but these were hardly important enough materially to affect the movement of the totals for eight roads.) The five series of annual totals for the respective categories constituted our "sample series" for 1855–71.

TABLE 12

"Sample List" of Steam Railroads, 1855–71: Totals by Fiscal Years

Year	Gross earnings (unit: one million dollars)	Tons (unit: one thousand tons)	Passengers (unit: one thousand passengers)	Ton-miles (unit: one million ton-miles)	Passenger-miles (unit: one million passenger-miles)
1855	26.96	3,662	9,306	520	468
1856	30.92	4,513	9,622	646	478
1857	29.86	5,033	9,840	651	478
1858	26.66	5,102	8,537	691	426
1859	26.86	5,795	9,072	762	435
1860	30.36	7,352	9,497	991	438
1861	33.86	7,992	9,021	1,198	428
1862	44.64	9,697	9,726	1,534	476
1863	54.80	10,818	12,292	1,707	621
1864	68.30	11,663	16,347	1,743	845
1865	78.48	11,263	18,380	1,619	1,006
1866	78.70	14,372	18,835	2,026	915
1867	77.15	15,640	19,582	2,228	845
1868	80.89	17,840	20,797	2,563	869
1869	86.31	19,858	24,023	3,049	926
1870	87.45	23,224	26,566	3,569	953
1871	93.91	26,802	28,088	4,162	945

CHART 6

"Sample List" of Steam Railroads, 1855–71:
Totals by Fiscal Years*

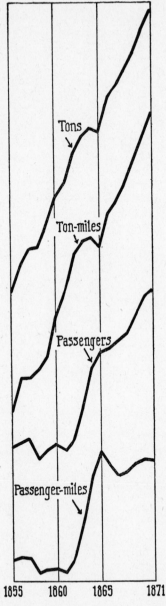

* Logarithmic vertical scales. For explanation, see accompanying text.

The annual series for each of the five categories are given in Table 12, and the totals pertaining to the four traffic series are presented graphically in Chart 6.

Because of the absence of desired basic data, our sampling process here is less satisfactory than in the 1866–90 period, and we cannot feel equal confidence as to the representativeness of the series obtained. Nevertheless, for the overlapping years 1866–71 our present series, though less comprehensive, show in each case relative fluctuations closely similar to those exhibited by the series resulting from the 1866–90 investigation.[16] On the whole, we have perhaps made as good an approximation as could have been readily obtained from the available material.

---

[16] The question of correction for possible long-run bias over the years 1855–66 is discussed in the next chapter.

CHAPTER VI

TRANSPORTATION AND COMMUNICATION: THE STEAM-RAILROAD SERIES—(B) RECTIFICATION AND TESTS

IN THIS CHAPTER we describe processes of rectification which were applied to our steam-railroad data, and certain tests which were carried out.

THE "CROSS-SECTION" TOTALS FOR 1871, AND RECTIFIED SERIES FOR 1866–90

While a considerable amount of thought and effort had been devoted to the development of our "sample series" for the period 1866–90, a possible source of error had to be considered. Even granting that our sampling procedure had yielded us an acceptable picture of the form of fluctuation for series indicative of steam-railroad traffic, this picture might nevertheless give an incorrect impression in a respect which was decidedly vital. Quite possibly, that is, our various series might have gradual biases over time: it might be that the proportionate size of the sample totals, as compared with the corresponding national aggregates, exhibited progressive changes, and that our series, therefore, little by little drifted away from a true representation.

In order to avoid error from this source we desired to compare our annual series at certain points against comprehensive "cross-section" estimates, and to develop suitable rectifications for drifts over time in the sampling proportion—or, in other words, to correct for "growth biases" which might be present in our annual series, due to sampling difficulties.

For the final year of the period 1866–90, the desired comprehensive "cross-section" totals were readily obtainable, for all four traffic series; we could simply use the 1890 aggregates presented in the summary tables of *Poor's Manual of Railroads,* for by 1890 the Poor's aggregates were virtually inclusive of all railroads in the United States.[1] For the earlier part of the period 1866–90, on the other hand, no such all-inclusive aggregates were available. Fortunately, however, it was found that for the year 1871 *Poor's Manual of Railroads* had published elaborate tabulations, giving a substantial amount of basic statistical data for individual roads.[2] Needless to say, these tabulations constitute an exceedingly valuable body of material for research workers in the fields of economic history and economic statistics. The year 1871 was sufficiently near the beginning of the period 1866–90 to make it usable for the purposes of judging the general tendencies over the period.

For two of the four categories of traffic statistics—ton-miles and passenger-miles—the tabulated 1871 data were clearly inadequate for making the desired over-all "cross-section" estimates; the extensive development of ton-mile and passenger-mile statistics did not come until somewhat later in our period of analysis. But for the other two categories—tons and passengers—the 1871 data were quite extensive and, further, were so well dispersed geographically and industrially as to make feasible the development of "cross-section" estimates.[3]

We next proceeded to the development of rectified annual series, 1866–90, for tons and passengers, taking the two series in turn.

For tons, the adjustment though not large was clearly perceptible. Going forward from 1871 toward 1890, the average annual ratio of change indicated by the two "cross-section" totals— the 1871 aggregate developed from the Poor's tabulations for individual roads, just referred to, and the Poor's reported total for 1890—was a little lower than the corresponding ratio for our "sample series": the first of these two ratios stood to the second in the proportion 0.9953 to 1 (or, if one reversed the direction of movement, and measured *backward* from 1890 toward 1871, the

[1] See fn. 3 of Chapter V.
[2] See *Poor's Manual of Railroads* for 1872–73, pp. xxxiv ff. The tabulations were continued in subsequent years.
[3] For description of the methods employed in securing the estimates, see Appendix E, Part Two.

proportionate annual discrepancy would be, of course, the recipro-
cal of 0.9953, or 1.0047).[4]

Accordingly, in developing our annual series of estimated
all-inclusive totals for tonnage, to be used in extending backward from 1890 toward 1871 the annual totals which we had
already transcribed for 1890–1914, we took account of the indicated annual discrepancy just computed. More explicitly, the
actual ratio of change, $\dfrac{1889}{1890}$, for our "sample series" totals was
$\dfrac{218.9 \text{ million tons}}{247.4 \text{ million tons}}$, or 0.8848; in estimating the 1889 all-inclusive
total, we multiplied the Poor's total for 1890 (691.3 million tons)
not by this ratio 0.8848, but by a modified ratio which took account of the discrepancy indicator previously derived: that is, we
multiplied the Poor's 1890 total by $\dfrac{0.8848}{0.9953}$, or 0.8890. We thus obtained 0.8890 x 691.3 million tons, or 614.6 million tons, as our
estimated all-inclusive total for the year 1889.

Proceeding, we found the actual $\dfrac{1888}{1889}$ ratio of change for the
"sample series" totals to be $\dfrac{211.8 \text{ million tons}}{218.9 \text{ million tons}}$, or 0.9676; in estimating the 1888 all-inclusive total we multiplied the 1889 all-
inclusive total (previously estimated, as described in the preceding paragraph) of 614.6 million tons, *not* by this ratio 0.9676, but
by the modified ratio $\dfrac{0.9676}{0.9953}$, or 0.9721. We thus obtained 0.9721
x 614.6 million tons, or 597.4 million tons, as our estimated all-
inclusive total for 1888.

This process was continued, going backward until the year 1871
was reached. The 1871 estimated all-inclusive total derived by this
procedure agreed precisely with the 1871 "cross-section" total
which had previously been obtained; this coincidence of results

---

[4] Roughly, one might say that the indicated discrepancy in year-to-year movement was one-half of one per cent.

was, of course, not accidental, but was a matter of mathematical necessity.[5]

The question next arose as to the procedure to be employed in extending our series of estimated all-inclusive totals, going backward from 1871 toward 1866. In the absence of any direct "cross-section" estimate for 1866, the best policy seemed to be to continue the discrepancy allowance which had been used in going backward from 1890 toward 1871; that is, to continue to divide the year-to-year ratios of change exhibited by the "sample series," going backward from 1871 toward 1866, by 0.9953 in estimating the all-inclusive totals over the interval.

The methods for developing our annual estimates of all-inclusive totals for the passenger series, going backward from 1890 toward 1871 and thence to 1866, were precisely analogous to those just described for the tonnage series. For the passenger series, however, the check-up of the relative changes between the two years 1871 and 1890 of our "sample series," and the previously obtained "cross-section" estimates was almost perfect; almost no "drift," or tendency toward long-run bias, appeared. In view of this fact, formal correction for long-run bias could indeed have been dispensed with, so far as essential accuracy was concerned. However, for the sake of uniformity of procedure with that of the tonnage series, it seemed best to go through the formal process of correction—even though little alteration was thereby produced.

Such discrepancy as existed was in the opposite direction from that in the tonnage case. Going forward from 1871 toward 1890 for the passenger series, the average annual ratio of change indicated by the two "cross-section" totals was very slightly higher than the corresponding ratio for our "sample series": the first of these ratios stood to the second in the proportion 1.0002 to 1 (or, in the reverse direction, 0.9998 to 1).[6]

[5] The operations described in the preceding three paragraphs are—as the attentive reader has no doubt already observed—simply an adaptation of the "post method" described in the earlier pages of Chapter IV.

[6] Again speaking roughly, one might say that the indicated discrepancy in year-to-year movement was two-hundredths of 1 per cent.

By means of these rectifications we had now extended back our annual series for tons and passengers so that these series covered the interval from 1866 to 1914. It was very much regretted that similar rectifications could not have been performed for ton-miles and passenger-miles, but the necessary basic data were simply not available.

The "Cross-Section" Totals for 1855, and Rectified Series for 1855–66

The rectification of the annual series for tons and passengers was thus completed for our period of principal interest, 1866–1914. We turned next to consider the possibilities for extending the rectification of the two series to cover our period of incidental interest, 1860–65.

So far as the termination of this latter period was concerned, the natural solution—inasmuch as no basic data for making direct estimates of totals for all railroads were available—was, for each of the two series, to take the estimated 1866 total which had just been obtained by the process of rectification as the best approximation to the desired 1866 "cross-section" aggregate. But with respect to the other end of this time interval—the year 1860—we were not able to find any published "cross-section" estimates, nor any material from which such estimates might be derived.

We were, however, fortunate in discovering estimates of all-inclusive totals, for both tons and passengers, pertaining to the year 1855. These figures, given in *Poor's Manual of Railroads* for 1900, page xxxiii, were as follows:

> Tons of freight moved 23,319,449
> Passengers carried 37,815,110

In order to take advantage of these highly valuable "cross-section" totals, we modified our procedure somewhat. We took as the period of immediate analysis the interval *1855–66*. For each of the two series tons and passengers, we adopted the previously derived 1866 rectified total as the "cross-section" estimate for

1866 and the figure given by Poor's as the "cross-section" estimate for 1855.

The method followed in rectifying the two series, going backward from 1866 toward 1855, was altogether comparable to that previously employed in the corresponding rectification going backward from 1890 toward 1871. No detailed description of the procedure need, therefore, be given. Since here the "sample list" of constituent railroads, because of paucity of fundamental data, presumably was less representative than the "sample list" for 1866–90, our confidence regarding the short-run movements of the 1855–66 rectified series cannot be as high as that for the 1866–90 series, but the 1855–66 series probably does at least portray the main tendencies over that twelve-year interval.

Through the set of operations described on preceding pages of this chapter, we obtained for each of the two series tons and passengers a continuous set of rectified totals, by years, 1855–1914. These items are shown in Table 13. The figures, it will be remembered, pertain to fiscal years.[7]

These two rectified series were adopted as the steam-railroad components of our transportation and communication index over the period 1860–1914. On grounds of principle, ton-miles and passenger-miles would have been preferable—as constituting more direct measurements of the volume of transportation activity, inasmuch as each is a compound of number of units transported and distance—but the impossibility of rectifying these latter series made their use impracticable.[8]

TESTING VALIDITY OF SHORT-RUN MOVEMENTS: "SAMPLING BY SIZE OF ROAD"

We came next to testing from a particular viewpoint the two series which had finally been set up, as described above, to represent the volume of production for the steam-railroad industry.

[7] For discussion of the problem of fiscal-year dating, see the next chapter.

[8] In the ton-miles and passenger-miles series, available data were inadequate for 1871 "cross section" estimates, as was indicated on an earlier page of this chapter.

TABLE 13

RECTIFIED SERIES FOR STEAM-RAILROAD TONS AND PASSENGERS:
BY FISCAL YEARS, 1855–1914

Year	Tons (unit: one million tons)	Passengers (unit: one million passengers)	Year	Tons (unit: one million tons)	Passengers (unit: one million passengers)
1855	23.3	37.8			
1856	28.7	40.3	1886	491	394
1857	31.9	42.4	1887	570	434
1858	32.3	38.0	1888	597	467
1859	36.7	41.7	1889	615	490
1860	46.5	44.9	1890	691	520
1861	50.5	44.0	1891	704	556
1862	61.2	48.9	1892	731	576
1863	68.3	63.7	1893	757	597
1864	73.4	87.5	1894	675	570
1865	70.9	101.3	1895	756	530
1866	90.3	107.2	1896	774	535
1867	98.9	111.6	1897	788	504
1868	112.3	122.3	1898	913	515
1869	128.6	136.1	1899	976	538
1870	147.6	150.4	1900	1,081	576
1871	170.0	160.0	1901	1,089	607
1872	190.2	167.9	1902	1,200	649
1873	213	182.3	1903	1,304	694
1874	213	188.7	1904	1,309	715
1875	204	190.1	1905	1,427	738
1876	218	208.8	1906	1,631	797
1877	231	180.0	1907	1,796	873
1878	244	178.1	1908	1,532	890
1879	297	187.6	1909	1,556	891
1880	338	222	1910	1,849	971
1881	400	258	1911	1,781	997
1882	430	297	1912	1,844	1,004
1883	432	319	1913	*2,058	1,043
1884	435	348	1914	2,002	1,063
1885	451	364			

* See fn. 6 of Chapter V.

We had here to do with a question of sampling, and hence our problem had relevance only for the period before 1890 (inasmuch as beginning with 1890 our totals were practically all-inclusive, as was earlier set forth). For years prior to 1890, our totals were based upon samples, and these samples from practical necessity related to the larger railroad systems. The question therefore arose as to *sampling by size of road.* Could the movements of our series before 1890 be taken as denotative of fluctuations in activity for the whole industry?

We began with consideration of the *tonnage* figures. We were able to obtain two sets of data which were suitable for the purposes of testing short-run movements. Both pertained to the decade of the eighteen-eighties.

The first set of data consisted of certain figures presented in the United States Census of 1890, by years, 1881–90.[9] The Census series are not completely inclusive of all railroads in the United States, but do embrace 90 to 95 per cent of total mileage. These figures, moreover, are widely comprehensive in their geographical and industrial coverage, and include many small railroads. The Census data, then, though from the long-range point of view less homogeneous than our series, were usable for the purpose of comparison of short-run movements with those of our series.

Inasmuch as the composition (i.e., list of constituent roads) of the Census series varied somewhat from year to year, the first step was to put the series on a "per-mile-of-road" basis; while this was by no means a completely satisfactory adjustment for variation in composition, even for short-run movements, nevertheless worth-while improvement was doubtless produced in this respect. Next, our own series—though homogeneous as to composition— was also, for the sake of comparability, put on a "per-mile-of-road" basis.

Even upon a "per-mile-of-road" basis, both series showed decided upward secular movements over the decade 1881–90. It seemed desirable, therefore, to adjust the two series for secular

---

[9] United States Department of the Interior, Census Office, *Eleventh Census of the United States: 1890,* vol. XIV, *Transportation,* part 1, *Transportation by Land* (Washington: Government Printing Office, 1895), pp. 53, 623.

trend, in order that the cyclical and other short-run movements might stand out in clear relief. Adjustment was made, in each case, by fitting a compound-interest curve—a straight line upon logarithmic vertical scale—to the period 1882–90.[10] The annual

TABLE 14

COMPARISON OF TREND-RATIOS, BY FISCAL YEARS, 1881–90*

(*Unit: one per cent*)

Year	Tons				Passengers				Weighted average of tons and passengers	
	Our series	Composite series	Census series	Poor's series	Our series	Composite series	Census series	Poor's series	Our series	Composite series
	(1)	(2)	(3)	(4)	(5)	(6)	(7)	(8)	(9)	(10)
1881	115	114	114	..	100	100	100	..	111	110
1882	110	106	107	105	102	104	104	104	108	106
1883	103	101	100	103	101	99	98	100	102	101
1884	93	95	95	95	99	99	99	99	95	96
1885	93	95	95	94	97	96	98	95	94	95
1886	95	99	99	99	99	100	99	100	96	99
1887	102	102	102	102	100	100	99	101	101	101
1888	100	100	100	101	100	99	99	99	100	100
1889	99	99	100	98	100	101	101	101	99	99
1890	107	104	103	104	101	102	102	102	105	103

* For explanation, see accompanying text.

trend-ratios for each of the two series were then computed (i.e., ratios of the successive annual items to the corresponding ordinates of trend). These trend-ratios are shown in Columns 1 and 3 of Table 14.

The main impression obtained from a comparison of the two sets of trend-ratios is that of generally close correspondence as

[10] No more complicated procedure seemed called for with respect to these data over this short period. If fitting of trends to these series for somewhat longer periods were required, quite probably broken lines or more complicated curved lines would be required—perhaps arrived at by the methods discussed in the writer's *Economic Fluctuations in the United States* (Cambridge, Mass.: Harvard University Press, 1942), chaps. XIII–XV.

The trend interval was started with *1882*, rather than 1881, in order to make possible comparability of results with those for the Poor's totals (presently to be brought into the computations), which were available only beginning with 1882. For the two present series, the trends were extrapolated back to 1881.

to *form* of cyclical variation, with our series exhibiting a moderately higher *amplitude* of cyclical variation.[11]

When the computations pertaining to the comparison with the Census series had been completed, we turned to the second set of data alluded to above—certain annual series of totals, 1882–90, originally presented in *Poor's Manual of Railroads*.[12] These series, also, are widely comprehensive in their geographical coverage, and include many small railroads. The Poor's data, 1882–90, were thus highly valuable for the purpose of testing the short-run movements of our own series.[13] Computations were carried out for the Poor's tonnage series (Table 14, Column 4), analogous to those previously made for the corresponding Census series. The results were broadly similar, though here and there individualistic differences appear. Comparison of our own series of trend-ratios with the Poor's series led to much the same conclusions, with reference to form and amplitude of cyclical variation, as those above stated for the comparison of our series with the Census series.

It now seemed desirable to epitomize the information afforded by the trend-ratios for the Census and Poor's series. Accordingly, a new series was set up, 1881–90, consisting simply of annual means of the Census and Poor's trend-ratios—except for 1881, where the Census trend-ratio alone was used (the Poor's series being unavailable). This new set of figures (Column 2 of Table 14) we designated as the "composite series for tons."

Comparison of this new composite series of trend-ratios for tonnage with our own series (cf. Columns 1 and 2 of Table 14) indicated a very high degree of correlation in form of cyclical

---

[11] There are also, to be sure, certain detailed differences of behavior. However, these are not necessarily always indicative of fault in *our* series: they may arise also owing to differences in fiscal-year dating as between the two series; or may be ascribable to some defect of the Census data, say lack of uniformity as to list of constituent railroads.

[12] The immediate source of these figures was United States Interstate Commerce Commission, Bureau of Statistics, *Railway Statistics Before 1890* [Statement No. 32151, File No. 323–A–1] (Washington: December 1932), p. 3 for mileage statistics, p. 9 for passenger statistics, p. 10 for freight statistics. A note says that "the attached tables have been copied for convenient use from the various annual issues of Poor's Manual of Railroads for the years 1869 to 1900."

[13] It will be remembered that beginning with 1890 we used the Poor's totals as our all-inclusive annual series (cf. Chapter V).

movement (the coefficient of correlation, in fact, was +0.96).
And here, as in the comparison with each of the two components
of the composite series, our series showed a perceptibly higher
amplitude of cyclical variation.

We next gave attention to data for *passengers carried*. Using
the same basic sources as for tonnage, we arrived at an analogous
set of results (Columns 5–8 of Table 14). Examination of these
results indicated that while there was correspondence as to general
cyclical sweep, more difference appeared with respect to detail of
movement. Nevertheless, the correlation between the trend-ratios
for our series and the composite series (Columns 5 and 6 of the
table) was even here high (the correlation coefficient being
+0.85). Both series showed rather narrow amplitude of cyclical
movement.

We finally came to the test which was definitely pertinent to our
immediate main problem—the problem, that is, of building up the
combined index of transportation and communication. The specific issue which we now considered related to the sampling reliability of our tonnage and passenger series, with respect to short-
run movements before 1890.[14]

The computation process here involved the taking of two sets
of weighted averages of the trend-ratios for tons and passengers,
by years, 1881–90: (i) for our own series, and (ii) for the composite series, respectively.[15] These two sets of weighted averages
are shown in Table 14 (compare Columns 9 and 10 of this table).

The correlation between the two sets of weighted trend-ratios
is very close (the coefficient of correlation is +0.98); the *form* of
cyclical movement exhibits decided similarity as between the two
series. The *amplitude* of cyclical movement is somewhat greater
for our weighted series (the standard deviations are 5.3 per cent

---

[14] Beginning with 1890, as was earlier indicated, no question arises as to sampling,
inasmuch as our series are virtually all-inclusive.

[15] The weights were those of Table 16, presented in the next chapter (see Column
5 of this table).

for our weighted series, 4.2 per cent for the weighted composite series).[16]

Our tests for the period 1881–90, then, suggest the conclusion that from the point of view of short-run fluctuations the two series, based upon sample data, which we have set up to represent fluctuations in the volume of traffic in the railroad industry before 1890 may be taken as substantially dependable as regards sampling reliability—especially for the purpose of computing the combined annual index for transportation and communication.[17]

In this chapter, we have performed processes of rectification and set up certain tests, relating to the tonnage and passengers series. The results of these operations tend to substantiate the view that our final series for these two entities, even though they were made up from figures pertaining to the larger railroad systems, may be accepted without too great reservations as denotative of movements for the United States as a whole.

[16] Cf. the corresponding conclusions, stated above, for tonnage (the more heavily weighted component of the averages).

[17] Indeed, from the point of view of the combined index of transportation and communication presented in the next chapter, even the moderately higher amplitude of cyclical variation, referred to just above, may turn out to be a good fault, in view of the fact that in the derivation of this combined index we were obliged to make certain estimates and interpolations whose effect was in the direction of some *understatement* of the amplitude of cyclical variation (cf. Appendix C and fn. 4 of the next chapter).

CHAPTER VII

WHEN THE DERIVATION of the series for steam-railroad transportation had been carried out, as described in the two preceding chapters, we turned our attention to other series indicative of the volume of transportation and communication in the United States over our period of analysis.

BASIC DATA FOR SERIES OTHER THAN STEAM-RAILROAD

For certain fields, we were able to find statistical series which were directly indicative of the volume of service: Great Lakes traffic (represented by tonnage moved through the canals at Sault Ste. Marie, Michigan and Ontario); New York canals traffic (represented by tonnage moved through New York canals); telephone service (represented by number of completed telephone conversations); telegraph service (represented by number of telegraph messages transmitted); postal service (represented by two series—issue of postage stamps, stamped envelopes, and the like; and postal money orders issued).

For two fields, both relating to foreign trade, the representation was somewhat less direct, in that our measurements were based upon the capacity of vessels entered during the year, rather than upon the volume of traffic itself: shipping services rendered by American vessels in foreign trade (represented by tonnage of American vessels entered); and harborage services—such as towing—rendered to foreign shipping in American ports (represented by tonnage of foreign vessels entered).

For two other fields, we had to resort to still more indirect representation: automobile transportation (represented by estimated number of automobiles in use as of June 30); and coastal traffic (represented by gross tonnage of vessels licensed for domestic commerce and outstanding as of June 30).

For the field of street-railway transportation, the situation was mixed: from 1890 onward, we used the Census data for the number of passengers carried where such figures were available, and estimated inter-censal totals on the basis of year-to-year changes in the number of employees; prior to 1890, we made estimates based upon mileage data.

Appendix C gives detailed information regarding sources and methods of derivation for the several individual series relating to transportation and communication other than steam-railroad. These series, as we finally set them up after research and computation, are shown in Table 15.

For transportation and communication, as for manufacture, it is necessary to record that—in spite of the fact that a great deal of care and effort was devoted to the derivation of the fundamental data for the individual series—many defects and limitations still remain; the basic materials are subject to numerous defects and limitations which are irremediable, regardless of any ingenuity and effort devoted to them. And while here, as before, there can be no thought of suggesting that the index finally arrived at is from all points of view unimpeachable, nevertheless we may perhaps claim for our index of transportation and communication some degree of merit, relative to that which is practically possible —especially with regard to the qualities of continuity and comparability over time.

WEIGHTS FOR THE COMBINED ANNUAL INDEX

In the derivation of our combined index of production for transportation and communication, we so far as possible followed the general procedure previously adopted for the index of manufacturing production. We again employed the weighted arithmetic mean of quantity relatives (which is under certain simple conditions equivalent to the aggregative); and we computed the index with the year 1899 as base and with 1899 weights.[1] In one respect,

---

[1] Cf. the discussion for manufacture, in the earlier pages of Chapter II.

TABLE 15

Before making use of the items for these series, the reader should refer to the detailed descriptions in the several sections of Appendix C, or perhaps even to the original sources. The approach to precision of the measurements differs from series to series, and from time to time. Some series pertain to calendar years, some to fiscal.

Year	(1) Street railways: revenue passengers carried* (unit: one million passengers)	(2) Automobiles in use (unit: one thousand automobiles)	(3) Sault Ste. Marie canals traffic (unit: one thousand short tons)	(4) New York canals traffic (unit: one thousand short tons)	(5) Coastal trade: gross tonnage of vessels documented (unit: one thousand gross tons)	(6) Foreign trade: tonnage of American vessels entered (unit: one thousand net tons)	(7) Foreign trade: tonnage of foreign vessels entered (unit: one thousand net tons)
1860	175	..	154	4,650	2,645	5,921	2,354
1861	..	..	88	4,508	2,705	5,024	2,218
1862	..	..	162	5,599	2,617	5,118	2,245
1863	..	..	237	5,558	2,961	4,615	2,640
1864	..	..	284	4,853	3,245	3,066	3,471
1865	..	..	182	4,730	3,382	2,944	3,217
1866	..	..	240	5,775	2,720	3,372	4,410
1867	..	..	325	5,688	2,660	3,455	4,319
1868	..	..	299	6,442	2,702	3,551	4,495
1869	..	..	368	5,859	2,516	3,403	5,348
1870	455	..	540	6,174	2,638	3,486	5,670
1871	..	..	586	6,468	2,765	3,743	6,266
1872	..	..	746	6,673	2,930	3,712	7,095
1873	..	..	888	6,365	3,163	3,613	8,083
1874	..	..	655	5,805	3,293	3,894	9,198
1875	..	..	833	4,860	3,220	3,574	8,119
1876	..	..	1,074	4,172	2,599	3,611	8,899
1877	..	..	913	4,956	2,540	3,663	9,791
1878	..	..	937	5,171	2,497	3,642	10,821
1879	..	..	1,051	5,362	2,598	3,415	12,778
1880	700	..	1,322	6,458	2,638	3,437	14,574
1881	735	..	1,568	5,179	2,646	3,254	15,066
1882	786	..	2,030	5,467	2,796	3,341	14,260
1883	850	..	2,267	5,664	2,838	3,256	13,126
1884	908	..	2,875	5,009	2,884	3,202	11,867
1885	985	..	3,257	4,732	2,895	3,132	12,173

For footnote, see end of table.

TABLE 15 (*Continued*)

Year	(1) Street railways: revenue passengers carried* (*unit: one million passengers*)	(2) Automobiles in use (*unit: one thousand automobiles*)	(3) Sault Ste. Marie canals traffic (*unit: one thousand short tons*)	(4) New York canals traffic (*unit: one thousand short tons*)	(5) Coastal trade: gross tonnage of vessels documented (*unit: one thousand gross tons*)	(6) Foreign trade: tonnage of American vessels entered (*unit: one thousand net tons*)	(7) Foreign trade: tonnage of foreign vessels entered (*unit: one thousand net tons*)
1886	1,086	..	4,528	5,294	2,939	3,232	11,904
1887	1,255	..	5,495	5,554	3,011	3,366	12,451
1888	1,469	..	6,411	4,943	3,172	3,367	12,026
1889	1,710	..	7,516	5,370	3,211	3,724	12,228
1890	2,097	..	9,041	5,246	3,409	4,083	14,024
1891	2,254	..	8,889	4,563	3,610	4,381	13,823
1892	2,514	..	11,214	4,282	3,701	4,470	16,543
1893	2,713	..	10,797	4,332	3,855	4,359	15,223
1894	2,818	..	13,196	3,883	3,696	4,655	15,335
1895	3,128	..	15,063	3,500	3,729	4,473	14,822
1896	3,412	..	16,239	3,715	3,790	5,196	15,793
1897	3,598	..	18,983	3,618	3,897	5,525	18,235
1898	3,896	..	21,235	3,360	3,960	5,240	20,339
1899	4,129	6.3	25,256	3,686	3,965	5,341	20,770
1900	4,367	10.8	25,643	3,346	4,287	6,136	22,027
1901	4,722	16.4	28,403	3,421	4,583	6,381	23,387
1902	4,971	23.5	35,961	3,275	4,859	6,961	23,693
1903	5,509	31.3	34,674	3,615	5,141	6,907	24,187
1904	6,146	43.8	31,546	3,139	5,335	6,679	23,273
1905	6,625	62.6	44,271	3,227	5,442	7,081	23,903
1906	7,093	85.3	51,751	3,541	5,674	7,613	26,543
1907	7,441	115.4	58,217	3,408	6,011	8,116	28,507
1908	7,750	157.9	41,391	3,052	6,372	8,473	30,076
1909	7,954	232.4	57,895	3,117	6,451	8,771	30,287
1910	8,561	358.3	62,363	3,073	6,669	8,888	31,347
1911	9,103	511.4	53,477	3,097	6,720	9,693	32,982
1912	9,546	698.4	72,473	2,606	6,737	11,257	34,901
1913	9,845	1,007.4	79,718	2,602	6,817	13,073	37,567
1914	9,995	1,450.0	55,370	2,081	6,818	13,730	39,659

For footnote, see end of table.

TABLE 15 (*Continued*)

Year	(8) Telephone conversations completed (*unit: one million messages*)	(9) Telegraph messages transmitted (*unit: one million messages*)	(10) Postage stamps: revenue (*unit: one million dollars*)	(11) Postal money orders issued (*unit: one million orders*)
1860...........	..	..	6.9	..
1861...........	..	..	6.7	..
1862...........	..	..	7.8	..
1863...........	..	..	10.3	..
1864...........	..	..	11.0	..
1865...........	..	..	12.8	..
1866...........	..	12.9	12.0	0.24
1867...........	..	..	13.4	0.47
1868...........	..	..	13.9	0.83
1869...........	..	..	15.1	1.26
1870...........	..	..	16.6	1.67
1871...........	..	..	17.7	2.2
1872...........	..	..	19.0	2.6
1873...........	..	..	20.3	3.4
1874...........	..	..	23.4	4.5
1875...........	..	..	24.5	5.1
1876...........	..	..	26.9	5.1
1877...........	..	..	25.8	5.0
1878...........	..	..	27.4	5.7
1879...........	..	..	28.1	6.5
1880...........	80	40.0	31.5	7.5
1881...........	121	..	34.8	8.0
1882...........	142	..	39.7	8.8
1883...........	184	..	43.0	9.3
1884...........	198	∴.	40.7	12.0
1885...........	212	..	40.1	13.2
1886...........	244	..	41.4	14.4
1887...........	274	..	45.7	16.2
1888...........	298	..	49.5	17.4
1889...........	350	..	53.0	17.8
1890...........	405	..	57.7	18.4
1891...........	458	..	62.6	19.2
1892...........	537	..	67.4	20.1
1893...........	536	..	72.4	22.1
1894...........	618	..	70.2	23.0
1895...........	734	..	73.5	22.9

For footnote, see end of table.

TABLE 15 (*Continued*)

Year	(8) Telephone conversations completed (*unit: one million messages*)	(9) Telegraph messages transmitted (*unit: one million messages*)	(10) Postage stamps: revenue (*unit: one million dollars*)	(11) Postal money orders issued (*unit: one million orders*)
1896..........	858	..	78.4	24.9
1897..........	1,083	..	79.0	26.1
1898..........	1,468	..	85.0	28.8
1899..........	2,210	..	87.3	30.0
1900..........	2,623	85.0	94.0	33.2
1901..........	3,683	..	102.0	36.8
1902..........	4,769	90.8	112.2	41.8
1903..........	5,186	..	123.5	47.9
1904......,....	5,888	..	131.9	52.6
1905..........	7,214	88.0	140.5	55.9
1906..........	8,633	..	154.0	61.5
1907..........	9,912	97.9	168.5	65.7
1908..........	10,649	..	176.4	68.6
1909..........	11,234	98.0	188.4	72.5
1910..........	12,035	100.0	206.5	81.4
1911..........	12,697	..	218.7	86.0
1912..........	13,515	103.5	227.0	89.0
1913..........	13,635	114.0	245.8	95.3
1914..........	13,656	115.0	265.1	108.6

* Prior to 1890, these figures are estimates based upon changes in street-railway mileage (cf. the appropriate section of Appendix C).

however, we were forced to depart from the earlier procedure. For most of the industries in the transportation and communication field, 1899 value-added figures were not available, at least not readily. Resort was had, then, to another criterion of economic importance—gross income.[2] This alteration in procedure was regretted, with respect to both theoretical principle and comparability with the manufacture index. However, it is believed that the combined index of transportation and communication as finally set up is not appreciably different from that which would have been secured had the desired value-added weights been available.

[2] Cf. the practice of United States Department of Commerce, Bureau of Foreign and Domestic Commerce, *Survey of Current Business*, XXII (September 1942), 20–28.

Even for the gross-income data, a variety of expedients had to be employed. For some series—including the important steam-railroad series—the 1899 gross-income figures were indeed easily obtainable, directly from official reports. For certain other series, gross-income figures were available only for years other than 1899, and the 1899 item could only be approximated. For a few series, presenting individualistic difficulties, special processes of estimation had to be worked out.

Full details regarding the derivation of the weights for the transportation and communication index are set forth in Appendix D. The weighting figures as finally adopted are presented in Table 16; Columns 2 and 3 of this table show the basic gross-income data, and Columns 4 and 5 show the percentage weights derived therefrom.

TABLE 16

DERIVATION OF WEIGHTS FOR TRANSPORTATION AND COMMUNICATION INDEX

(For general explanation, see accompanying text; for details, see Appendix D)

Individual series	Basic data for weighting: gross income, 1899* (unit: $1,000,000)		Weights (percentage basis)	
(1)	(2)	(3)	(4)	(5)
All Series Included................	1,906.2	..	100.00	..
Steam railroads....................	1,313.6	..	68.90	..
(A) Freight tonnage carried........	..	918.0	..	51.98
(B) Passengers carried.............	..	298.8	..	16.92
Street railways: revenue passengers carried.............................	194.8	..	10.22	..
Automobiles in use.................	1.3†	..	0.07	..
Sault Ste. Marie canals traffic.........	32.0	..	1.68	..
New York canals traffic.............	5.8	..	0.30	..
Coastal trade: gross tonnage of vessels documented......................	145.8	..	7.65	..
Foreign trade: tonnage of American vessels entered.......................	8.0	..	0.42	..
Foreign trade: tonnage of foreign vessels entered.......................	16.5	..	0.87	..
Telephone conversations completed....	57.2	..	3.00	..
Telegraph messages transmitted.......	36.2	..	1.91	..
Postage stamps: revenue.............	93.7	..	4.91	..
Postal money orders issued..........	1.3	..	0.07	..

* Many of these gross-income figures are estimated, and the closeness to precision of the estimates varies from series to series. For details, see the text of Appendix D.

† Obtained by a special method; see the section on automobiles in use, Appendix D.

With respect to the gross-income items in Table 16, a word of caution is necessary. As has just been indicated, many of these items are estimates, and the approach to precision of the estimates varies from series to series. Taking any particular case by itself, the margin of error may be appreciable. Nevertheless, the writer is reasonably confident that, from the point of view of the combined index, the net effect of these errors is not of any great significance. The 1899 gross-income figures for the highly important steam-railroad industry (which has a weight of nearly seven-tenths of the total—cf. Column 4 of Table 16) are presumably quite reliable. No one of the other constituents has a very heavy weight; and we may fairly conclude that any errors of approximation in the gross-income estimates for these other series can hardly have affected the combined index in any essential way.

Here, as in the manufacture index, we employed the "imputed-weighting" system. Thus, for example, the tonnage of freight moved through the canals at Sault Ste. Marie was taken as an indicator of fluctuations of a much broader entity—the volume of traffic on the Great Lakes system; the tonnage of *foreign* vessels entered in the foreign trade of the United States was (as previously set forth) taken as an indicator of fluctuations in the volume of harborage services—such as towing—rendered in American ports.

On the whole, the "imputed-weighting" system seemed for the present index much more nearly justifiable than the rival "earned-weighting" principle.[3] However, it was particularly noted that the railroad-traffic series would in either case have a predominant weight, and that the magnitude of the gross-income figure for this group would not differ materially as between the two systems—the figure was 1313.6 million dollars on the "imputed-weighting" basis, and would be 1216.8 million dollars on the "earned-weighting" basis (cf. the steam-railroad section of Appendix D). All in all, it did not seem likely that, for the combined index, material difference would appear as between the results for the two systems. This impression was confirmed by actual calculation. Experimen-

[3] Cf. the concluding pages of Chapter II, and the references in the final footnote to that chapter.

tal computations revealed only unimportant differences between the two sets of results.

COMPUTATION OF THE COMBINED ANNUAL INDEX

For each of the thirteen constituent series—the two steam-railroad series, freight and passengers, together with the eleven series of Table 15—annual quantity relatives to the base 1899 were computed, 1860–1914.[4] Next a *preliminary* combined annual index was computed, 1860–1914, such index being calculated as annual weighted arithmetic means of the relatives to base 1899 for the individual component series, employing the weights shown in Columns 4 and 5 of Table 16.

THE CALENDAR-YEAR ADJUSTMENT

The index as so far developed was, in the main, upon a *fiscal-year* basis: the steam-railroad series—whose weight constituted almost seven-tenths of the total (cf. Table 16)—pertained to fiscal years, as well as several of the other constituents (cf. Appendix C). Adjustment of the index to a calendar-year basis, as accurately as might be, was highly desirable.

In making this adjustment, we adapted methods which had previously been employed in particular phases of the construction of the manufacture index (see the section of Chapter III headed "Transference of Certain Fiscal-Year Series to a Calendar-Year Basis").

With respect to the choice of series to be used as basis for making the calendar-year adjustment in the present case, the best decision seemed to be to utilize the available monthly series on gross earnings of steam railroads.[5] This was a logical series to use for

---

[4] It was necessary to make a few interpolations and extrapolations to fill certain gaps in the array of original items for constituent series (cf. Table 15); the procedure generally employed was straight-line logarithmic interpolation. The series for automobiles in use entered the index only beginning with 1899. (For further discussion, see later pages of this chapter.)

[5] Once more, we were indebted to Dr. Arthur H. Cole for the use of the data presented in his article "A Monthly Index of Railroad Earnings, 1866–1914," *Review of Economic Statistics*, XVIII (February 1936), 31–41.

the purposes of the short-run adjustment here contemplated, especially in view of the very high weight of steam-railroad activity in
the combined index. Moreover, if due allowance was made for
the difference in time reference as between the two series—the
preliminary transportation and communication index, as we had
just computed it; and steam-railroad gross earnings—these short-
time fluctuations were found to correlate quite well.

Our first step was, from a survey of the available information,
to arrive at as good an approximation as was feasible concerning
the changes over time in the *average dating*[6] of the fiscal-year
figures for our steam-railroad traffic series. Investigation suggested that in the reports which railroads made to *Poor's Manual
of Railroads* opposite tendencies were present over time: prior to
1890, the average date for the ending of fiscal years fell in the
latter part of October;[7] in 1890, the average date moved rather
abruptly back to about September 30, and from 1890 on, this date
shifted steadily backward.[8] These changes in 1890 and subsequent
years were, of course, occasioned by the requirement of reports to
the Interstate Commerce Commission for years ending June 30.
The Interstate Commerce Commission's own reported figures
pertain to fiscal years ending June 30, from 1890 through the end
of our period of analysis.

For the purpose of applying calendar-year adjustments, then,
we up to 1890 thought in terms of fiscal years ending October 31;

[6] In our computation of average dating of fiscal years we computed weighted
averages, weighting the several roads by their gross earnings for the current fiscal
period.

A closer approach to precision would, of course, have been obtained by dealing with the individual roads *separately*, adjusting the figures for each road individually, in accordance with its own particular dating system. The expense of
this latter procedure was, however, prohibitive—especially considering that many
of the constituent roads embraced subsidiaries that would have had to be in-
vestigated each in its own right.

[7] This was true for both of our "sample lists"—the list pertaining to 1855–71
and that pertaining to 1866–90.

[8] Cf. passages in *Poor's Manual of Railroads* (for statement regarding full designation of this source, see fn. 3, Chapter V, above): *Manual* for 1891, p. vi; *Manual*
for 1892, p. xxviii; *Manual* for 1895, p. x.

for 1890–95, in terms of fiscal years ending September 30; for 1896–99, in terms of fiscal years ending August 31; and after 1899 —when, it will be remembered, we made a transition to the Interstate Commerce Commission data—in terms of fiscal years ending June 30.

The procedure followed in redistributing the successive items of our fiscal-year index between calendar years followed the principle upon which the calendar-year adjustments for manufacture were founded (see again the section of Chapter III to which reference is made just above). In detail, the methodology for the series vessels produced is most nearly comparable. That is to say, the successive steps here were: (1) to redistribute the items of our fiscal-year index between calendar years on the basis of the short-time movements of Dr. Cole's railroad earnings series;[9] and (2) to reduce the series just derived to the base 1899 (i.e., to the base, *calendar year* 1899 = 100), by dividing this series through by its 1899 item.[10]

Our combined annual index, 1860–1914, shifted to the calendar-year basis by the method which has been described, is presented in Table 17, and is shown graphically as the third curve on Chart 2.[11]

THE "CONTINUITY" OF THE INDEX

A few words may be added as to the "continuity" of the index— with respect, that is, to the list of constituent series.

One series, automobiles in use, comes into the combined index only beginning with 1899. This is not regarded as a "discon-

[9] For years prior to 1866, when Dr. Cole's series was not available, we could do no better than to resort to the rough expedient (thinking in terms of fiscal years ending October 31, as indicated in the text, just above), of allocating five-sixths of each fiscal-year item to the corresponding calendar year, and the remaining one-sixth to the *preceding* calendar year.

[10] In the present application of the procedure, we did not trouble with secular-trend adjustments, since both series involved had strong upward secular movements and for any given year-to-year comparison the magnitude of the relative secular movements did not differ markedly as between the two series.

[11] Here, as for manufacture, it must be recorded that over 1860–65, the index, for a variety of reasons, is less reliable than in later years.

tinuity," however, since the introduction of this series represented the emergence of a new form of transportation service.[12]

Here, as previously for the manufacture index (cf. the pertinent parts of Chapters III and IV), we were obliged to make some interpolations and extrapolations to fill certain gaps which appeared in the array of original items for constituent series (cf. again

TABLE 17

INDEX OF PRODUCTION FOR TRANSPORTATION AND COMMUNICATION: BY YEARS, 1860–1914

(*Base: 1899*)

Year	Index	Year	Index	Year	Index
1860	10	1879	32	1897	86
		1880	36	1898	92
1861	11			1899	100
1862	12	1881	40	1900	106
1863	14	1882	44		
1864	15	1883	45	1901	116
1865	16	1884	46	1902	126
		1885	46	1903	136
1866	16			1904	138
1867	17	1886	51	1905	156
1868	18	1887	59		
1869	20	1888	60	1906	172
1870	21	1889	65	1907	180
		1890	70	1908	164
1871	23			1909	188
1872	25	1891	74	1910	200
1873	27	1892	78		
1874	28	1893	78	1911	200
1875	27	1894	74	1912	220
		1895	80	1913	228
1876	27			1914	220
1877	27	1896	80		
1878	28				

Table 15). Once again, attention may be expressly directed to the fact that these interpolations and extrapolations were developed solely for the purposes of index-number calculation, and were not, in any given case, put forth as necessarily being approximations to the unknown missing items of the series itself. This distinction may properly be once more stressed: very often an interpolated

---

[12] Cf. the corresponding discussion for automobile production, in the manufacture index (Chapter III).

or extrapolated figure—even when decidedly untrustworthy as an estimate of the missing value itself—may be quite adequate for the purposes of the general computation process of which the interpolation or extrapolation is a part.

These general statements may appropriately be applied to the case at hand. The interpolations and extrapolations made in the course of the computation of our combined index of transportation and communication could not, the writer is confident, have interfered in any essential way with the validity of the movements shown by this index.[13]

The Final Combined Index Adjusted for Secular Trend

As is more fully set forth in Chapter IV of this volume, the present writer in an earlier study reached the conclusion that for a number of production indexes—including the new index of transportation and communication—the secular trend over our pre-war period (i.e., up to 1914) could be represented with reasonably close approach to precision by a logarithmic parabola.[14]

The logarithmic-parabola secular trend fitted to the new transportation and communication index is shown on Chart 2 (which is constructed with logarithmic vertical scale) as a dotted line drawn through the curve. This secular trend indicates a rapid average rate of growth (5.82 per cent per year) accompanied by comparatively slight retardation in relative growth (0.014 per cent per year).[15]

The "annual index of production for transportation and communication, adjusted for secular trend"—obtained by dividing the successive items of the actual index-number series through by

[13] Cf. fn. 17, in Chapter VI.

[14] In lieu of extended statement here, regarding the basis for this conclusion and the properties of the logarithmic parabola, the reader is referred to the discussion at the end of Chapter IV, above, and the references therein contained.

[15] On a chart constructed with logarithmic vertical scale (as in Chart 2), a constant rate of growth results in an upward-sloping straight line, and upon any given logarithmic scale the larger the rate of growth, the steeper the slope of the line; retardation in ratio of growth manifests itself in curvature away from a straight-line movement—the line, that is, is convex upward—and upon any given logarithmic scale the more rapid the rate of retardation in relative growth, the greater is the curvature.

TABLE 18

INDEX OF PRODUCTION FOR TRANSPORTATION AND COMMUNICATION,
ADJUSTED FOR SECULAR TREND: BY YEARS, 1860–1914

(*Unit: one per cent*)

Year	Adjusted Index	Year	Adjusted Index	Year	Adjusted Index
1860	93	1879	92	1897	90
		1880	98	1898	91
1861	92			1899	93
1862	93	1881	103	1900	94
1863	102	1882	106		
1864	106	1883	102	1901	97
1865	108	1884	99	1902	99
		1885	94	1903	102
1866	101			1904	98
1867	101	1886	99	1905	105
1868	98	1887	107		
1869	102	1888	104	1906	110
1870	104	1889	106	1907	109
		1890	108	1908	94
1871	105			1909	102
1872	107	1891	108	1910	103
1873	112	1892	107		
1874	106	1893	102	1911	98
1875	98	1894	91	1912	102
		1895	94	1913	100
1876	94			1914	92
1877	88	1896	88		
1878	86				

the corresponding trend values ("ordinates of secular trend")—
is given in Table 18, and is shown as the third curve on Chart 3.

AN ESTIMATED MONTHLY INDEX, ADJUSTED FOR SECULAR TREND AND SEASONAL VARIATION

Table 19 and Chart 7 show the results of a special computation,
carried out with a view to utilizing certain supplementary information which fortunately was available concerning the cyclical fluctuations of railroad earnings over our period of analysis, and thus
securing a more detailed picture of the short-time movements of
production in the field of transportation and communication.

The monthly items presented in Table 19 and Chart 7 are estimates, secured by superimposing, upon the annual index of trans-

TABLE 19

INDEX OF PRODUCTION FOR TRANSPORTATION AND COMMUNICATION, ADJUSTED FOR SECULAR TREND AND SEASONAL VARIATION: BY MONTHS, JANUARY 1866 TO JUNE 1914

(Unit: one per cent)

Year	Jan.	Feb.	Mar.	Apr.	May	June	July	Aug.	Sept.	Oct.	Nov.	Dec.
1866	105	100	99	95	104	105	103	100	97	100	101	94
1867	101	96	94	99	98	95	100	104	107	105	105	97
1868	98	99	93	98	97	97	97	100	100	100	96	96
1869	100	99	103	100	103	106	104	102	102	104	107	103
1870	101	104	102	104	107	106	103	106	103	103	105	103
1871	103	102	105	103	106	105	105	105	105	102	104	102
1872	110	108	105	107	107	106	106	106	105	109	106	103
1873	112	114	115	116	116	116	113	111	114	109	104	108
1874	112	108	105	108	108	107	106	105	102	103	100	104
1875	101	95	99	101	98	98	102	96	98	96	97	96
1876	95	97	93	94	95	96	92	92	94	94	93	90
1877	88	88	88	86	88	87	81	87	90	90	88	87
1878	91	89	86	87	86	82	84	86	85	86	89	85
1879	88	90	88	88	88	86	90	89	94	95	95	99
1880	99	101	99	98	96	97	99	96	96	98	104	100
1881	99	96	101	103	103	108	105	105	101	97	102	108
1882	108	106	105	103	103	104	105	107	106	105	107	107
1883	104	103	109	101	102	101	102	105	104	102	104	100
1884	98	99	101	102	101	97	99	99	99	97	96	98
1885	95	93	98	94	92	91	91	89	96	97	97	98
1886	88	97	99	95	95	98	102	100	101	101	101	102
1887	102	105	109	108	106	107	106	107	107	106	109	109
1888	101	107	102	103	104	106	104	104	103	103	102	103
1889	104	104	101	103	105	101	107	110	106	109	107	110
1890	109	110	106	111	113	105	109	108	108	107	106	107
1891	113	106	102	106	104	105	110	108	109	109	108	111
1892	106	114	104	106	104	107	106	107	108	106	107	108
1893	104	107	108	106	108	108	101	94	98	102	97	95
1894	93	92	93	91	88	87	84	94	90	93	94	92
1895	91	90	91	91	91	91	92	94	91	98	98	96
1896	95	94	89	88	88	88	88	84	85	89	86	89
1897	87	90	87	85	86	89	90	90	90	92	93	92
1898	92	95	92	91	93	88	85	88	89	90	92	94
1899	92	86	91	89	93	94	94	93	94	94	96	95
1900	99	96	94	93	93	94	92	93	91	94	94	98

TABLE 19 (*Continued*)

Year	Jan.	Feb.	Mar.	Apr.	May	June	July	Aug.	Sept.	Oct.	Nov.	Dec.
1901	102	98	94	96	98	97	99	98	95	98	98	96
1902	104	97	95	100	101	99	100	98	97	98	98	100
1903	107	103	104	108	104	104	106	100	99	99	98	99
1904	98	101	98	99	97	98	95	96	98	96	101	101
1905	100	93	104	103	104	106	104	104	105	103	109	111
1906	118	115	110	106	110	111	110	107	104	105	107	111
1907	115	112	111	116	117	114	115	110	106	108	103	96
1908	93	92	91	90	87	91	96	94	96	96	96	101
1909	97	96	98	98	98	102	104	103	103	103	107	100
1910	104	106	108	106	106	105	102	102	101	98	103	102
1911	101	98	96	97	102	99	97	97	96	95	97	98
1912	94	103	98	98	101	102	103	103	100	103	105	105
1913	107	104	96	98	104	102	104	100	99	99	97	97
1914	96	90	94	94	92	96	..	..	..	..	..	..

portation and communication adjusted for secular trend, the form of short-time movement exhibited by monthly railroad earnings adjusted for secular trend and seasonal variation.[16] We may describe the new series as our estimated monthly combined index of production in the field of transportation and communication, adjusted for secular trend and seasonal variation, January 1866 to June 1914.

As has just been stated, the short-run fluctuations shown by our new monthly index represent the result of estimates, rather than of direct measurement (which is, of course, impossible from existing data). The indication of cyclical and other short-run movements for the combined index of transportation and communication may, therefore, fail of complete accuracy. However, in view of the generally high correlation between the short-run movements of steam-railroad transportation and steam-railroad earnings—together with the further considerations that the steam-railroad

[16] In this analysis, we employed the series for monthly railroad earnings adjusted for seasonal variation which was developed by Dr. A. H. Cole and described in his article, "A Monthly Index of Railroad Earnings, 1866–1914," *Review of Economic Statistics*, xviii (February 1936), 31–41. Adjustment of these figures for secular trend was carried out by the present writer—cf. Edwin Frickey, *Economic Fluctuations in the United States* (Cambridge, Mass.: Harvard University Press, 1942), *passim*, especially chap. xv including Table 15 and Chart 34.

CHART 7

INDEX OF PRODUCTION FOR TRANSPORTATION AND COMMUNICATION, ADJUSTED FOR SECULAR
TREND AND SEASONAL VARIATION: BY MONTHS, JANUARY 1866 TO JUNE 1914*

(*Unit: one per cent*)

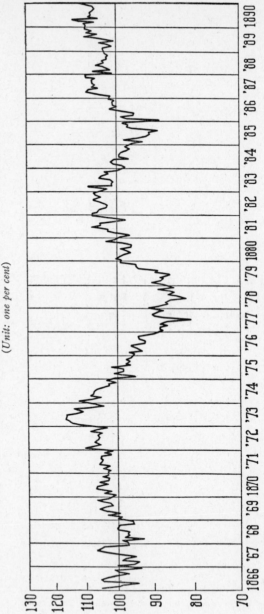

* Logarithmic vertical scale. For explanation, see accompanying text.

CHART 7 (Continued)

INDEX OF PRODUCTION FOR TRANSPORTATION AND COMMUNICATION, ADJUSTED FOR SECULAR
TREND AND SEASONAL VARIATION: BY MONTHS, JANUARY 1866 TO JUNE 1914*

(Unit: one per cent)

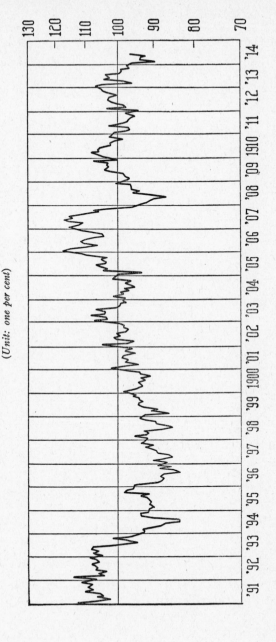

series have a very high weight in the combined index (between them, almost seven-tenths of the total), and that the cyclical fluctuations of the other constituents of the index are in general comparatively narrow in amplitude—it would appear that the estimate afforded by our new monthly index for transportation and communication constitutes at least a reasonably close approach to the truth.

CHAPTER VIII

AN INDEX OF INDUSTRIAL AND COMMERCIAL PRODUCTION

As a final task, we undertook the development for our period of analysis of an annual index of industrial and commercial production.[1]

THE MODE OF ATTACK

It was immediately evident that for the period 1860–1914 we could not hope to obtain the desired index number through the straightforward process of building up a composite by combination of series representing various components of the broad economic entity—"industrial and commercial production." The lacunae in the statistical material were too numerous and too serious to make this line of approach feasible.

We had resort, then, to a different mode of attack. We endeavored to find "points of observation," so to speak, upon which to stand and review the passage of economic activity. And for this purpose, we made use of the two indexes which we had previously developed: the new index of manufacture and the new index of transportation and communication. These two indexes, it will be remembered, had been constructed with special attention to the highly important qualities of continuity and comparability over time.

Furthermore, from the economic point of view the selection of the two fields—manufacture, and transportation and communication—appeared appropriate with reference to the observation of the flow of industrial and commercial production. As regards manufacture, it is true that practically all the elements connected with industrial and commercial production pass through the manu-

---

[1] This chapter is adapted from certain passages in the writer's *Economic Fluctuations in the United States* (Cambridge, Mass.: Harvard University Press, 1942); cf. pp. 202–204 and pp. 274–276 in this earlier volume.

facturing process, and so we were able to set up a "checking station" at this part of the economic system. The following remarks by Dr. Edmund E. Day—though stated formally with respect to the concept, "the national real income"—were pertinent here. "So far as the national real income is embodied in goods, the most important single barometer of changes in the size of the income is the physical volume of output in manufacture. This follows from the fact that the great bulk of modern articles of consumption pass at one stage or another through factory processes. Even our foodstuffs—our flour, meat, sugar, coffee—emerge in finished form from industrial plants. Only a few commodities—fresh vegetables and fruits, milk, household coal—are not regarded as in any way manufactured. The production of all others—the bulk of our food, our clothing, our shelter—involves manufacture." [2] Likewise, the formation of producers' capital goods is closely interconnected with the manufacturing process. It is also true that, by and large, the elements connected with industrial and commercial production pass through the nation's widespread system of transportation and communication, and consequently we were here again enabled to set up a "checking station" for observation of the flow of economic activity.

We made the new index, then, by averaging, year by year, 1860–1914, our indexes for manufacture and for transportation and communication, derived as described on preceding pages. Since, all things considered, there seemed little ground for discrimination between these two indexes with regard to intrinsic merit as indicators of the economic entity in which we were here interested, we assigned them equal weight. For the purposes at hand, the choice of form of average was not of any essential importance. We selected the geometric average, for the reason that we thus made it possible to simplify somewhat certain technical comparisons connected with measurements of relative growth and retardation (which are, of course, worked out on a geometrical-progres-

---

[2] Edmund E. Day, "The Measurement of Variations in the National Real Income," *Quarterly Publication of the American Statistical Association*, xvii (March 1921), 553–554.

sion basis); however, had the arithmetic average been employed instead, the results—except for very slight alteration in the indicated rates of growth and retardation—would have been virtually the same.[3]

TABLE 20

INDEX OF INDUSTRIAL AND COMMERCIAL PRODUCTION:
BY YEARS, 1860–1914

(*Base: 1899*)

Year	Index	Year	Index	Year	Index
1860	13	1879	34	1897	83
		1880	39	1898	92
1861	13			1899	100
1862	13	1881	43	1900	103
1863	15	1882	46		
1864	17	1883	48	1901	114
1865	17	1884	47	1902	126
		1885	46	1903	131
				1904	129
1866	19			1905	148
1867	19	1886	54		
1868	20	1887	60		
1869	22	1888	61	1906	162
1870	23	1889	65	1907	168
		1890	71	1908	144
				1909	177
1871	25			1910	186
1872	28	1891	74		
1873	29	1892	78		
1874	28	1893	74	1911	180
1875	28	1894	71	1912	206
		1895	81	1913	215
1876	28			1914	206
1877	29	1896	77		
1878	30				

Our new index of industrial and commercial production is presented in Table 20, and is shown graphically as the first curve on Chart 2.[4]

THE NEW INDEX ADJUSTED FOR SECULAR TREND

As is more fully set forth in Chapter IV of this volume, the present writer, in an earlier study, reached the conclusion that for

[3] On the concepts of growth and retardation, see pp. 59, 118.
[4] The items for 1860–65 are less reliable than those for subsequent years.

a number of production indexes (including, among others, the new index of industrial and commercial production), the secular trend over our pre-war period (i.e., up to 1914) could be represented with reasonably close approach to precision by a logarithmic parabola.[5]

TABLE 21

INDEX OF INDUSTRIAL AND COMMERCIAL PRODUCTION, ADJUSTED FOR SECULAR TREND: BY YEARS, 1860–1914

(Unit: one per cent)

Year	Adjusted Index	Year	Adjusted Index	Year	Adjusted Index
1860	99	1879	93	1897	89
		1880	102	1898	93
1861	96			1899	96
1862	90	1881	106	1900	94
1863	98	1882	109		
1864	102	1883	106	1901	99
1865	98	1884	98	1902	104
		1885	93	1903	103
1866	102			1904	96
1867	101	1886	103	1905	104
1868	100	1887	107		
1869	104	1888	104	1906	109
1870	102	1889	106	1907	107
		1890	109	1908	88
1871	103			1909	102
1872	110	1891	107	1910	102
1873	109	1892	108		
1874	102	1893	97	1911	94
1875	94	1894	88	1912	102
		1895	96	1913	101
1876	90			1914	92
1877	87	1896	86		
1878	87				

The logarithmic-parabola secular trend fitted to the new index of industrial and commercial production is shown on Chart 2 (which is constructed with logarithmic vertical scale) as a dotted line drawn through the curve. This secular trend indicates a rapid average annual rate of growth (5.38 per cent per year),

[5] Once more, in lieu of extended statement regarding the basis for this conclusion and the properties of the logarithmic parabola, we refer the reader to the discussions in the closing pages of Chapter IV and Chapter VII, respectively, and the references therein contained.

accompanied by rather slight retardation in relative growth (0.007 per cent per year).[6]

The "annual index of industrial and commercial production, adjusted for secular trend"—obtained by dividing the successive items of the actual index-number series through by the corresponding trend values ("ordinates of secular trend")—is presented in Table 21, and is shown as the first curve on Chart 3.

[6] The series thus exhibits—as would, of course, be expected—properties intermediate between those of its two constituents.

APPENDICES

APPENDIX A

MANUFACTURE INDEX—CONSTITUENT SERIES

Detailed descriptions of the series used in the manufacture index are given on the following pages; and for most of the series, the sources from which the data were obtained are stated fully in the descriptive notes. Some governmental publications, however, underwent several changes in titles and in issuing departments over the years. Details concerning these source materials, all of which have been published by the Government Printing Office, are as follows.

1. *Statistical Abstract of the United States*—referred to in the descriptive notes below as *Statistical Abstract*—was prepared for the years 1878–1902 by the Bureau of Statistics, Treasury Department; for 1903–11, by the Bureau of Statistics, Department of Commerce and Labor; for 1912–37, by the Bureau of Foreign and Domestic Commerce, Department of Commerce; and for 1938–date, by the Bureau of the Census, Department of Commerce.

2. *Mineral Resources of the United States*, for the years 1882–1923, was issued by the United States Geological Survey, Department of the Interior; for 1924–33, by the Bureau of Mines, Department of Commerce; and for 1934–date, by the Bureau of Mines, Department of the Interior. Beginning in 1933, the title was changed to *Minerals Yearbook*.

3. *Commerce and Navigation of the United States* through the year 1865 was issued annually by the Register of the Treasury, Treasury Department; and for 1866–1911, by the Bureau of Statistics, Treasury Department. Beginning 1912, the issuing body became the Bureau of Foreign and Domes-

tic Commerce, Department of Commerce, and the title was changed to *Foreign Commerce and Navigation of the United States*.

4. Monthly publications on foreign trade were issued by the Bureau of Statistics, Treasury Department, under varying titles as indicated below.

   (a) *Monthly Report of the Director of the Bureau of Statistics*, November 15, 1866 to August 22, 1868. The report was "suspended then because of causes resulting in a change of direction."

   (b) *Monthly Report of the Deputy Special Commissioner of the Revenue, in Charge of the Bureau of Statistics*, January 1869 to January 1870. At times this report has been called *Monthly Report on the Commerce and Navigation of the United States*.

   (c) *Monthly Report of the Chief of the Bureau of Statistics*, February 1870 to June 1875.

   (d) *Summary Statement of the Imports and Exports of the United States*, July 1875 to December 1894.

   (e) *Finance, Commerce, and Immigration of the United States*, January 1895 to December 1895.

   (f) *Monthly Summary of Finance and Commerce of the United States*, January 1896 to June 1898.

   (g) *Monthly Summary of Commerce and Finance of the United States*, July 1898 to June 1903. This publication was continued under the same title through June 1914, but the issuing authority changed several times, as follows: July 1903 to June 1912, Bureau of Statistics, Department of Commerce and Labor; July 1912 to June 1914, Bureau of Foreign and Domestic Commerce, Department of Commerce. In July 1914, the title was changed to *Monthly Summary of Foreign Commerce of the United States*, but the report was still issued by the Bureau of Foreign and Domestic Commerce through April 1941. In May 1941 it appeared under the auspices of the Bureau of the Census, Division of Foreign Trade Statistics, Department of Commerce, and continued through September 1941, when publication ceased for the duration of the war.

In the selection of sources for some of the manufacture series, we were aided by information secured from Arthur F. Burns, *Production Trends in the United States since 1870* (New York: National Bureau of Economic Research, Inc., 1934). We have also taken from this publication certain of the import series, as is more fully indicated below.

The actual items for annual series, 1860–1914, are presented in Table 1; the items for certain census-year series, 1859–1914, are presented in Table 2.

WHEAT FLOUR PRODUCED

The period 1880–1914. Our series for wheat-flour production by calendar years, 1880–1914, has been patterned after data published in *Wheat Studies of the Food Research Institute* of Stanford University. In the publication of December 1927, a series was developed for wheat-flour output during the crop years 1880–1914.[1] In this study estimates were made to "fill the gaps" between census years; for census years, fairly complete data on flour production are available in the United States Census of Manufactures.

The estimates for flour production, published in *Wheat Studies,* were based on the fact that "actual consumption of flour, per capita, in the United States apparently changes very little from year to year, except with the gradual change in consumption habits . . . Given the per capita consumption of flour in each year, it is a simple matter to calculate the total domestic consumption. The total production in any period must obviously equal the domestic consumption plus the exports in the same period,

[1] A crop year covers the twelve-month period ending June; e.g., the crop year from July 1879 through June 1880 is dated 1880. For a detailed description of the series, see "Statistics of American Wheat Milling and Flour Disposition Since 1879," *Wheat Studies of the Food Research Institute,* IV (December 1927), 63–102.

neglecting differences in total stocks of flour at the beginning and at the end of the period." [2]

The Institute's first step in obtaining the desired figures was to calculate the estimated total consumption in census years.[3] These total-consumption figures divided by population figures yielded estimates of per-capita consumption of wheat flour in census years. For estimates of per-capita consumption in intercensal years from 1879 to 1902, the Institute adopted a horizontal straight line "at the level indicated by the average for the three census years 1879 to 1899 inclusive." [4] In other words, they concluded that annual per-capita consumption of wheat flour for crop years from 1880 to 1902 could be taken as essentially constant throughout the period, and as equal to the average of the estimated per-capita consumption figures for the census years 1879, 1889, and 1899. From 1903 to 1914, however, the estimates of annual per-capita consumption were read off as ordinates of trend from a line fitted by the least-squares method to the census figures for 1904, 1909, and 1914.[5] These annual estimates of per-capita consumption were multiplied by population figures, as of January 1 each year, to secure data for total consumption of wheat flour in each crop year, 1880–1914.[6]

The Institute then made estimates of wheat-flour production in each crop year, 1880–1914, by adding, year by year, the estimates of flour consumption (described above) to figures for net exports and shipments of flour.[7] In this calculation, differences in total stocks of flour at the beginning and end of the period were neglected; but, according to *Wheat Studies*, the method of calcula-

---

[2] *Wheat Studies*, IV, 64.

[3] These estimates were based upon production as reported in the Census of Manufactures for census years, estimated unreported production, imports, exports, and changes in stocks. See *Wheat Studies*, IV, 85–87.

[4] *Wheat Studies*, IV, 87.

[5] *Loc. cit.*

[6] The population figures as of January 1 each year, 1880–1908, "are means of successive census estimates for July 1, from U. S. Statistical Abstract, 1914"; for 1909–14, they are "estimates of National Bureau of Economic Research, *News Bulletin*, April 20, 1925." See *Wheat Studies*, II (June 1926), 261, footnote *e* to Table II.

[7] Figures for flour consumption, net exports, shipments, and output have been published in *Wheat Studies*, IV, 101.

tion yielded estimates "with an error probably never over 3 per cent and usually under 1 or 2 per cent." [8]

Our desire was to obtain *calendar-year data* for wheat-flour production; accordingly, for the period 1880–1914 we patterned our procedure after that of *Wheat Studies* for crop years, just described. That is to say, for each year, 1880–1914, we added (1) wheat-flour consumption for calendar years, obtained by straight-line interpolation upon the smooth curve of the *Wheat Studies* crop-year estimates, to (2) exports of wheat flour for calendar years, secured from various monthly publications on foreign trade issued by the United States Treasury Department and the Department of Commerce.[9] No account was taken of either imports or re-exports of wheat flour, since their net effect was found to be negligible.[10] Our series, like the *Wheat Studies* crop-year series of wheat-flour production, does not take into account changes in stocks. According to *Wheat Studies*, flour stocks on January 1 are subject to more variation than are stocks on July 1;[11] for this reason, our calendar-year series is probably somewhat less accurate than the Institute's crop-year series, so far as year-to-year movements are concerned. (The Food Research Institute—*op. cit.*, page 91—considers its estimates of annual flour production "to be seldom, if ever, more than 1.5 per cent wide of the facts.") But for the purpose of our particular study calendar-year estimates—even though not so nearly precise as crop-year estimates —are preferred, since our aim is to use figures for wheat-flour production along with calendar-year data obtainable for other series, in order to make our combined production index apply as nearly as possible to calendar years.

The period 1860–79. We have estimated wheat-flour consumption for 1860–79, first by crop years, following the general method described above for the period 1880–1914. The Food Research

---

[8] *Wheat Studies*, IV, 65.

[9] For a detailed description of the sources of the foreign-trade data, see the introduction to this Appendix.

[10] Data on imports, exports, and re-exports of wheat flour for years ending June 30, 1880–1927, may be found in *Wheat Studies*, IV, 101.

[11] *Wheat Studies*, IV, 91.

Institute gives 5.600 bushels as the annual per-capita consumption of wheat for food purposes in each crop year from 1867 through 1880;[12] and the United States Department of Agriculture has calculated that 4.85 bushels of wheat were used in making a barrel of flour in the census year 1879.[13] By dividing the number of bushels of wheat consumed per capita by the number of bushels of wheat per barrel, we derived a figure for per-capita wheat-flour consumption in barrels over the period 1860–79. (The estimate was obtained as follows: $\dfrac{5.600}{4.85} = 1.155$. Note that this figure differs only slightly—0.7 per cent—from the figure—1.147—used by the Food Research Institute for the period 1880 to 1902.) We then multiplied this per-capita wheat-flour consumption figure by the population on January 1 of each crop year, to secure estimates for total wheat-flour consumption in the several crop years, 1860–79.[14]

Finally, we obtained the calendar-year series of wheat-flour production, 1860–79, by adding (1) wheat-flour consumption by calendar years, derived by straight-line interpolation between crop-year figures, as before, to (2) exports of wheat flour by calendar years (as in the compilation for the period 1880–1914, imports and re-exports of wheat flour were not taken into account). Calendar-year exports, 1867–79, were secured directly from

[12] *Wheat Studies,* II, 263. "In view of the uniformity of per capita consumption of flour from year to year, as indicated by the close agreement of the figures for most census years and as supported by common observation, it appears not only that the figures derived from the census give a reliable statement of consumption in these years but also that the lines connecting the figures for census years probably give a reasonably accurate picture of per capita consumption of wheat in the form of flour in the intervening years." (*Ibid.,* p. 241.) See, also, *Wheat Studies,* IV, 81.

[13] *Wheat Studies,* II, 250, and United States Department of Agriculture, *Crops and Markets,* III, Supplement No. 4 (April 1926), p. 108. Although the Institute considers the figure of 4.85 bushels to be somewhat high (cf. *Wheat Studies,* II, 249–250), we have used it in our calculations, since it is an official figure available for the early period, and the results obtained can, at best, be only rough estimates.

[14] The population figures used for the period 1867–79 were taken from *Wheat Studies,* II, 263. For the years 1860–66, we interpolated the figures from data in *Statistical Abstract,* 1914, p. 628, following the method used by the Food Research Institute, as described in the above discussion of 1880–1914 data. (For a detailed description of the *Statistical Abstract,* see the introduction to this Appendix.)

various monthly publications on foreign trade issued by the Bureau of Statistics, United States Treasury Department. Prior to 1867, these exports data are published only for fiscal years ending June 30; we approximated calendar-year totals, 1860–66, by straight-line interpolation.[15]

REFINED SUGAR PRODUCED

Since no figures for the total output of refined sugar in the United States by calendar years are available for our period of study, we have derived an estimated series, as described below. In our compilations we have used data for sugar cane and sugar beets, which yield products that serve identical purposes.[16]

The period 1888–1914. We developed a series for this period by adding (1) cane-sugar meltings of United States refiners, by calendar years,[17] to (2) domestic refined beet-sugar production, by years beginning July 1. The sugar-meltings data were furnished by Willett and Gray, Sugar Statisticians, of New York City; and figures for beet-sugar production were taken from United States Department of Agriculture, *Agriculture Yearbook,* 1923 (Washington: Government Printing Office, 1924), page 845, where the series is designated as "beet sugar (chiefly refined)."

Although the series for beet-sugar production is formally dated as of the year beginning July 1, the figures may practically be considered nearly equivalent to calendar-year data. The beet-

[15] Fiscal-year data were obtained from annual issues of *Commerce and Navigation of the United States.* For a detailed description of the foreign-trade sources, see the introduction to this Appendix.

[16] Cf. *The Encyclopaedia Britannica,* Fourteenth Edition, XXI (London: The Encyclopaedia Britannica Company, Ltd.; New York: Encyclopaedia Britannica, Inc., 1929), 523, which, in a discussion of cane sugar and beet sugar, states: "These impurities [derived from the plant juices] account for differences in colour, odour, and flavour of raw cane and beet sugars. When refined these sugars are colourless and odourless, have equal sweetening power, contain about 99.8% of sucrose, and cannot be distinguished by chemical analysis. After further purification in the laboratory, they both contain 100% of sucrose."

[17] Sugar melting is one of the basic operations in the refining of sugar. *The Encyclopaedia Britannica* states that sugar refining "consists of three main operations: (1) dissolving [or 'melting'] the raw sugar in water; (2) decolourizing the resulting solution; and (3) re-crystallization." See Fourteenth Edition, XXI (1929), 527. Cf. also *The Encyclopedia Americana,* XXV (New York and Chicago: Americana Corporation, 1936), 801: "The refining of sugar consists in washing, melting, purifying, evaporating and recrystallizing."

sugar "campaign" extends somewhat into the calendar year succeeding the season in which most of the sugar beets are harvested and processed, but most of the season's output of refined beet sugar takes place prior to the end of the calendar year.[18] Thus, for example, by using the data for the year beginning July 1, 1900 as representative of the calendar year 1900, we obtain a good approximation to the actual calendar-year production; the net error of this approximation is equal to the difference between beet-sugar production in the early part of the calendar year 1900 and that in the early part of the calendar year 1901. In view of the comparatively small amount of beet-sugar production at the beginning of a calendar year, such net error would hardly be significant in our study, particularly because of the relatively greater importance of cane sugar over the period of analysis.

The period 1860–87. Since data for cane-sugar meltings are not available prior to 1888, we estimated the amount of raw cane sugar available for cane-sugar meltings, and then multiplied this amount by a conversion factor typical of the ratio between sugar meltings and their raw material. To this converted series representing cane-sugar meltings, we added (as before) refined beet-sugar production for years beginning July 1.

The amount of cane sugar available for cane-sugar meltings was estimated for each calendar year by securing the sum of (1) domestic cane-sugar production for the year beginning July 1, and (2) net raw-sugar imports for the calendar year (including shipments from noncontiguous territories), which latter formed by far the greater part of the total. Although the available figures for domestic cane-sugar production pertain to years beginning July 1, figures so dated may be assumed to yield a close approximation to calendar-year production for refining purposes, since

---

[18] Cf. also *The Encyclopedia Americana,* XXV (1936 edition), 800. "The harvesting [of sugar beets] is begun in different sections of the country at different periods, depending upon the climatic conditions. In some portions of California harvesting may begin in August while in sections where the temperature is not so favorable it is begun in September and October. The harvesting extends from two to four months." See also *Agriculture Yearbook,* 1923, p. 843, Table 356, which states that the average length of the beet-sugar campaign, over the period 1914–20, was 83 days.

domestic cane sugar "was largely melted before December 31." [19]

Data covering domestic production of raw cane sugar, for years beginning July 1, 1864–87, were obtained from *Statistical Abstract,* 1916, page 528; and data for 1860–63, also for years beginning July 1, were taken from *Statistical Abstract,* 1901, page 350.[20]

The series for net raw-sugar imports was secured by computing the difference between imports—including shipments received from noncontiguous territories (insular possessions)—and reexports. Virtually no domestic cane sugar was exported in raw form. The imports series of raw sugar seems to have varied in designation during the long period 1860–1914. For 1862–64, some of the figures are described as "brown and partially refined"; for 1865–66, "not above No. 15 Dutch." In general, from 1860 to 1881, the figures pertain to brown sugar. For 1882, the description of the series is "not above No. 20"; for 1883–90, "under No. 13 Dutch"; and for 1891–1912, "under No. 16 Dutch." Despite these differences, the imports series appears to be substantially homogeneous throughout the entire period. The foreign-trade data for the calendar years 1867–87 were taken from various monthly publications on foreign trade issued by the Bureau of Statistics, United States Treasury Department. For the period 1860–66, no calendar-year figures were available, but rough approximations were arrived at by straight-line interpolation between fiscal-year figures secured from annual issues of *Commerce and Navigation of the United States.*[21]

The sum of domestic raw cane-sugar production and net raw-sugar imports yielded a calendar-year series of raw cane sugar available for domestic melting and refining; we shall refer to this

---

[19] For this information we are indebted to Willett and Gray, Sugar Statisticians, of New York City.

[20] For a detailed description of the sources, see the introduction to this Appendix.

For a clear picture of the effect of the Civil War on domestic cane-sugar production and the slowness of the recovery, see the chart on p. 157 of *Agriculture Yearbook,* 1923, which presents domestic raw cane-sugar production, 1823–1922, and also domestic beet-sugar production, 1879–1922.

[21] For a detailed description of the sources of foreign-trade data, see the introduction to this Appendix.

series as the "raw materials" series. To render the series comparable to the sugar-meltings series which was used for the period 1888–1914, we multiplied the "raw materials" data for each year by the factor 0.9413. This conversion factor is the ratio of sugar meltings to raw cane sugar available for refining in the year 1899. The 1899 ratio was chosen because it is about equal to the average ratio for the entire pre-war period over which meltings data are available (1888–1914); throughout this period, no trend was apparent in the ratio.[22] The validity of this decision was confirmed by graphic comparison, using charts with logarithmic vertical scale, of sugar meltings and "raw materials" data developed for 1888–1914. (The method used for developing the 1888–1914 data was the same as that described above for 1860–87 data.)

We also employed this graphic method to test, from several points of view, the propriety of using our "raw materials" series to represent sugar meltings. Sugar meltings for calendar years were compared with various dating combinations of "raw materials" for the period 1888–1914 (for example, imports and domestic cane-sugar production, both for years ending June 30, were combined in one experiment). These tests indicated conclusively: (1) that the "raw materials" series based on the dating system which we had adopted conformed in its year-to-year fluctuations more closely to meltings (taking into account both timing and form of movement) than did "raw materials" series based on various other experimental dating systems; (2) that the annual ratio between the "raw materials" and meltings series was roughly constant during the entire period, 1888–1914; and (3) that the trends of the two series were almost parallel throughout the period.

Nevertheless, as might be expected, moderate discrepancies do exist between year-to-year fluctuations of meltings and of our "raw materials" series. These differences are probably ascribable mainly to the lag between imports of raw cane sugar and their

[22] This factor may be compared with that given in United States Department of Agriculture, *Yearbook of Agriculture*, 1932 (Washington: Government Printing Office, 1932), p. 676, Table 153, fn. 1: "Cane sugar, raw, converted to refined basis by multiplying by the following factors: United States, 0.932; Porto Rico, 0.9393; Hawaii, 0.9358; Philippine Islands, 0.95."

melting, and to changes from one year-end to another in the level of raw-sugar stocks. In addition, as noted above, our domestic raw cane-sugar production series is not precisely on a calendar-year basis.

As the final step in obtaining an annual series indicative of total production of refined sugar prior to 1888, we added, year by year, 1860–87, domestic production of refined beet sugar for years beginning July 1 to our estimated data for sugar meltings. The figures for beet-sugar production, 1866–87, were taken from *Agriculture Yearbook*, 1923, page 845; for earlier years, no data are available, but production of beet sugar clearly was negligible.[23]

COFFEE IMPORTED

Data for this series were obtained from the following sources: 1860–66, from annual issues of *Commerce and Navigation of the United States;* 1867–69, from various issues of *Monthly Report* of the Bureau of Statistics;[24] 1870–1914, from Arthur F. Burns, *Production Trends in the United States since 1870* (New York; National Bureau of Economic Research, Inc., 1934), pages 292–293.

The series throughout consists of net imports (i.e., general imports minus foreign exports) of coffee. Data for 1867–1914 were available by calendar years, in the sources noted above. For 1860–66, however, reports were given for fiscal years ending June 30; we applied straight-line interpolation to the fiscal-year data in order to secure estimates for calendar years. Although the estimates thus obtained may not measure accurately the year-to-year fluctuations, they do provide an indication of the general drift of the series over the period. Moreover, taking into account the small weight of the series in the combined index of manufacture,

---

[23] Cf. *Agriculture Yearbook*, 1923, p. 156. "The establishment of the sugar-beet industry on a paying basis has been a comparatively recent development in American agriculture. Attempts to launch the industry were made as early as 1838, but all efforts met with failure until 1879, when a factory erected at Alvarado, Calif., proved to be a profitable undertaking." From the year beginning July 1, 1866 through the year beginning July 1, 1878, the annual domestic production of refined beet sugar at no time exceeded 2 million pounds, whereas during the same period our estimates of the annual production of refined sugar ranged from a low of 841.3 million pounds in 1867 to a high of 1777.9 million pounds in 1878.

[24] For a detailed description of these two sources, see the introduction to this Appendix.

the expenditures necessary to attempt possible greater refine-
ment of the data did not seem justified.

Cocoa Imported

The sources from which these data were obtained, and the
methods followed, are the same as those used for coffee imports,
described above. Net imports of crude cocoa (general imports
minus foreign exports) were taken throughout the period.

Raw Cotton Consumed

As a measure of the annual output of cotton cloths (plus other
primary products of raw cotton), over the years 1860–1912, we
have used data for raw cotton consumed, compiled by the United
States Department of Commerce, since no sufficiently comprehensive figures on the actual output of cotton products are obtainable.
An exact description of the composition of this cotton-consump-
tion series is not available.

The series for raw cotton consumed, 1860–1912, has been taken
directly from the United States Department of Commerce, Bureau
of the Census, Bulletin 166, *Cotton Production and Distribution*,
Season of 1928–29 (Washington: Government Printing Office,
1929), Table 31, pages 57–58. Information from the Department
of Commerce indicates that the data in this table have been "compiled from a number of sources," and that "in the absence of
exact statistics those presented in this table as a ready reference
are believed to be reasonably close approximations." [25]

These figures relate to the twelve-month period ending August
31, during which the crop of the specified year was marketed. It
seems probable, however, that the crop-year data for raw cotton
consumed are fairly well representative of calendar-year production of cotton cloths and other primary cotton goods. We should
in general expect a lag of some months to occur between the production of raw cotton and the manufacture of cotton goods therefrom. And, more important, a comparison of the crop-year figures

[25] From correspondence with Mr. Harvey J. Zimmerman, United States Department of Commerce, Bureau of the Census. The author is most grateful to Mr.
Zimmerman for his replies to queries concerning the raw-cotton data.

for raw cotton consumed with calendar-year indicators of general business activity indicates a rather close correlation between the short-run movements of the two series.

For the years 1913–14, figures for raw cotton consumed on a calendar-year basis are available in United States Department of Commerce, Bureau of the Census, *Record Book of Business Statistics,* Textiles Section (Washington: Government Printing Office, 1927), page 20. These data are based upon reports from individual cotton-consuming plants; the consumption figures "are taken as the bales of cotton are opened at the mills" (*loc. cit.*), and thus anticipate somewhat actual output of products.

Raw Cotton Consumed, Adjusted for Foreign Trade in Cotton Goods

As an indicator of the output of articles manufactured from cotton cloths (as well as from other primary products of raw cotton), we have employed figures for raw cotton consumed, adjusted for foreign trade in cotton goods. The consumption figures are those described in the preceding section. Foreign-trade data, covering imports and exports of countable cotton cloths for years ending June 30, were supplied by Mr. W. A. Graham Clark of the United States Tariff Commission.[26] Annual figures for the quantity of cotton cloths imported are available beginning with the year 1861; and for cotton cloths exported, with 1864.

The cotton consumption figures, which pertain to *raw* cotton, are reported in units of bales of raw material, while the foreign-trade data are obtainable in units of yards of fabricated products —those for imports in units of square yards and those for exports in units of linear yards. Obviously, the consumption and foreign-trade data had to be put in comparable units before a combination of the figures could be made.

To secure conversion factors, we made use of figures for the

[26] The author wishes to acknowledge his indebtedness to Mr. Clark for his aid. The receipt of these data in tabular form made unnecessary the compilation of figures from several sources, and thus time and expense were saved. Mr. Clark also rendered assistance and gave advice concerning factors that might be used to convert yards of cotton cloths to pounds. In this latter problem, Mr. Russell T. Fisher, Secretary of the National Association of Cotton Manufacturers, also furnished assistance.

1920's and 1930's, since data for this purpose were not obtainable over the period covered by our study. Imports data for the years 1923–35 were secured in units of both square yards and pounds, and these figures indicated that a pound of imported fabric would contain approximately five square yards. For exports, the records were in units of square yards only; but *production* of countable cotton cloths in units of pounds and square yards was obtained, biennially, from 1919 through 1933. In those years, approximately four square yards equaled one pound of fabric. We have converted our foreign-trade data for countable cotton cloths from yards to pounds by assuming that a pound of imported fabric would contain five square yards and that a pound of exported fabric would contain four linear yards.[27]

Further adjustment was necessary, however, before the foreign-trade data could be compared with *raw-cotton* figures. Both exports and imports of cotton cloths converted to pounds were raised by 15 per cent,[28] the increase representing the dirt, leaf, etc., taken out of the raw cotton in the cleansing process. The excess of exports over imports—both raised to the raw-cotton level—was next computed; and the resulting figures were converted to bales, assuming 500 pounds of raw cotton per bale. Finally, these converted figures in bales were subtracted from the figures for raw cotton consumed, described in the preceding section, to obtain a series adjusted for foreign trade in cotton goods, by years, 1864–1914.

The series just derived pertains approximately to crop years.[29] But here, as for raw cotton consumed itself (cf. the preceding sec-

---

[27] That imports of cotton cloths averaged lighter than domestic production is indicated in a report of the United States Tariff Commission, which states: "The bulk of the exported cloths are woven of coarse or medium numbers of yarns, whereas the bulk of the imported cloths are woven of fine yarns." See 68th Congress, 1st Session, Senate Document No. 150, *Cotton Cloth Industry: Letter from the Chairman of the United States Tariff Commission, Transmitting in Response to a Senate Resolution of May 12, 1924, a Report on the Present Depression in, and the Effect of Imports Upon, the Cotton-Cloth Industry* (Washington: Government Printing Office, 1924), p. 8.

[28] This factor was obtained through correspondence with the National Association of Cotton Manufacturers.

[29] As stated above, the foreign-trade data pertain to years ending June 30 and the consumption data in the main to years ending August 31.

tion), there are reasons for believing that the crop-year data are fairly representative of fluctuations in calendar-year output of fabricated products. Here also, a lag in production of fabricated articles would be expected (and, correspondingly, the statistical lag for the data used is here on the average somewhat longer— for, as set forth in a preceding footnote, the foreign-trade data pertain to years ending *June 30*—which is appropriate, since we are now dealing with goods in a later stage of fabrication than in the preceding case); and the correlation of short-run movements with those of indicators of general business activity is again high.

RAW WOOL CONSUMED

As a measure of the annual output of wool cloths (plus other primary products of raw wool), we have in general used data on raw wool consumed, since no sufficiently comprehensive figures on the actual output of wool products are obtainable. The series for raw wool consumed was secured by adding net imports of raw wool in each fiscal year, 1861–93 and 1900–14, to domestic production in the preceding calendar year. A different procedure, described below, was followed for the interval 1894–99.

The years 1861–93 and 1900–14. Figures for net imports (i.e., general imports minus exports of foreign wool and of domestic wool) for fiscal years ending June 30, 1861–93, were computed from data secured from two published sources: (1) general imports minus exports of foreign wool, from Worthington C. Ford, Bureau of Statistics, Treasury Department, *Wool and Manufactures of Wool* (Washington: Government Printing Office, 1894), pages 317–318; and (2) domestic exports, from Caroline G. Gries, *Foreign Trade of the United States, Annual, 1790–1929: Sheep, Mutton, Lamb and Wool* (United States Department of Agriculture, Bureau of Agricultural Economics, Division of Statistical and Historical Research, Report F. S. 49, June 1930, mimeographed), pages 26 and 30. Net imports for the fiscal years 1900–14 were taken directly from the publication of Caroline G. Gries, pages 32 and 36. Production figures for the calendar years 1860–69 were obtained from *Statistical Abstract*, 1910, page 703;[30]

[30] For a detailed description of this source, see the introduction to this Appendix.

and those for the years 1870–92 and 1899–1913, from United States Department of Agriculture, *Agriculture Yearbook*, 1923 (Washington: Government Printing Office, 1924), pages 1001–1002.

Net imports for the fiscal year ending June 30 were added to domestic production for the preceding calendar year, and the resulting total was assumed to represent raw wool made available for consumption in the fiscal year ending June 30.[31] For our period of investigation, it was not possible to take account of changes in stocks of raw wool.

The wool-consumption series is, then, intended to represent raw wool made available for consumption during the fiscal year. To what extent the series can be taken as an indicator of the actual output of primary wool products for the corresponding calendar year is uncertain. The evidence is less clear than in the corresponding case for cotton (cf. the section on raw cotton consumed, above). To be sure, we should here also expect some lag, but whether as much as six months, or more, is doubtful. And the correlation between the short-run movements of fiscal-year figures for raw wool consumed and calendar-year indicators of general business activity, though fairly good, is appreciably less close than the analogous correlation in the case of cotton. But, all things taken into account, it would appear that in general we have, in the fluctuations of the raw-wool consumption series just described, as good an approximation to an indicator of year-to-year changes in the calendar-year output of primary wool products as can readily be arrived at from the available data.[32]

The years 1894–99. For the period 1894–99, however, the method above described would clearly give extremely erroneous results, because of the pronounced tariff changes and the resulting

---

[31] This method of computing fiscal-year data was approved by Mr. Preston Richards, Division of Statistical and Historical Research, Bureau of Agricultural Economics, United States Department of Agriculture. The author is indebted to Mr. Richards for his assistance in clarifying certain discrepancies in the wool data appearing in various published sources.

[32] For discussion of general qualifications of production data with respect to various points—e.g., changes in quality or degree of fabrication—see the publications referred to in fns. 11 and 12 of Chapter IV.

dislocation of normal imports due to speculative buying. The situation is well summarized by Professor F. W. Taussig. "Among the extraordinary fluctuations [in wool imports] some are obviously accounted for by the tariff changes of 1894–97. The free admission of wool in 1894 and the re-imposition of duties three years later necessarily caused great shifts. In the year just before the act of 1894, when it was almost certain that wool would become free, imports naturally shrank almost to nothing. They then rose abruptly as soon as the abolition of the duty went into effect. Again, after the election of McKinley in the autumn of 1896 it became in turn almost certain that the duty would be restored. Consequently during the fiscal year 1896–1897, imports were rushed in from every possible quarter while wool was still free. They then fell abruptly after the passage of the tariff act of 1897. For several years after 1897 the stocks of wool from these heavy importations weighed on the market, and prevented the price of wool from rising as promptly and fully as had been expected. During the interval imports were naturally small, and confined to special qualities. Not till 1900 were the effects of this abnormal situation out of the way." [33] Obviously, some allowance had to be made for these great changes in stocks if our statistical indicator of the annual volume of production of wool goods was to be at all dependable.

In our search for a substitute method, over the period 1894–99, we made use of certain readily available data on the year-to-year fluctuations of *employment* in the woolen and worsted industries of Massachusetts. These data were especially helpful in view of the fact that throughout this period Massachusetts was one of the leading states in such manufacture.

The basic data for Massachusetts employment were taken from the successive issues of Commonwealth of Massachusetts, Bureau of Statistics of Labor, *The Annual Statistics of Manufactures* (Boston: Wright and Potter Printing Company, State Printers). In this source, data are presented beginning with 1889 in homogeneous pairs for overlapping years. The first pair is for 1889

[33] F. W. Taussig, *Some Aspects of the Tariff Question* (third edition, Cambridge, Mass.: Harvard University Press, 1934), p. 299. See also the chart on p. 298.

and 1890. The data are homogeneous in that for each pair of years statistics are presented for the same number of reporting establishments.

We were concerned only with the interval starting with the 1893–94 comparison and ending with that for 1899–1900. Over this interval, since in each case data are given by months and separately for sub-groups, we first computed monthly totals of employment in the woolen and worsted industries combined, and then annual totals of the monthly figures. These annual totals, also, pertained to homogeneous pairs for overlapping years, 1893–94 to 1899–1900. We next, from these annual totals for homogeneous pairs of overlapping years, computed link relatives—percentage ratios of year-to-year change—in Massachusetts employment for the woolen and worsted industries, starting with the $\dfrac{1894}{1893}$ link relative and ending with that for $\dfrac{1900}{1899}$.

The basic notion of our substitute method was to use the employment link relatives in estimating the substitute series over the interval between 1893 and 1900. But first a slight modification had to be applied to the employment link relatives. Since the *average* annual rate of growth between 1893 and 1900 was somewhat less for the reported series of raw-wool consumption than for the employment series, the employment link relatives were each slightly lowered (in an appropriate uniform ratio).

Finally, the substitute series itself was developed, 1894–99. We took the reported raw-wool consumption figure for 1893 (see the earlier part of this section) as a starting point. Then we multiplied this 1893 figure by the $\dfrac{1894}{1893}$ link relative for employment (modified as just set forth), to secure the 1894 substitute figure; multiplied this 1894 figure by the $\dfrac{1895}{1894}$ modified link relative for employment, to secure the 1895 substitute figure; and so on, until the substitute figure for 1900 was reached—when of necessity (because of the adjustment previously applied to the employment link relatives) the substitute series coincided precisely with the reported series.[34]

It is clear, of course, that this method for filling in substitute figures between 1893 and 1900—based, as it was, upon *employment* data for a *single state* (even as important a state as Massachusetts in the wool-goods industry)—could give only an approximation to the desired indicator: that of year-to-year changes in the output of wool goods in the United States, 1894–99. But, granting all the elements of approximation involved in the substitute method, it seemed clear that the results of this method were most decidedly to be preferred to those which would be secured by using over this interval the greatly disturbed, and therefore highly misleading, reported series for "raw wool consumed" (in which no account was taken of changes in stocks).

In 1895, 1896, and 1897, the substitute series is lower than the reported series; this is to be anticipated, in view of the speculative imports consequent upon the abolition of the duty on wool. In 1898 and 1899, the substitute series is higher than the reported series; this is, of course, ascribable to the fact that imports during these two years were low while the accumulated stocks of raw wool were being consumed.

RAW WOOL CONSUMED, ADJUSTED FOR FOREIGN TRADE IN WOOL GOODS

As an indicator of the output of articles manufactured from wool cloths (as well as from other primary products of raw wool), we have employed figures for raw wool consumed (described in the preceding section), adjusted for imports of wool fabrics.[35]

---

[34] The procedure here followed represents a special case of the "post method," discussed in the early pages of Chapter IV.

[35] The United States *exports* of wool fabrics have always been small. [See United States Tariff Commission, Tariff Information Surveys, *Woven Fabrics of Wool* (Washington: Government Printing Office, 1927), p. 4, and Table 16, p. 134.] In the year ending June 30, 1870, the value of the export trade of total wool manufactures (which includes carpets, wearing apparel, etc., as well as wool fabrics) amounted to $124,000; in 1880, it was $217,000; in 1900, $1,300,000; in 1910, $2,360,000. (Source: *Statistical Abstract*, 1879, 1909, 1919.) Because of the small size of exports, no adjustment for the export trade in wool fabrics has been attempted for this study.

Quantities of wool fabrics imported into the United States for consumption have been published in reports issued by the United States Treasury Department and the United States Tariff Commission.[36] The first year for which these data are available is the fiscal year ending June 30, 1867. In the publications of the Treasury Department, the data are listed according to the valuation of the product; and for any one fabric, several sets of data for one year are reported. In order to secure a total figure for one fabric, annually, the figures for the various classifications must be combined. Such summary figures for the fiscal years 1867–94 have been compiled and published by the National Association of Wool Manufacturers;[37] and by the United States Tariff Commission for the period subsequent to 1894.[38] The data in both sources include cloths, flannels, dress goods, and yarns, and they are reported in units of pounds for all the series except dress goods. (Beginning 1898, flannels weighing not over four ounces per square yard were reported in units of square yards instead of pounds. For the present study, these data were converted to pounds by assuming that three ounces equaled one square yard.) For dress goods, the figures are given in units of square yards. They have, however, been converted to pounds by Dr. A. H. Cole, and through his courtesy the converted figures have been made available to the present writer. The data were published in graphic form only in Dr. Cole's study. See Arthur H. Cole, *The American Wool Manufacture,* II (Cambridge, Mass.: Harvard University Press, 1926), 40. The tabulated figures were secured from his research files.

To secure a total figure for imports of wool fabrics, the four series, in units of pounds, were added together. But—since these data were to be combined with figures for raw wool consumed,

[36] United States Treasury Department, Bureau of Statistics, *Wool and Manufactures of Wool* (Washington: Government Printing Office, 1887), pp. 52–103; Worthington C. Ford, Bureau of Statistics, Treasury Department, *Wool and Manufactures of Wool* (Washington: Government Printing Office, 1894), pp. 348–431; United States Tariff Commission, *Textile Imports and Exports, 1891–1927* (Washington: Government Printing Office, 1929), pp. 198–211.

[37] S. N. D. North, *The Wool Book* (Boston: The Rockwell and Churchill Press, 1895), pp. 53–56.

[38] *Textile Imports and Exports,* pp. 198–211.

and since the latter were reported on a grease basis—further adjustments of the imports data were essential. The figures for the total weight of wool fabrics imported were multiplied by the factor 1.4 to secure figures for scoured wool; these figures in turn were multiplied by the factor 2 in order to obtain an approximation to grease wool used in imported wool fabrics.[39] The final step was to add these adjusted figures for imports of wool fabrics to our series for raw wool consumed (derived as described in the preceding section; note in particular the substitute figures for 1894–99).

As to the relation of the present series, which has been formally derived upon approximately a fiscal-year basis, to output for corresponding calendar years of articles made from wool fabrics and other primary products of raw wool, compare what is said regarding the analogous point for raw wool consumed, in the preceding section.

RAW SILK AND SPUN SILK IMPORTED

For the period 1870–1914, this series was obtained by adding net imports of raw silk (i.e., general imports minus exports of foreign merchandise) and imports of spun silk. " 'Raw silk' proper is . . . the continuous thread reeled from the interior of the cocoon. The exterior hull of the cocoon, however, has broken fibres; in the innermost part of the cocoon, the fibre becomes so attenuated as not to be unwound profitably; and there are also pierced and imperfect cocoons whose filaments are broken. These 'waste' fibres, as well as some other 'wastes,' are used in making spun silk." [40] As is to be expected, the value per pound of spun silk is substantially less than that of raw silk (cf. quantities and values of imports of raw and spun silk in sources given below).

No separate data are available for imports of spun silk prior to 1870; therefore, the series used in the index for the period 1860–69 is composed solely of net imports of raw silk. But, since

---

[39] The conversion factors were supplied by Mr. Walter Humphreys, Secretary of the National Association of Wool Manufacturers, whose assistance has been throughout of great value to the author in the preparation of this study.

[40] F. W. Taussig, *Some Aspects of the Tariff Question* (third edition, Cambridge, Mass.: Harvard University Press, 1934), p. 226.

spun-silk imports were relatively small in these early years, it is unlikely that their omission for 1860–69 affects the accuracy of our series in any essential respect. For example, in the calendar year 1870 spun-silk imports were 1.4 per cent of raw-silk and spun-silk imports combined; and in 1880, 1.1 per cent. These figures may be contrasted with 12.0 per cent for 1890, and 8.1 per cent for 1897.

Raw-silk imports. Net imports of raw silk for calendar years, 1870–1914, were obtained from Arthur F. Burns, *Production Trends in the United States since 1870* (New York: National Bureau of Economic Research, Inc., 1934), pages 294-295; and those for calendar years, 1867–69, from various issues of *Monthly Report* of the Bureau of Statistics.[41] The series covers raw-silk imports only; that is, it excludes silk waste, cocoons, silk worms, and eggs of silk worms.

Net imports for fiscal years ending June 30, 1864–66, were transcribed from successive annual issues of *Commerce and Navigation of the United States*.[42] No quantity figures for 1861–63 were available; but a quantity figure for the fiscal year 1860 was secured from United States Department of the Interior, *Twelfth Census of the United States,* 1900, volume IX, *Manufactures,* part III, *Special Reports on Selected Industries* (Washington: United States Census Office, 1902), page 202.[43] We obtained fiscal-year estimates for 1861–63 by straight-line interpolation between the fiscal-year figures for 1860 and 1864. Finally, we interpolated between the data for successive fiscal years to secure estimates by calendar years, 1860–66. These calendar-year estimates may furnish a satisfactory indication of the general drift of the series, but probably they do not measure accurately the year-to-year movements.

[41] For a detailed description of the sources used here, see the introduction to this Appendix.

[42] For a detailed description of the sources used here, see the introduction to this Appendix. Official statistics are available for only the *values* of imports and of exports in the three fiscal years 1861–63. An attempt to estimate quantity figures from these value data did not produce satisfactory results.

[43] A footnote to the 1860 figure states: "Estimated from current prices, only the value being on record."

Spun-silk imports. As indicated above, data for spun-silk imports are not available prior to the year 1870. The figures used for the period 1870–1914 were obtained from a number of sources.

For fiscal years ending June 30, 1870 and 1880–97, data were secured from *Twelfth Census of the United States,* 1900, volume IX, *Manufactures,* part III, page 202. Estimates for the fiscal years 1871–79 were obtained by straight-line interpolation between the fiscal-year figures for 1870 and 1880. Likewise, calendar-year estimates for the entire period, 1870–97, were secured by straight-line interpolation between the data for successive fiscal years. These interpolated data undoubtedly indicate the general drift of the spun-silk imports over the period studied, but no claim of accurate measurement of the year-to-year fluctuations can be made (however, as to the effect of possible errors here upon the total for raw-silk and spun-silk imports combined, cf. the figures given in the second paragraph of this section, indicative of the relative importance of spun silk up to 1897).

For the period 1898–1914, calendar-year figures were transcribed directly from various issues of *Monthly Summary of Commerce and Finance of the United States.*[44]

MINOR FIBERS IMPORTED

The series for imports of minor fibers is a composite, consisting of the sum of imports of jute, Manila hemp, and sisal;[45] the figures have been obtained from various sources, as described below. The data pertain to fiscal years ending June 30 during the period 1861–90, and to calendar years, 1891–1914. Because of the large irregular fluctuations of the series over the period 1861–90, and the lack of conformity with any standard indicator of general economic or industrial activity, no attempt was made to put the data on a calendar-year basis. In any case, devoting time and expense in an attempt to secure calendar-year estimates would hardly have been

[44] For a detailed description of the sources used here, see the introduction to this Appendix.

[45] The data are net imports (i.e., total imports minus exports of foreign merchandise) for the years 1861–66 and 1891-1914, and imports entered for consumption, 1867–90.

justified, in view of the comparatively minor importance of the series in the index of total manufacture.

The composite series for minor-fibers imports over the period 1870–1914 was transcribed from Arthur F. Burns, *Production Trends in the United States since 1870* (New York: National Bureau of Economic Research, Inc., 1934), pages 294–295.

To carry the composite series back through the year 1861, we compiled data which would be as nearly homogeneous as possible with the data secured from *Production Trends*. Our first step in obtaining the desired series was to transcribe, from annual issues of *Commerce and Navigation of the United States*,[46] total imports and exports of foreign merchandise for each of the three series—jute, Manila hemp, and sisal—in the period 1861–66. For each series, we then computed net imports by deducting "foreign exports" from total imports. The composite net-imports series was secured by adding together the net-imports data for the three individual series.[47]

Imports entered for consumption, 1867–69, for each of the three series were transcribed from annual issues of *Commerce and Navigation of the United States;* and these data were added together, year by year, to secure the composite series.

[46] For a detailed description of the sources used here, see the introduction to this Appendix.

[47] Foreign exports of jute are not available for 1861 and 1864; and foreign exports of sisal could not be obtained for 1862, 1863, 1865, and 1866. We therefore assumed that the net imports figures were the same as those for total imports. The lack of data on foreign exports in the years cited is unimportant in our particular problem, since data available for adjacent years indicate that foreign exports in the early period were practically negligible.

The reported figures for foreign exports of jute and of Manila hemp in the year 1863, and of sisal in the year 1864, appeared obviously in error when comparisons were made with total imports in those years and with foreign exports in adjacent years. For example, foreign exports of jute in 1863 are reported as four times larger than total imports of jute in the same year. The unit for the series, although given as tons, apparently should have been given as hundredweights; we have assumed this to be true in our use of the data.

The total-imports data for each of the three series are reported in units of hundredweights for the years 1868 and 1869. Before making use of the figures, we converted them from hundredweights to tons.

The 1861 figure for jute imports includes sisal. Manila hemp imports for the same year are described as "hemp, unmanufactured," and they may have included some Russian hemp. Both imports and foreign exports of sisal, 1862–64, are described as "sisal and other cordage material not specified."

PIG IRON PRODUCED

Calendar-year data for 1860–66 were obtained from "Iron Ore, Coal, Pig Iron, and Steel in All Countries," *Statistics of the American and Foreign Iron Trades for 1894, Annual Statistical Report of the American Iron and Steel Association*, Supplement (Philadelphia: The American Iron and Steel Association, 1895), page 8; and for 1867–1914, from *Annual Statistical Report of the American Iron and Steel Institute*, 1914 (Philadelphia: American Iron and Steel Institute, 1915), pages 11–12. Production of ferro alloys, which was small throughout the entire period, was included.

STEEL INGOTS AND CASTINGS PRODUCED

Statistics covering the production of steel ingots and castings for calendar years, 1860 and 1863–82, were obtained from "Iron Ore, Coal, Pig Iron, and Steel in All Countries," *Statistics of the American and Foreign Iron Trades for 1894, Annual Statistical Report of the American Iron and Steel Association*, Supplement (Philadelphia: The American Iron and Steel Association, 1895), page 10; those for calendar years, 1883–1914, were taken from *Annual Statistical Report of the American Iron and Steel Institute*, 1914 (Philadelphia: American Iron and Steel Institute, 1915), page 27.

RAILS PRODUCED

For the period 1860–73, calendar-year figures were transcribed from "Iron Ore, Coal, Pig Iron, and Steel in All Countries," *Statistics of the American and Foreign Iron Trades for 1894, Annual Statistical Report of the American Iron and Steel Association*, Supplement (Philadelphia: The American Iron and Steel Association, 1895), pages 12–13; and for the period 1874–1914, from *Annual Statistical Report of the American Iron and Steel Institute*, 1914 (Philadelphia: Bureau of Statistics, American Iron and Steel Institute, 1915), page 47.

Prior to 1867, the series consists of production of iron rails only; subsequently, both iron and steel rails are included. "The manufacture of Bessemer steel rails in the United States as a commercial product dates from 1867, although they had been made experimentally in the two preceding years." [48]

STRUCTURAL IRON AND STEEL PRODUCED

For the period 1892–1914, calendar-year data were secured from *Annual Statistical Report of the American Iron and Steel Institute,* 1914 (Philadelphia: American Iron and Steel Institute, 1915), page 48; and for the census years 1879 and 1889, figures were obtained from United States Department of the Interior, *Twelfth Census of the United States,* 1900, volume X, *Manufactures,* part IV, *Special Reports on Selected Industries* (Washington: United States Census Office, 1902), page 61. The census year 1879 covers the twelve-month period ending May 31, 1880; and the census year 1889, the twelve-month period ending June 30, 1890.

IRON AND STEEL "END PRODUCTS," OTHER THAN RAILS AND STRUCTURAL IRON AND STEEL

The major group designated by the Census as "Iron and Steel and Their Products" covers a wide range of operations and products. "This group is intended to cover the manufacture of crude iron and steel and its conversion into finished products. Some of the finished products included, such as rails, plates, pipe, and wire, are of a relatively simple character. Others are highly elaborated products, for which the mere cost of the iron and steel as such is but a small proportion of the total cost. Many of these highly elaborated products may be roughly grouped under the terms 'machinery' and 'tools.' " [49]

The making of elementary materials, iron and steel, is directly represented in the physical-quantity statistics over our period of analysis by the two series, pig iron produced and steel ingots and

---

[48] *Statistics of the American and Foreign Iron Trades for 1894, Annual Statistical Report of the American Iron and Steel Association,* Supplement, p. 13.

[49] Cf. United States Department of Commerce, Bureau of the Census, *Abstract of the Census of Manufactures,* 1914 (Washington: Government Printing Office, 1917). The quotation is from p. 95. For a list of the industries included in this group, see pp. 96–97.

castings produced, respectively. But the remainder of the iron and steel group—and particularly that part comprised by the highly important "end products"—is only slightly represented in statistics of output (and data on input are highly fragmentary).

The only feasible method over our period for representing production in the iron and steel group beyond the stages of making pig iron and steel is the use of some series on *basic materials consumed*. It has become customary to use pig-iron consumption (or, less appropriately, pig-iron production) for this purpose.[50] But in this connection pig-iron consumption has numerous defects— both from the point of view of long-run, secular-trend movements and from the point of view of cyclical and other short-run fluctuations. Let us first consider the *secular-trend* defects of pig-iron consumption as representative of the output of "end products" of the iron and steel group.

SECULAR DEFECTS OF PIG-IRON CONSUMPTION

(1) Over our period of analysis (as well as in later years) the use of *scrap* to supplement pig iron as "original basic material" of the industry has tended, in a proportion varying over time, to make the tonnage of "original basic material" embodied in the "end products" of the iron and steel group greater than the tonnage of the pig iron consumed.

(2) Opposed to the preceding, there has been, again in a proportion varying over time, a tendency for tonnage *shrinkages* to appear as between the original "basic material" consumed (pig iron and scrap), and the amount of such "original basic material" embodied in the final "end products" classified by the Census under the iron and steel group. These shrinkages have occurred partly in the making of steel, partly in other ways.

(3) Another element interfering with a simple correspondence between pig iron consumed and "end products" produced is *foreign trade in partially-fabricated iron and steel goods*—sometimes a net import, sometimes a net export.

[50] With respect to the statistical series for pig iron consumed, 1860–1914, see the detailed statement at the close of this section.

(4) The *weighting* problem, also, is involved. If, over our period of analysis, we take pig-iron consumption to represent the whole iron and steel group beyond the earlier stages of making pig iron and steel, we must correspondingly give to pig-iron consumption the total value-added weight of the group, less the comparatively small part of such weight which may be assigned to the making of pig iron and steel. This means, in effect, that each ton of pig iron consumed is given the same weight, regardless of its destination. But if we fix our attention upon any selected time interval which may be chosen as period of reference for weighting (in the present study the year 1899 was so selected), we know that in fact there are great differences among the several "end products" as regards value added per unit of "original basic material" consumed—such differences being to a very considerable extent ascribable to differences in degree of fabrication. The more highly fabricated products will then in effect be underweighted, and the less highly fabricated overweighted. Such implicit weighting may lead to a secular bias in the computed production index for the group: if, for example, the production of highly fabricated "end products" increases faster over the period of analysis than that of the slightly fabricated, the computed index will have a downward secular bias.

(5) Further, quite aside from the question of comparative weighting, many of the various individual "end products" have undergone decided change in *quality* (over and above, that is, those changes which might be ascribed to mere alteration in the quantity of "original basic material" per unit of product). These quality changes are, of course, not reflected in the tonnage statistics.[51]

---

[51] Two other defects of pig-iron consumption may be mentioned: (6) the available statistics are faulty in that they fail of full proper adjustment for *changes in stocks on hand,* as between the beginning and end of the year; (7) there is necessarily in fact a *time lag,* on the average, between the consumption of pig iron and the performance of productive acts in the various stages leading to the emergence of the "end product," and the conventional handling of the statistics ignores this lag. These two defects are in the main important with respect to cyclical and other short-run changes. The time-lag criticism, however, has some relevance even for secular changes (cf. fn. 61, p. 167).

ADJUSTMENT FOR FOREIGN TRADE IN PARTIALLY-FABRICATED IRON
AND STEEL GOODS

With respect to Point 3 of the preceding enumeration, it was possible to make a reasonably satisfactory adjustment. We developed over our period of analysis, 1860–1914, an annual tonnage series for net imports (or net exports, as the case might be) of partially-fabricated iron and steel goods.[52] Next, the annual figures for tonnage of pig-iron consumption, year by year, 1860–1914, were adjusted by adding such net imports (or subtracting such net exports, as the case might be), to obtain an annual series for pig-iron consumption adjusted for foreign trade in partially-fabricated iron and steel goods.[53] This adjustment was desirable and worth while, for net imports of partially-fabricated goods amounted to a fairly high percentage of pig-iron consumption in the earlier years (19 per cent in 1860), but subsequently declined and after 1896 a net export appeared.

"SAVING THROUGH SCRAP" VERSUS "SHRINKAGE"

We turn now to consider Points 1 and 2 of the preceding enumeration. Let us take first Point 1, relating to the saving in "original basic material" through the use of scrap in place of pig iron. The obtainable evidence upon this point, taken from the United States Census records, is scanty; Table 22 summarizes the evidence derived from the Census. If we set aside the data for 1880, which are exceptional because of cyclical perturbations,[54]

[52] For extended description of procedure, see concluding pages of this section.

[53] Strictly, the data for partially-fabricated goods should have been corrected for "shrinkage"—cf. the discussions of "shrinkages" on immediately following pages— but the absence of such correction can hardly have led to any significant error in the final results of our calculation, as later arrived at.

[54] Cf. the following quotation from United States Department of the Interior, Census Office, *Report on the Manufactures of the United States at the Tenth Census,* 1880 (Washington: Government Printing Office, 1883), monograph compiled by James M. Swank, entitled "Statistics of the Iron and Steel Production of the United States," p. 4.

"The total consumption of old iron rails and scrap iron in the rolling mills in 1880 was abnormal, and was the result mainly of the great scarcity of pig iron which followed the sudden revival of demand for iron and steel products in the summer of 1879."

the figures tabulated in the right-hand side of the table suggest that over the period the ratio of (a) to $(a + b)$—where (a) is consumption of pig iron and (b) is consumption of scrap—averaged around 0.75, and that the secular trend of this ratio was not far from horizontal. Are we now to infer from these suggestions that for our period of analysis the "saving-through-scrap ratio" may (so far as *secular* movements are concerned) be taken as sensibly constant at a value of about 0.75?

Such a conclusion would be open to serious reservation, on two grounds. In the first place, the Census figures here employed refer not to the whole iron and steel industry, but only to a sample; the sample throughout is large—in the sense that its constituent industries account for more than a major fraction of total pig iron consumed—but it nevertheless falls short of complete coverage, and may not be representative. In the second place, the Census totals for scrap consumed, tabulated in Table 22, may include, in unknown and perhaps variable proportion, an amount of what we have called "intermediate scrap"—that is, scrap produced and consumed within the iron and steel industry. Such "intermediate scrap" we, of course, should not want to include in our calculations, for it does not constitute a part of the "original basic material"; its inclusion would mean multiple counting—double counting or worse.[55]

Now it is true that the Census figures quoted in Table 22 appear to exclude scrap made and consumed in the same works (for all of the census years included in the table, except 1870, this inference is definitely confirmed by the Census notation; cf. the stub of Table 22: so far as the census year 1870 is concerned, there is no specific statement, but—since the Census tabulations give dollar amounts in direct conjunction with the physical-quantity figures— the implication is that the exclusion is made in 1870 also). How-

---

[55] To use a homely analogy, a housewife may prepare twenty-one ounces of biscuit dough; then, with a circular cutter, stamp out sixteen biscuits each weighing one ounce; next, after combining the five ounces of "scrap" remaining, stamp out four more biscuits each weighing one ounce; and, finally, assemble the "scrap" left over from this last operation, fashioning it by hand to form one more one-ounce biscuit. The "original basic material" consumed is *not* twenty-seven ounces (twenty-one ounces plus five ounces plus one ounce); it is simply twenty-one ounces. The five ounces and the one ounce are "intermediate scrap"—should not be counted.

ever, presumably the data in the main body of Table 22 *do include* consumption of scrap "produced by consumer in other works"; and judging from certain figures which are available for 1910 and 1915 only (cf. footnote ¶ to Table 22), this is a factor of at least moderate importance. And, further, we must infer that the Census figures include scrap purchased from *other firms* within the broad limits of the iron and steel group as a whole.

What is the effect of the two reservations we have just considered? With reference to the accuracy of the suggested average "saving-through-scrap ratio" of 0.75, the first reservation—that connected with the sampling aspect—does not point directly to any definite conclusion; the second reservation—that connected with the "intermediate-scrap" aspect—does, however, suggest that the ratio of 0.75 is, as an average, too low; it seems reasonable to suppose that an average around (say) 0.80 would come nearer the truth than one of 0.75. And both of the reservations throw doubt upon the suggestion that the secular trend of the ratio may be taken as very nearly horizontal.

We turn next to the question of the weight shrinkage as between the "original basic material" (pig iron and scrap), contrasted with the amount of such material embodied in the final "end products" of the iron and steel group, as that group is defined by the Census. There are several reasons for anticipating such shrinkage.[56]

First, we must speak of the shrinkage occurring in the steel-making operation. Here, for our period of analysis, two tendencies opposed each other. On the one hand, there was a persistent increase in the proportion of "original basic material" which went through the stage of steel making before being passed on toward the formation of "end products," and consequently in the proportion of "original basic material" which was subject to this form of shrinkage. But, on the other hand, the open-hearth process, where the weight loss was relatively small, gained on and finally surpassed the Bessemer process, where the weight loss was relatively

[56] In the discussions immediately to follow, we ignore the element, foreign trade in partially fabricated iron and steel goods; for purposes of this discussion, we assume exports and imports of such products to offset each other.

TABLE 22

UNITED STATES CENSUS DATA ON CONSUMPTION OF PIG IRON AND SCRAP, WITH RATIOS COMPUTED THEREFROM*

Description	Consumption of materials, as given by the Census reports (unit: 1,000 tons†) Census years‡							Ratios computed by us $\left(\dfrac{a}{a+b}\right)$ Census years‡						
	1870	1880	1890	1900	1905	1910	1915	1870	1880	1890	1900	1905	1910	1915
Data from Census of 1870:														
[Summation of materials for the following five industries: "iron blooms"; "iron, rolled"; "iron, forged"; "iron, cast"; "steel"]														
(a) Pig iron....................	2,328	..	..	..	..	..	..	..	..	..	..	..	..	..
(b) Scrap iron..................	630	..	..	..	..	..	..	..	..	..	..	..	..	..
Ratio of (a) to (a + b).........	..	..	..	..	..	..	..	0.79	..	..	..	..	..	..
Data from Census of 1905:														
"Quantity of materials purchased and consumed by steel works and rolling mills and forges and bloomeries"														
(a) "Pig iron, spiegeleisen, ferro-manganese, and all other pig iron"..................	..	2,395	5,854	10,411	12,191	..	..	..	..	..	..	..	..	..
(b) "Old iron or steel rails, and other scrap iron or steel".......... ("The scrap iron and steel embraces only purchased material, and does not include scrap produced by iron and steel plants and consumed by the producing establishment")	..	1,207	1,748	4,127	5,124	..	..	..	..	..	..	..	..	..
Ratio of (a) to (a + b).............	..	..	..	..	..	..	..	..	0.66	0.77	0.72	0.70	..	..

Data from Census of 1915:¶

"Materials consumed by steel works and rolling mills"

"For furnaces and hot rolls"

(a) "Pig iron, including ferro-alloys"	10,411	12,191	19,077	17,430
(b) "Scrap, including old rails, not intended for rerolling— from outside sources"	4,127	5,124	4,804	5,071
Ratio of (a) to (a + b)	0.72	0.70	0.80	0.77

---

* The sources of the figures on consumption of pig iron and scrap are as follows:

Census of 1870. United States Department of the Interior, Census Office, *Compendium of the Ninth Census, 1870* (Washington: Government Printing Office, 1872), pp. 905–913, 924–925.

Census of 1905. United States Department of Commerce and Labor, Bureau of the Census, *Census of Manufactures*, 1905, part IV (Washington: Government Printing Office, 1908), p. 13.

Census of 1915. United States Department of Commerce, Bureau of the Census, *Census of Manufactures*, 1914, vol. II (Washington: Government Printing Office, 1919), p. 226.

† For 1880 and subsequent years, long tons of 2,240 pounds; for 1870, no indication in source, but probably short tons of 2,000 pounds.

‡ As is indicated in the reports, the exact time reference of the census year varies from census to census.

¶ The 1915 Census of Manufactures also gives, for the census years 1910 and 1915 only, the following data, under the heading "scrap, including old rails, not intended for rerolling" (unit: 1,000 long tons):

	1910	1915
Produced by consumer in other works	774	899
Purchased	4,030	4,172

If we take, for each of the two years, the ratio of (a) pig iron to (a + b) pig iron plus *purchased* scrap, we obtain:

	1910	1915
Ratio	0.83	0.81

large. In a book published during our period of analysis, Bradley
Stoughton says, speaking of the acid Bessemer process, that "the
difference in weight between the pig iron charged into the con-
verter and the steel ingots made will be 8 per cent in good practice,
although running above that (say to 10 per cent) in some mills." [57]
The weight loss under the open-hearth process, as between the
metal charged and the steel produced, has been variously stated
as ranging from 3 to 7 per cent, depending on the exact procedure
employed, the proportion of pig iron used, the extent to which the
carbon was eliminated before tapping, etc.[58]

Second, shrinkages in basic iron content are involved in con-
verting through various stages until the final "end products" are
reached. It is very difficult to form even an approximate idea of
the relative magnitude of these shrinkages. To be sure, numerous
statements can readily be found in various manuals to the effect
that in a particular industry there is a weight loss of, say, 20 or 30
per cent between the pig iron or steel ingot and the finished
product. But these weight losses do not constitute the shrinkage
we are after, for they include the creation of what we have called
"intermediate scrap"; and, since we have previously refused to
count "intermediate scrap" as a part of the "original basic material" of the industry, we must now, to be consistent, refrain from
speaking of the creation of "intermediate scrap" as a shrinkage.[59]

Third, a considerable tonnage outgo occurs of "original basic
material" to a number of industries which are not classified by the
Census under the group "Iron and Steel and Their Products," but
which nevertheless use iron and steel largely as materials; among
these were, over our period of analysis: steam-railroad cars; automobiles; railroad repair shops; agricultural implements; electrical

[57] Bradley Stoughton, *The Metallurgy of Iron and Steel* (Second Edition, New
York: McGraw-Hill Book Co., Inc., and London: Hill Publishing Co., Ltd., 1913),
p. 102. (On p. 108, he indicates that, for the basic Bessemer process, "the loss of
metal will be much higher than in the acid process, averaging perhaps 13 to 17 per
cent," but he states, on p. 110, that the basic process "is no longer in use in Amer-
ica because this country does not produce the desired grade of pig iron in sufficiently large quantities.")

[58] Cf., for example, Stoughton, *The Metallurgy of Iron and Steel,* pp. 135, 142.

[59] To return to the biscuit-dough analogy of an earlier footnote, we do not refer
to the five ounces and the one ounce as shrinkages, inasmuch as we do not count
them as "original basic material."

machinery, apparatus and supplies; and ship building.[60] The shrinkage ascribable to this element undoubtedly is appreciable.[61]

It is difficult to draw any very definite conclusion as to the magnitude of the total shrinkage. However, taking into account all of the various sources of shrinkage, one might hazard the guess that the "shrinkage ratio"—that is the ratio of (i) "original basic material" (pig iron and scrap) embodied in "end products" of the iron and steel industry as defined by the Census, to (ii) "original basic material" consumed (pig-iron consumption plus scrap consumption)—may over our period of analysis be somewhere around 0.80, in the sense that it is probably nearer that figure than 0.70 or 0.90. So far as a possible secular trend in this ratio is concerned, our information does not warrant us in making any assumption.

We next came to the problem of the application to our actual statistical data of Points 1 and 2, taken jointly. What should be the *conversion factor* by which we should multiply (x) our series (earlier derived) for the tonnage of pig-iron consumption adjusted for foreign trade in partially-fabricated goods, in order to obtain (y) the estimated tonnage of "original basic material" embodied in "end products"? Obviously, this conversion factor depended on the comparative size of the "saving-through-scrap ratio" and the "shrinkage ratio," as these terms have been defined: if these ratios are equal, then the conversion factor is unity; if the "shrink-

---

[60] Cf. *1914 Abstract,* p. 95.

[61] An opposing element to these "shrinkages" must be mentioned, though such opposing element has its origin in a technical statistical consideration. As is set forth above (fn. 51, p. 160), if one uses pig-iron consumption to represent the production of "end products," one thus neglects the *time lag* between the consumption of pig iron and the performance of productive acts in the various stages leading to the emergence of the "end products." Now pig-iron consumption has a very rapid secular increase over our period of analysis; the average monthly rate is about $\frac{1}{2}$ per cent. Given this figure, the magnitude of the average error introduced into the computations by the neglect of time lag will vary, of course, depending upon the length of the average time lag. To illustrate, if the average time lag were one month, the error would be simply $100(1.005-1)$ per cent, or 0.5 per cent, indicating an annual average overstatement of 0.5 per cent; if the average time lag were three months, the error would be $100(1.005^3-1)$ per cent, indicating an annual average overstatement of 1.51 per cent; and so on.

age ratio" is above (below) the "saving-through-scrap ratio," the conversion factor is more (less) than unity.

Fixing our attention on the secular-trend aspects (and thus setting aside, for the time being, the cyclical and other short-run aspects), what judgment could we make regarding the magnitude of the conversion factor during our period of analysis? First, as to the *average size* of this factor.[62] Our earlier considerations, as presented on immediately preceding pages, while not leading to any precise conclusion, suggested that the average "saving-through-scrap ratio" over the period might not differ too greatly from the average "shrinkage ratio"; the equality of these two average ratios would indicate an average conversion factor of unity. But this conclusion was open to an appreciable margin of error: on the basis of our evidence, the average conversion factor might easily be anywhere between 0.90 and 1.10, and perhaps depart even somewhat farther from unity.

Next, as to the *average annual rate of growth* in the conversion factor over our period of analysis. Here, as we have seen, the evidence points to no certain conclusion. The trend of the conversion factor might approximate the horizontal, or might depart somewhat therefrom: it did not seem probable, however, that any violent upward or downward slope was present.[63]

Taking all things into account, our decision was simply to use a constant conversion factor of unity: that is to say, the annual

---

[62] Though decision was scarcely required from the point of view of precision in calculation (our judgments being of necessity only very rough), it was nevertheless desirable to meet the question of *principle* as to what was the proper form of average (e.g., arithmetic, geometric, harmonic) to be employed in calculating the average size of the ratio, or its average annual rate of growth (referred to, in the text just below). Inasmuch as we had been dealing with relative movements in an entity over time, it seemed that the geometric average would be most appropriate— or, rather perhaps, that variant of the geometrical process of averaging which is involved in fitting the exponential curve. [If still closer approach to precision in trend determination is required, going on to the logarithmic parabola may be indicated. Cf. a discussion by the present writer: Edwin Frickey, *Economic Fluctuations in the United States* (Cambridge, Mass.: Harvard University Press, 1942), pp. 143 ff.]

[63] So far as still more sophisticated characteristics of secular trend are concerned —e.g., average annual rate of acceleration or retardation (cf. Frickey, *Economic Fluctuations*, pp. 144–146)—it was hardly possible to form any judgment from the information available.

series of pig-iron consumption adjusted for foreign trade in partially-fabricated goods (previously derived as described on an
earlier page) was used to represent our estimate of "original basic
material" embodied in the "end products" of the iron and steel
group as defined by the Census. It did not appear that on the
basis of the information available to us we were justified in setting
up any more complicated arrangement with respect to the conversion factor. In a later sub-section we shall discuss in some detail
the probable reliability of the results obtained by this procedure.

THE PROBLEM OF THE COMPARATIVE WEIGHTING OF VARIOUS "END PRODUCTS"

We came next to consider Point 4, relating to a problem of weighting (as set forth above). Applying the issue there discussed to the
present situation, we wished to avoid so far as possible any bias
which might arise through mere blanket imputation of weight to
an aggregate "end-products" series—that is, to avoid bias arising
because of the fact that under this blanket-imputation system
each ton of "original basic material" would in effect be given the
same weight regardless of whether that ton was embodied in an
"end product" with a high degree of fabrication (which ought to
be weighted relatively higher) or in an "end product" with a low
degree of fabrication (which ought to be weighted relatively
lower).

While paucity of physical-quantity data made it impossible for
us to do anything about this matter in any thoroughgoing way, we
were able to separate out two important "end products" which
were subject to a relatively low degree of fabrication (and hence
had a relatively small value added per ton). The annual statistical
series pertaining to these two "end products" were rails produced,
and structural iron and steel produced, respectively (the derivation
of these series is described in the appropriate sections of this
Appendix, above).

The next step, then, in our formal procedure was to split our
estimated "end-products" series, year by year, 1860–1914, into
three parts. This was accomplished by taking our annual series
for estimated tonnage of total "end products" (previously derived,

as set forth just above) and reducing it by the sum of the tonnages for the rails and structural iron and steel series, thus obtaining a new annual series for "iron and steel 'end products,' other than rails and structural iron and steel" (cf. Table 1).[64] The splitting of the total "end-products" series into three parts, thus accomplished, represented a definite improvement in procedure, as it made possible differentiation of value-added weighting with respect to two important constituents—rails, and structural iron and steel.

CONCLUSIONS AS TO THE RELIABILITY OF OUR PROCEDURE FROM THE POINT OF VIEW OF LONG-RUN, OR SECULAR-TREND, MOVEMENTS

Let us now consider—from the point of view of long-run, or secular-trend, movements—the reliability of the newly-developed annual series, 1860–1914, for "tonnage of 'original basic material' embodied in 'end products' of the Census iron and steel group, other than rails and structural iron and steel" (which we shall, from here on, designate briefly as the "other-end-products series") taking in order the various points formally enumerated on an earlier page.

Take first Points 1 and 2. These two points have been discussed at length above. In this connection, it will be remembered, we made two decisions regarding the conversion factor by which we were to multiply (x) our series for the tonnage of pig-iron consumption adjusted for foreign trade in partially-fabricated goods, in order to obtain (y) the estimated tonnage of "original basic material" embodied in "end products." These two decisions were: first, to take the average size of the conversion factor over our period of analysis as unity; and, second, to assume a constant value of the factor—a horizontal trend over time.

As has been pointed out on an earlier page, both of these decisions are open to an appreciable margin of error. It therefore now becomes pertinent to inquire into the effect of possible errors from this source upon the reliability of the new "other-end-products

[64] With respect to certain (quantitatively unimportant) interpolations and extrapolations for the series structural iron and steel, see the appropriate part of Appendix E, Part One.

CHART 8

"END-PRODUCTS" EXPERIMENTS: ANNUAL FIGURES, 1860–1914*

A "Other-end-products series" as actually computed.
B Experimental computation, with conversion factor of 1.20.
C Experimental computation, with conversion factor of 0.80.
D Experimental computation, with conversion factor gradually varying from 0.80 to 1.20.

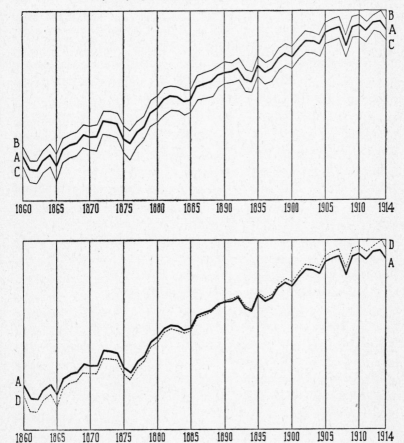

* Logarithmic vertical scales. For explanation, see accompanying text.

series." Chart 8, drawn with logarithmic vertical scale, presents some pertinent evidence upon this question. Curve A (plotted in both the upper and lower sections of the chart) represents the "other-end-products series" as it was actually computed, using a constant conversion factor of unity. Curves B and C (in the upper section) show the results of recomputations using constant conversion factors of 1.20 and 0.80, respectively. This exhibition of curves clearly indicates that, so long as we assume the conversion factor to be constant, an error in its value—while perhaps of considerable importance with reference to the *absolute size* (the tonnage totals) of the "other-end-products series"—will have almost negligible effect upon the *relative movements* of the series (which alone are important in our index-number construction).

Curve D—the dotted line on Chart 8 (lower section)—exhibits the result of a different kind of experiment: this curve shows the "other-end-products series" computed by assuming a compound-interest *secular trend* in the conversion factor, starting with 0.80 at the beginning of the period and moving by geometrical progression to 1.20 at the end of the period. The results of this experiment (cf. the chart) suggest that a trend in the conversion factor *will* bring about some alteration in the relative rate of upward growth of the "other-end-products series"; but these results also suggest that, within any limits of secular variation for the factor which seem reasonably plausible, such alteration is likely to constitute little more than a moderate deflection of the rapid upward growth which is intrinsically present in the "other-end-products series."

Now let us bring into the picture Point 5 of our earlier enumeration (relating to the highly important element of changes in the *quality* of the various individual "end products")—a point which has not been discussed in our previous statement of statistical procedure, simply because there appears to be no way of applying a statistical adjustment for this element. Considering Points 1 and 2 in conjunction with Point 5, it seems practically certain that any secular bias which may be present in our "other-end-products series," on account of secular error involved in assuming a constant conversion factor of unity, is of minor importance as compared with the downward growth bias which exists in the "other-end-products series" because of our inability to take account statistically of improvements in quality of individual products.[65]

To sum up, as regards the *secular-trend* aspects. By our new procedure we have been able to bring about appreciable and worthwhile improvements upon the conventional practice of simply letting the series pig-iron consumption stand for all production in the iron and steel group beyond the making of pig iron and steel. Specifically, with respect to Point 3, relating to foreign trade in partially-fabricated iron and steel goods, we have obtained a reasonably satisfactory adjustment; with respect to Point 4, the problem of the comparative weighting of the various "end products," though paucity of physical-quantity data rendered it impossible for us to reach a complete solution we nevertheless effected a definite improvement in procedure by "shearing off" the two series, rails and structural iron and steel; with respect to Points 1 and 2, relating to the "saving-through-scrap ratio" and the "shrinkage ratio," and hence to the conversion factor, we have through our investigations and experiments established a more logical ground for the use of a constant conversion factor of unity (which has conventionally been assumed without consideration and investigation), and have presented evidence that any secular bias attributable to error in such conversion factor of unity is for our purposes probably not serious. With respect to Point 5, relating to changes over the period in quality of the various individual "end products," we have not been able to improve upon the conventional procedure.

All in all, we have from the secular-trend point of view succeeded in bringing about a considerable improvement over the conventional practice as regards iron and steel "end products." But on balance there is still, in all probability, an appreciable downward growth bias in our "other-end-products series"—such bias being largely ascribable to improvements in quality of "end products" over the period of analysis, and being irremediable by direct statistical procedure.[66]

[65] Over and above, that is, improvements which emerge merely through increased *quantity* of basic material embodied per unit of final product.

[66] Any statistical procedure which could be devised would have to rest upon arbitrary assumptions of one sort or another.

A word now as to *cyclical* and other *short-run* aspects of the problem. Here, we have not been able to effect anything more than a very moderate improvement of the conventional use of pig-iron consumption. To be sure, the measurements have been bettered somewhat by our foreign-trade adjustment (Point 3) and by our splitting of the "end-products" series into three parts (Point 4); but the other defects still remain (cf. the various points listed on pages 159–160, including footnote 51, page 160).[67]

SUPPLEMENTARY NOTE ON THE STATISTICAL SERIES FOR PIG IRON CONSUMED

Throughout the period 1860–1914, this series consists of domestic production of pig iron plus imports minus exports—except for the interval 1874–1904, when stocks unsold on January 1 of each year were added and stocks on December 31 were deducted. For 1905–14, no adjustment for stocks was made.

Calendar-year data for 1860 and for 1870–93 were obtained from *Statistics of the American and Foreign Iron Trade for 1904, Annual Statistical Report of the American Iron and Steel Association* (Philadelphia: The American Iron and Steel Association, 1905), page 96;[68] and for 1894–1914, from *Annual Statistical Report of the American Iron and Steel Institute, 1914* (Philadelphia: American Iron and Steel Institute, 1915), page 17.

Since the American Iron and Steel Association did not publish figures on pig iron consumed for 1861–69, we extended the series back to 1860, following their procedure (domestic production plus imports minus exports). The sources for the components of this series, 1861–69, are as follows.

Domestic production: see section on "pig iron produced," in this Appendix.

Exports (domestic and foreign) and imports: fiscal-year data (years ending June 30) for 1861–67 were obtained from various

---

[67] In bringing this statement of conclusions to a close, we may finally point out that for the "other-end-products series"—as for many of the constituent series of the manufacture index—the figures are appreciably less trustworthy, especially as regards year-to-year movements, in the period prior to 1866 than subsequently.

[68] It is stated here that "except in some of the earlier years the exports of pig iron have been deducted."

issues of *Commerce and Navigation of the United States;* and calendar-year data for 1867–69, from various issues of *Monthly Report of the Chief of the Bureau of Statistics.*[69] To improve the homogeneity of the series, 1861–67, the import and export data (available only for fiscal years) were roughly converted to a calendar-year basis by straight-line interpolation between successive fiscal years.

SUPPLEMENTARY NOTE ON THE STATISTICAL SERIES FOR FOREIGN TRADE IN PARTIALLY-FABRICATED IRON AND STEEL GOODS

Throughout the period 1860–1914, our data are stated in terms of long tons; in many years it was necessary for us to convert short tons or pounds (as given in the sources) into long tons. Finished products such as rails and machinery were excluded throughout, as was tinplate.

(a) *The period 1860–70.* For this period, we computed total imports of (1) rolled iron other than rails ("bar, rod, hoop, sheet, and plate iron"), and (2) steel "ingots, bars, sheets, or wire." Data on rolled iron were taken from *Statistics of the American and Foreign Iron Trades, Annual Report of the Secretary of the American Iron and Steel Association, Containing Statistics of the American Iron Trade to January 1, 1877* (Philadelphia: The American Iron and Steel Association, 1877), page 46.[70] Data on steel "ingots, bars, sheets, or wire" were taken from various issues of *Commerce and Navigation of the United States.* The original data for both iron and steel pertain to fiscal years ending June 30. We effected a rough conversion to calendar-year basis by straight-line interpolation between successive fiscal years. Exports were negligible in these years, and hence were neglected in the calculation.

(b) *The period 1871–83.* For this period, net imports of rolled iron (again, excluding rails) were estimated from data in *Statistics of the American and Foreign Iron Trades, Annual Report of the*

---

[69] For a detailed description of the sources of the foreign-trade data, see the introduction to this Appendix.

[70] According to the dating system followed in later years by the American Iron and Steel Association, this particular report would be identified as that for 1876.

Secretary of the American Iron and Steel Association, Containing Statistics of the American Iron Trade to January 1, 1877, page 18 (data for 1871–76); *Statistics of the American and Foreign Iron Trades in 1880, Annual Report of the Secretary of the American Iron and Steel Association* (Philadelphia: The American Iron and Steel Association, 1881), pages 51 and 53 (data for 1877–80); *Statistics of the American and Foreign Iron Trades in 1883* (Philadelphia: The American Iron and Steel Association, 1884), pages 62–63 (data for 1881–83). The designations of specific commodities imported varied slightly from year to year, but among them were "bar iron," "band, hoop, and scroll iron," and "sheet iron."

For the period 1871–82, quantity data for imports of steel "ingots, bars, sheets, and wire" were not available. However, the value of imports was available by years, and we estimated quantity imports by dividing the value of imports in each year by the average yearly price of Bessemer steel rails at works in Pennsylvania. The price as given was lowered by 10 per cent in each year, to compensate roughly for the fact that rails, being fabricated, were more expensive than (say) ingots. For the period 1871–80 value data were taken from *Statistics of the American and Foreign Iron Trades in 1880*, pages 50 and 51; price data, from page 55. For 1881–82, value data were taken from *Statistics of the American and Foreign Iron Trades in 1883*, pages 62–63; price data, from page 58. In each year, the data (which pertain to calendar years) for (1) rolled iron and (2) steel ingots, bars, sheets, and wire, were totaled to obtain aggregate net imports.

For 1883, quantity figures for imports of "steel ingots, blooms, bars, etc.," and for "iron and steel wire rods" were available for the six months ending December 31, 1883 in *Statistics of the American and Foreign Iron Trades in 1883*, page 17. We roughly estimated imports for the year as a whole by doubling this half-year total. This estimate was then added to net imports of rolled iron, to obtain estimated total imports of partially-fabricated iron and steel goods.

(c) *The period 1884–1914.* Import and export data for calendar years were obtained from various issues of *Statistics of the American and Foreign Iron Trades, Annual Statistical Report of the American Iron and Steel Association,* and of the *Annual Statistical Report of the American Iron and Steel Institute.*[71] In some cases, when exports or imports were negligible, they were omitted from our computations. The data as given in the Reports are divided into several categories, which we totaled to obtain net imports, or net exports, for each year. The designations of these categories vary slightly from time to time; among those taken off by us were "bar iron," "steel hoops, plates, and sheets," "steel ingots, blooms, billets, bars, etc.," "wire rods, of iron or steel," "steel plates and sheets," "steel bars or rods, except wire rods," etc.

LUMBER PRODUCED

Calendar-year data, based on reports of the Bureau of the Census, decennially, 1859–99, and annually, 1904–14, were secured from 73rd Congress, 1st Session, Senate Document No. 12, volume I, The Report of the Forest Service of the Agricultural Department on the Forest Problem of the United States, *A National Plan for American Forestry* (Washington: Government Printing Office, 1933), pages 247–248. The figures cover the production of sawed softwood and hardwood, and include the output of custom mills as well as that of sawmills.

LUMBER CONSUMED

Calendar-year figures for lumber consumption—like those for lumber production—were obtained decennially, 1859–99, and annually, 1904–14, from 73rd Congress, 1st Session, Senate Document No. 12, volume I, The Report of the Forest Service of the Agricultural Department on the Forest Problem of the United States, *A National Plan for American Forestry* (Washington: Government Printing Office, 1933), pages 247–248. Production and consumption figures are identical for 1859; for subsequent

[71] The reports were prepared by the American Iron and Steel Institute starting with that for 1912. See the *Report* for 1912, pp. 9 ff.

years, consumption data were estimated by subtracting domestic exports from the combined figures for production and imports. No allowance has been made for changes in stocks.

PAPER PRODUCED

Total paper production for the calendar years 1859, 1869, 1879, 1889, 1899, 1904, 1909, and 1914 were furnished by R. E. Marsh, Chief of the Division of Forest Economics of the Department of Agriculture. These data consist of the aggregate production of newsprint, book, boards, wrapping, fine, and all other paper; and they were compiled or estimated by the Forest Service from Census reports prior to 1917. For 1889 and later years, production data are available for each type of paper; but, prior to 1889, such separate reports are not obtainable.

PAPER CONSUMED

Calendar-year data for 1859, 1869, 1879, 1889, 1899, 1904, 1909, and 1914 were taken from 73rd Congress, 1st Session, Senate Document No. 12, volume I, The Report of the Forest Service of the Agricultural Department on the Forest Problem of the United States, *A National Plan for American Forestry* (Washington: Government Printing Office, 1933), page 260. The series consists of production plus imports minus domestic exports of all kinds of paper (i.e., newsprint, book, boards, wrapping, fine, and all other paper), except the figure for 1859, which is for domestic production only. In that year, however, the value figures for imports and exports were approximately equal. (See *A National Plan for American Forestry*, page 260.)

FERMENTED LIQUORS PRODUCED

Figures for 1870–1901 were secured from *Annual Report of the Commissioner of Internal Revenue,* 1901 (Washington: Government Printing Office, 1901), pages 433, 440–443; and those for 1902–14, from United States Treasury Department, Bureau of Prohibition, *Statistics Concerning Intoxicating Liquors,* January 1930 (Washington: Government Printing Office, 1930), page 52. These data pertain to years ending June 30.[72]

The series is a by-product of the compilations of internal-revenue taxes, which were levied first in 1862 and continuously thereafter. Figures published for the fiscal years 1863–69—appearing in *Report of the Commissioner of Internal Revenue*, 1880 (Washington: Government Printing Office, 1880), page LXXXIX, and also in *Annual Report*, 1901, page 433—we have not used. It is likely that the collection system was least efficient in the earlier years of its operation and the calculated series for production of fermented liquors, based upon tax data, probably has an upward growth bias in the first few years over which tax data are available, because of the increasing efficiency of tax collection. In addition, the early figures behave erratically because of changes in the tax. The *Report of the Commissioner of Internal Revenue*, 1865 (Washington: Government Printing Office, 1865), page 6, states that: "From September 1, 1862, to March 3, 1863, the tax was one dollar per barrel, of not more than thirty-one gallons; from that date to April 1, 1864, sixty cents, and since that time one dollar."

DISTILLED LIQUORS PRODUCED

Figures for 1870–1901 were secured from *Annual Report of the Commissioner of Internal Revenue*, 1901, pages 428–429; and those for 1902–14, from *Statistics Concerning Intoxicating Liquors*, January 1930, page 3. (For additional details concerning these two sources, see the section on fermented liquors produced, just preceding.) The series includes all types of distilled liquors. The data pertain to years ending June 30.[73]

We have not used the data available for the fiscal years 1863–69 (published in *Annual Report of the Commissioner of Internal Revenue*, 1901, page 428), for reasons which were brought out in the discussion of fermented liquors produced. Tax receipts from

---

[72] The Liquors and Beverages group index, however, was adjusted to a calendar-year basis. See Chapter III, above.

[73] The Liquors and Beverages group index, however, was adjusted to a calendar-year basis. See Chapter III, above.

distilled liquors were reported to be several times greater in 1864 than in adjacent years, in large part because of legal tax avoidance. The *Report of the Commissioner of Internal Revenue*, 1865 (Washington: Government Printing Office, 1865), page 6, states that: "For the fiscal year 1864 the tax was twenty cents until March 7, after which it was sixty cents. From July 1, 1864, until January 1, 1865, it was $1.50 per gallon, and afterwards $2." In anticipation of the increased taxes there was a tremendous amount of speculative production (cf. *ibid.*, pages 6–7). Another possible partial explanation of the large figure for 1864 is that tax collection in that year may have been highly efficient. Producers who ordinarily might have been tempted to evade the tax may have decided to pay it because of the possibility of speculative profits.

PETROLEUM PRODUCED

Calendar-year figures for production of crude petroleum were obtained from *Mineral Resources of the United States*, as follows: for 1859–60, from the 1916 volume, part II, page 685; for 1861–1914, from the 1929 volume, part II, page 470.[74]

COKE PRODUCED

Calendar-year data for 1880–1914 were obtained from United States Department of Commerce, Bureau of Mines, *Mineral Resources of the United States*, 1929, part II (Washington: Government Printing Office, 1932), page 582. The series includes production of both beehive and by-product coke.

SUPERPHOSPHATE PRODUCED

Data for 1868–1914 were transcribed from K. D. Jacob and W. Arthur Shelton, "Development of Production of Superphosphate in the United States," *Proceedings of the Sixth Annual Convention of the National Fertilizer Association*, Held at Colorado Springs, Colorado, June 9, 10, 11, and 12, 1930 (published by the Association, 1930), pages 146–148. The figures pertain to years ending May 31 for the period 1868–85 (conversion to a calendar-year

[74] For a detailed description of the sources, see the introduction to this Appendix.

basis did not appear feasible, and in any case the weight of the series in the index was small); to calendar years for the period 1886–1914. The series was estimated by the authors from the quantity of phosphate-rock consumption that remained unaccounted for after deducting from total United States consumption the estimated consumption for (1) direct application to soil and (2) the manufacture of chemicals, etc. (For a more extended description of the method of estimate, see *Proceedings of the Sixth Annual Convention of the National Fertilizer Association,* pages 139–159, and especially pages 139–140, 141, 153–157.)

WHITE LEAD PRODUCED

Data for the census years 1859, 1869, and 1879—used in the census-year group index for Chemicals and Allied Products— were estimated as explained below; data for calendar years, 1884– 1914, were secured from various issues of *Mineral Resources of the United States,* [75] beginning with the issue for the year 1904, page 1115.

Census-year figures for white-lead production in the early period were not available, but data for 1860, 1870, and 1880 were reported by Mr. W. P. Thompson in "The Lead Industry," published in *One Hundred Years of American Commerce.*[76] This source also gives production data for 1887 and 1890, two of the years for which we secured figures from *Mineral Resources.* This overlap enabled us to adjust the level of Mr. Thompson's estimates to that of the series published in *Mineral Resources.* The adjustment was carried out as follows: for the year 1887 the ratio of the figure in *Mineral Resources* to the Thompson figure was 1.077; we accordingly multiplied the Thompson estimates for 1860, 1870, and 1880 by this ratio.[77] These adjusted Thompson

[75] For a detailed description of the sources used here, see the introduction to this Appendix.

[76] Chauncey M. Depew, Editor, *One Hundred Years of American Commerce,* II (New York: D. O. Haynes and Co., 1895), 439. Mr. Thompson's figures are cited in United States Department of the Interior, *Twelfth Census of the United States,* 1900, vol. X, *Manufactures,* part IV, *Special Reports on Selected Industries* (Washington: United States Census Office, 1902), p. 591.

[77] For 1890, the second year of the overlap, multiplication of the Thompson figure by this ratio gives 80.9 thousand tons; the figure for that year reported in *Mineral Resources* is 78.0 thousand tons—a reasonably close check.

figures were taken as approximations to production in the three census years 1859, 1869, and 1879, respectively (cf. Table 2).

FLAXSEED CONSUMED

This series consists of flaxseed production plus net imports (net imports include linseed oil in terms of seed). The data, 1879–1914, have been taken from Arthur F. Burns, *Production Trends in the United States since 1870* (New York: National Bureau of Economic Research, Inc., 1934), pages 298–299. The figures for this *raw-materials* series pertain to years beginning July 1; just how nearly they may indicate manufacture of *derived products* for the corresponding calendar years, it is difficult to say. In view of the relatively small weight of the series, however, it seems probable that any error attributable to this source must be minor.

COTTONSEED OIL PRODUCED

For the period 1872–74, data were secured from *Yearbook of the United States Department of Agriculture,* 1902 (Washington: Government Printing Office, 1903), page 815; and for 1875–1914, from United States Department of Commerce, Bureau of the Census, Bulletin 167, *Cotton Production and Distribution,* Season of 1929–30 (Washington: Government Printing Office, 1930), pages 72–73.[78] The series covers production of crude cottonseed oil, and pertains to years ending June 30, 1872–74, and to years ending July 31, 1875–1914. In view of the irregularity of year-to-year movements and the lack of correlation with indicators of the general cyclical movement over the years which we are studying, it did not seem feasible to attempt a conversion of the data to a calendar-year basis. The weight of the cottonseed-oil series in the group index for Chemicals and Allied Products is small, however, and therefore any error due to this cause would have little effect on the group index.

No figures for cottonseed oil produced are available prior to 1872. "It was not until after emancipation—not, indeed, until

---

[78] In the original source, the data for 1872–74 are given in units of gallons; we have converted these figures to units of pounds, to secure comparability with the data for 1875–1914 obtained from *Cotton Production and Distribution.*

after the cessation of the disturbed political and economic conditions of the reconstruction period in the South—that the seed of cotton was utilized to any important extent for industrial purposes . . . as late as 1867 the slow progress that the industry had made was attested by the fact that there were only four mills actually in operation in the United Sates." [79]

COTTONSEED CAKE AND MEAL PRODUCED

For statements concerning sources and availability of these data, see the discussion of cottonseed oil produced, in the section just preceding.

COPPER CONSUMED

Figures for the period 1860–86 were not secured directly from published sources, but were obtained by methods described below. For the years 1887–99, data were transcribed from Richard P. Rothwell, Editor, *The Mineral Industry*, volumes II–XI (New York: The Scientific Publishing Company, 1894–1903): and for 1900–14, from *Mineral Resources of the United States*, 1904, page 250; 1905, page 360; 1919, part 1, page 601; 1920, part 1, page 452.[80] All data pertain to calendar years.

In general, the figures for consumption given in *The Mineral Industry* were secured as follows: first, total supply was obtained by adding four series—(1) total domestic production of fine copper, (2) production from foreign ores, (3) refiners' stocks on January 1, and (4) imports of "bars, ingots, & old" copper—then from this supply total, data for copper exports (including copper ore) and refiners' stocks on December 31 were deducted to obtain estimates of consumption. (As indicated below, however, allowance was not made for refiners' stocks prior to the year 1884.)

The data in *Mineral Resources* were estimated by deducting, from total available supply, the quantity withdrawn from supply —letting the difference represent consumption. (See *Mineral Re-*

---

[79] *Yearbook of the United States Department of Agriculture*, 1901 (Washington: Government Printing Office, 1902), p. 285.

[80] For a detailed description of *Mineral Resources*, see the introduction to this Appendix.

sources of the United States, 1919, part I, page 600.) This method was followed for all the data that we have transcribed directly from *Mineral Resources.*

Throughout the entire period which we are studying, production of secondary copper and consumers' stocks of copper were not taken into account in the compilation of consumption data; beginning with the year 1884, allowance was made for refiners' stocks.

The period 1882–86. For these five years, data covering the total supply of copper and exports of copper are available in *The Mineral Industry,* II, 239. The exports for this period apparently include the full weight of the copper ore, although for the years 1887–90 (which are also given in this source) the fine-copper content of the ore was estimated, and beginning with the year 1891 (in the same source) the actual copper content of ore was reported.

Since the exports data had been used in the compilation of consumption figures, as indicated above, it clearly was desirable to obtain as homogeneous a series as possible, covering fine copper. On page 791 of *The Mineral Industry,* volume II, data for exports of copper ore are published; and on page 792, exports of pig, sheet, and old copper are given. We assumed that 55 per cent of exports of copper ore represented exports of fine copper;[81] and by applying this percentage figure to the published data for copper-ore exports, we obtained an estimate of the fine-copper content in such exports. To this estimated figure, we added exports of pig, sheet, and old copper to obtain an estimate of total exports of fine copper.

For the year 1882, we subtracted our estimate of copper exports from the figure for total supply, to obtain an estimate of copper consumption. No allowance was made for stocks in that year.

For the year 1883, the figure given in *The Mineral Industry*

[81] The use of the figure of 55 per cent follows the practice of *The Mineral Industry* for the years 1887–90. In *The Mineral Industry,* II, 239, fn., is the statement that "exports are calculated from official reports of exports, counting 'ore' as averaging 55% copper in 1887 to 1890, inclusive . . ." The adjustment factor of 55 per cent was also suggested to us by Mr. H. H. Wanders, Market Editor of *Engineering and Mining Journal.*

for supply did not include stocks on January 1 of that year; but in the calculation of consumption, stocks on December 31 were deducted from the figure for supply. The implication of this procedure is that copper stocks on January 1, 1883 were zero. Since this assumption appeared untenable, we recalculated the consumption figure, simply adding domestic production and imports, and then deducting our estimate for exports of fine copper (described above); thus no account was taken (and, of course, none could be taken) of changes in stocks during the year.

For the years 1884–86, we revised the copper-consumption figures reported in *The Mineral Industry*, deducting 55 per cent (rather than 100 per cent) of the exported ore from the figures reported for supply, in accordance with the analysis outlined above.

Our various recomputations for the years 1883–86 substantially raised the copper-consumption figures given in *The Mineral Industry*. The differences between the two sets of data are as follows (in units of million pounds):

Year	*Mineral Industry* figures	Revised figures
1883	37	84
1884	43	76
1885	52	87
1886	91	113

The revised figures for 1884, 1885, and 1886 agree fairly closely with figures reported for those years in *Mineral Resources of the United States*. For 1884, the figure in *Mineral Resources* is 80 million pounds; for 1885, it is 85–90 million pounds; for 1886, 108 million pounds. (Source for the 1884 and 1885 figures is *Mineral Resources*, 1885, page 224; for the 1896 figure, *Mineral Resources*, 1886, page 124.) No figure for 1883 was found in *Mineral Resources*.

The period 1864–81. We derived estimates of consumption in these years by adding net imports of copper to domestic production or by subtracting net exports of copper from domestic production, as the case might be. No data on copper stocks are available for this period.

Our main difficulty consisted in making proper allowance for the amount of fine copper in exports and imports of copper ore. We finally made the somewhat arbitrary assumptions that 25 per cent of the content of copper-ore imports, and 50 per cent of the content of copper-ore exports, represented fine copper.[82] A net import (+) or a net export (−) figure of ore converted to copper was obtained by the following method:

[(imports of copper ore—foreign exports of copper ore) × 0.25]—[domestic exports of copper ore × 0.50]

We then estimated figures for copper consumption, as follows:

(smelter copper produced in U. S.) + (imports of copper not in ore)

+ (net imports or exports of copper in ore, as calculated above)[83]

— (exports of copper not in ore).

The import and export data given in the original source pertain to calendar years, except for the period 1864–67, when they relate to fiscal years ending June 30. For these four years, we estimated calendar-year data by straight-line interpolation between successive fiscal years. This procedure affords a rough indication of the trend of copper consumption, although it does not, of course, yield a reliable measure of year-to-year fluctuations.

Data for copper production, 1864–81, were secured from *Mineral Resources*, 1929, part 1, page 535. Export and import data for fiscal years ending June 30, 1864–68, were obtained from *Commerce and Navigation of the United States;* for calendar years, 1868–81, from various issues of *Monthly Report* of the

[82] These figures, admittedly, are only rough approximations. The figure of 50 per cent for exports is about the same as that used for the period 1882–86 (see above). The percentage figure for imports is based upon a comparison of data covering fine copper in imports of copper ore during the years 1870–80, and figures for copper-ore imports in this same period. During these years, the fine-copper content of copper-ore imports averaged 23.4 per cent. Figures covering fine copper in imports of copper ore were secured from *The Mineral Industry*, I, 116.

[83] This, of course, could be either a positive or a negative figure.

Bureau of Statistics and from *Summary Statement of the Imports and Exports of the United States.*[84]

The period 1860–63. The available figures covering the quantity of imports and exports of copper during the years 1860–63 did not prove to be adequate for use in obtaining estimates of consumption data by the method followed for the period 1864–81. An attempt was made to develop a procedure for estimating quantities from value and price data, but the results were unsatisfactory when tested out for years in which both quantity and value data were available. Consequently, we have simply used smelter production of copper to represent copper consumption in 1860–63. A comparison of production and consumption data for years immediately following 1863 reveals that production data may serve as a general indicator of the trend of the consumption series over these early years, but not of the short-run changes. Figures for copper production, 1860–63, were transcribed from *Mineral Resources,* 1929, part 1, pages 535.

Lead Consumed

Figures for the years 1860–93 were secured from Walter Renton Ingalls, *Lead and Zinc in the United States* (New York and London: Hill Publishing Company, 1908), page 205; and for 1894–1914, from various issues of *Mineral Resources in the United States,*[85] beginning with the issue for 1903, page 250.

For 1860–93, the figures "represent simply the production plus the imports, minus the exports. For any single year they are likely to be incorrect, because statistics computed in this way fail to take into account the difference in stocks on hand at the beginning and end of the year, but over a series of years they indicate closely the actual progress in consumption." (See Ingalls, *Lead and Zinc,* page 204.) For the years 1894–1914, however—in addition to production, imports, and exports—producers' stocks were taken into account to some extent; but no account was taken of con-

---

[84] For a detailed description of the sources used here, see the introduction to this Appendix.

[85] For a detailed description of *Mineral Resources,* see the introduction to this Appendix.

sumers' stocks, and production of secondary lead was not included. (For statements concerning the variations in the series from which the "consumption" data are compiled, see issues of *Mineral Resources:* for example, the issues for 1907, pages 656–657; 1914, part 1, pages 820–822; and 1918, part 1, page 969.)

ZINC CONSUMED

For the period 1860–72 we computed a series for zinc consumption as described below. Data for 1873–94 were obtained from Walter Renton Ingalls, *Lead and Zinc in the United States* (New York and London: Hill Publishing Company, 1908), page 337; and for 1895–1914, from various issues of *Mineral Resources of the United States,* beginning with the issue for 1902, page 219. Figures pertain to calendar years throughout the entire period.

The series is composed of domestic production plus net imports,[86] with no account taken of stocks during the years 1860–94, but with smelter stocks taken into consideration in the period 1895–1914. Throughout the entire period 1860–1914, consumers' stocks are not taken account of, and secondary zinc is not included.

The series for 1860–72 was computed by adding net imports to production. Figures for calendar-year production in this period were obtained from United States Department of Commerce, Bureau of Mines, Economic Paper 2, *Summarized Data of Zinc Production* (Washington: Government Printing Office, 1929), page 19. Imports and exports for fiscal years ending June 30, 1859–66, were available in annual issues of *Commerce and Navigation in the United States;* but before being combined with calendar-year production, these fiscal-year figures were roughly adjusted to a calendar-year basis by straight-line interpolation between successive fiscal years. Imports and exports for the calendar years 1867–72 were obtained from various issues of *Monthly Report* of the Bureau of Statistics.[87]

---

[86] Imports, with domestic exports and foreign exports deducted. Foreign exports were negligible in all but the earliest years, and domestic exports were usually negligible prior to 1876.

[87] For a detailed description of the foreign-trade sources named above, see the introduction to this Appendix.

TIN IMPORTED

This series consists of net imports (i.e., general imports minus foreign exports). For years prior to 1870, we computed the series, based upon data secured from the sources described below; for the period 1870–1914, calendar-year figures were taken from Arthur F. Burns, *Production Trends in the United States since 1870* (New York: National Bureau of Economic Research, Inc., 1934), pages 296–297.

Figures for general imports and foreign exports (used as a basis for our series) during the fiscal years ending June 30, 1862, 1863, 1865, and 1866, were obtained from various issues of *Commerce and Navigation of the United States*. Because of the discontinuity of the series, no attempt was made to convert the fiscal-year data to a calendar-year basis.

The calendar-year figure for imports in 1867 was furnished by the Bureau of Foreign and Domestic Commerce, while the exports figure for the same year was obtained by totaling monthly items from various issues of the *Monthly Report* of the Bureau of Statistics of the Treasury Department. Imports and foreign exports for the calendar year 1868 were taken from *Monthly Report of the Deputy Special Commissioner of the Revenue*, No. 6, Series 1869–70, pages 231 and 236; and those for 1869 were secured from *Monthly Report of the Chief of the Bureau of Statistics*, No. 6, Series 1870–71, pages 175 and 180.[88]

For 1860, no quantity figures were discovered; and for 1861 and 1864, the available quantity data were so far out of line with those for adjacent years that they were rejected as unreliable.

CIGARS PRODUCED

Calendar-year figures for 1870–79 were estimated by us as described below, and those for 1880–1914 were transcribed from a mimeographed release of the Commissioner of Internal Revenue; this release had been compiled from the Commissioner's *Annual Reports*. The series consists of the production of cigars weighing more than three pounds per thousand.

[88] For a detailed description of the foreign-trade sources, see the introduction to this Appendix.

The data for tobacco, like those for liquor, are by-products of the internal-revenue taxes which were levied beginning with 1862.[89] For the earlier years of the period, production statistics have been based primarily on the various products brought to tax; and in so far as fraud and evasion prevailed, these figures are inaccurate.

Before 1870 the revenue taxes were changed frequently. Mr. Frank L. Olmstead has summarized the "experimental stage" prior to 1868 as follows: ". . . the returns for the first few years were disappointing. Direct fraud and evasion do not seem to have been so much to blame as the inertia of so great a system . . . Under the act of 1864 it can safely be said that the twenty millions of yearly revenue did not represent more than half the amount really due to the government."[90] This does not mean that reported quantity figures should be doubled, since fraud consisted in part in declaring products in a lower tax category than that in which they actually belonged.

Mr. Olmstead was of the opinion that the Act of July 20, 1868 (in which the stamp system was adopted) was the turning-point in tobacco-revenue history. He wrote: "The new system seemed to reach nearly its full effect in the first complete year of its trial; for the changes in the returns from it after 1870 were merely the results of natural growth and of the fluctuations of general trade . . . Almost all evidence of fraud had disappeared, and the system met general approval."

Large fluctuations in the output of tobacco products may be partially explained as ascribable to speculative manufacture caused by anticipation of tax changes. Allied to this is the possibility that increases in the tax may have resulted in some decrease of consumption.[91] Because of the unreliability of the tax-collection sta-

---

[89] The Act of July 1, 1862 went into operation September 1, 1862. For discussion of the liquors series, see earlier sections of this Appendix, on Fermented Liquors Produced and Distilled Liquors Produced, pp. 178–180.

[90] "The Tobacco Tax," *Quarterly Journal of Economics,* v (January 1891), 193–219. The various quotations given in the following description of the series have been taken from this source.

[91] Of some interest is the nature of tobacco consumption. Meyer Jacobstein in *The Tobacco Industry in the United States,* Studies in History, Economics, and Public Law, Edited by the Faculty of Political Science, Columbia University, xxvi,

tistics before 1870, we decided not to compile any data for cigars and other tobacco products for earlier years.

As stated above, figures for cigar production subsequent to 1880 have been published in reports of the Commissioner of Internal Revenue, but prior to 1880 no direct figures bearing on production are available. For the fiscal years ending June 30, 1863–79, however, the Commissioner of Internal Revenue has estimated the number of "cigars, large" brought to tax. This series is inaccurate as a measure of output, for it includes imports—which were taxed —and it does not include exports—which were not taxed. For our estimates of cigar production, therefore, we deducted net imports by fiscal years from cigars brought to tax.[92] While the published figures for exports are given in numbers of cigars, the data for imports and re-exports are stated in pounds. We therefore converted the imports and re-exports figures from pounds to number of cigars, letting thirteen and one-half pounds equal one thousand cigars.[93]

Next, we adjusted the fiscal-year data to a calendar-year basis by straight-line interpolation between data for successive fiscal years. In the absence of a fiscal-year figure for 1880, the 1879 calendar-year figure was obtained by straight-line interpolation between the estimated calendar-year figure for 1878 and the reported calendar-year figure for 1880. Since fiscal-year data for cigar production during the decade of the seventies showed a smooth and practically uninterrupted increase from year to year, our estimates of calendar-year data are probably quite reliable.

---

3 (New York: Columbia University Press, 1907), p. 45, wrote: "Until 1870 cigars and cigarettes were only in slight demand compared with smoking and chewing tobacco. More recently, however, the tendency has been strongly in favor of cigars and cigarettes, and more especially of the former."

[92] Data for cigars brought to tax through 1878 were obtained from *Annual Report of the Commissioner of Internal Revenue,* 1878 (Washington: Government Printing Office, 1878), p. lxiii; and those for 1879, from *Annual Report,* 1879 (Washington: Government Printing Office, 1879), p. lxxix. Data for exports, imports, and re-exports for 1870–78 were obtained from *Commerce and Navigation of the United States,* 1878, part 1; and those for 1879, from *Commerce and Navigation,* 1879. For a detailed description of *Commerce and Navigation,* see the introduction to this Appendix.

[93] This conversion factor was secured from *Annual Report of the Commissioner of Internal Revenue,* 1878, p. liv, where it was used for estimating the number of cigars imported during the fiscal year ending June 30, 1878.

Cigarettes Produced

For the years 1870–79, the series for the number of cigarettes brought to tax has been used to represent domestic production of cigarettes. First, data for fiscal years ending June 30 were obtained from *Annual Report of the Commissioner of Internal Revenue,* 1878 (Washington: Government Printing Office, 1878), page lxiii, and *Annual Report,* 1879, page lxxix. We then converted the fiscal-year figures to a calendar-year basis by the method used for cigar production (see the preceding section). Data for cigarette production in the calendar years 1880–1914 were transcribed directly from the mimeographed release of the Commissioner of Internal Revenue, described above in the section covering cigar production. The series consists of the production of all cigarettes and of cigars weighing not more than three pounds per thousand (before 1897, data for cigars weighing not more than three pounds per thousand are not segregated from cigarettes of the same designation).

A tax on cigarettes was levied as early as 1862, but during the years prior to 1870 the tax was usually included with "cigars, large," and hence cannot be segregated. Also, for the early years there is some doubt as to the homogeneity of the few individual figures that are available for "cigarettes brought to tax." For these reasons, and because of the incompleteness of tax-collection data (cf., again the preceding section), we decided not to attempt estimates of figures for cigarette production prior to 1870.

Manufactured Tobacco and Snuff Produced

For this series we estimated a figure for the fiscal year ending June 30, 1870 by adding (1) the total tobacco and snuff removed in bond for export, and (2) the quantity brought to tax for the year. This method is identical with that by which domestic production was calculated for several subsequent years by the Commissioner of Internal Revenue.[94] Basic data were obtained from

---

[94] See *Annual Report,* 1877, p. XII, and 1878, p. LIII. But also compare *Annual Report,* 1872, p. XI, where account is taken of the change in warehouse stocks.

Annual Report of the Commissioner of Internal Revenue, 1870 (Washington: Government Printing Office, 1870), page 11, and *Annual Report,* 1878, page LXI.

For fiscal years, 1871–79, data on the total production of manufactured tobacco and snuff (the individual products in this total series are plug, twist, fine-cut, scrap chewing, smoking, and snuff) were obtained from *Annual Report of the Commissioner of Internal Revenue* for various years from 1871 through 1880. Corresponding data for the calendar years, 1880–1914, were transcribed from the mimeographed release of the Commissioner of Internal Revenue, described above in the section covering cigar production.

The fiscal-year data obtainable for the period 1870-79 were converted to a calendar-year basis by the method used for cigar production, previously described.

RAILROAD FREIGHT CARS PRODUCED

This series, which extends from 1871 to 1914, measures domestic production of freight cars in the United States, exclusive of that in railroad repair shops. For the period 1899–1914, figures covering output for both domestic use and exports were secured from Dr. Edmund E. Day's study, "An Index of the Physical Volume of Production," *Review of Economic Statistics,* II (November 1920), 329. Dr. Day (*op. cit.,* page 332) commented as follows on this series: "Data on the production of *passenger cars* and *freight cars* are published regularly in the *Railway Age.* The figures as published for the period 1905–12 include, however, production in Canada as well as in the United States. The series excluding Canadian output have been kindly furnished by Mr. C. N. Foss, present associate editor of *Railway Age.*" We have used the figures compiled by Dr. Day for the period 1899–1914, except for the year 1912; for that year we made an additional adjustment. The 1912 figure in the series presented by Dr. Day included equipment built in railroad repair shops, which had been excluded for the other years in the period from 1899 onward. We therefore adjusted Dr. Day's figure for 1912 to eliminate cars built in railroad repair shops, basing our adjustment on data derived from the United States Census.

For the period 1888–98, figures for freight-car production were originally obtained through questionnaires circulated by the *Railroad Gazette* (predecessor of the *Railway Age*); data for these years were kindly furnished us by the *Railway Age*, which stated in correspondence, ". . . inclusive figures are shown for cars built by the builders and also by the railroads. From 1889 to 1898 the figures appear to cover builders' reports only. The number of builders reporting varies from year to year. Whether cars built for export are included in these reports we do not know." Since the data for 1888, provided by the *Railway Age*, were divided into cars built by builders and cars built by railroads, we were able to 'secure a figure for that year which would be comparable with the series also furnished for 1889–98, namely, production by "builders." Apparently, the *Railroad Gazette* attempted to reach all "builders" by questionnaire, although not all of them answered. For some years (1894, for example), a notation was made of the number of idle companies. The production figure for 1898 was based on twenty-eight reporting companies plus twenty-six estimated companies ("very small"). The number of reporting companies was smallest in 1892, when eighteen companies were included, but output in that year was almost as great as in 1891 when fifty companies reported, and very much greater than in 1893, when forty-three companies reported. From this internal evidence, we inferred that the coverage throughout the period 1888–98 was high, and that differences in the number of reporting companies were ascribable to inclusion or non-inclusion of the smaller companies (or companies which may have been idle). However, it is doubtful whether the data for this period are as reliable as those for the years 1899–1914.

In the *Railroad Gazette* for January 6, 1888, page 10, figures were published for the period 1880–87. A sharp break occurs, however, between these data and those for the period immediately following, apparently because the figures for 1880–87 were based

on a comparatively small sample of fifteen companies.[95] We estimated total production of freight cars, by years, 1880–87, utilizing
data on freight cars ordered by railroads, presented by John E.
Partington, in his *Railroad Purchasing and the Business Cycle*
(Washington, D. C.: The Brookings Institution, 1929), pages
219–226.

We first made a graphical comparison of data for freight-car
orders and freight-car production over the period 1888–1914. This
comparison showed that in general the fluctuations in freight-car
orders preceded those in freight-car production by about three-
quarters of a year. The second step was to estimate total production for the year 1887 by use of the following formula:

$$\text{(total production for 1887)} = \frac{\text{orders for twelve months ending with March 1887}}{\text{orders for twelve months ending with March 1888}} \times \left(\begin{array}{c} \text{total production} \\ \text{for 1888} \end{array} \right).$$

We then found that the ratio between this estimated total production for 1887 and the production shown by the sample of fifteen
companies for 1887 was 3.28. Finally, we multiplied the annual
figures of the sample for each year, 1880–86, by this ratio to secure annual estimates of total production. A comparison of these
estimates for production with the reported figures for orders
(proper adjustment being made for lag) revealed that the levels
of the two series were approximately the same.

Since we were unable to secure data covering output in the
period 1871–79, we estimated production, on the basis of data for
orders, taken from Partington's *Railroad Purchasing and the Business Cycle*. As stated above, graphical comparison of figures for
1888–1914 suggested that freight-car orders, suitably lagged, furnished a fairly accurate picture of year-to-year fluctuations in
production. To secure our estimates, we therefore adjusted the
level of the orders series to the level of the production series, also

[95] *Railroad Gazette*, January 6, 1888, p. 10, states: "The returns as to freight
cars are unfortunately not so complete as those relating to locomotives, and cannot
be taken to represent the total annual increase for the whole country. The relative increase in one year as compared with another is probably fairly shown." A
similar statement is made concerning the production of passenger cars, 1880–87.

taking account of the differences in timing between the two series. That is to say, we first computed the ratio of (a) our estimate of total production in the calendar year 1880 (derived as described in the preceding paragraph) to (b) total orders for the twelve months ending with March 1880; the ratio was found to be 0.861. Production for each calendar year, 1871–79, was then estimated by multiplying this ratio by orders for the twelve-month period ending with March of that calendar year. For example:

(estimated production for 1875) =
0.861 x (orders for the twelve months ending with March 1875).

Note that the difference in method of estimate between the period 1880–87 and the period 1871–79 is that estimates of the year-to-year fluctuations for 1880–87 are based on the *Railroad Gazette* sample, while for 1871–79 estimates of year-to-year fluctuations are based on orders, suitably lagged.

RAILROAD PASSENGER CARS PRODUCED

Figures for the domestic production of railroad passenger cars in the period 1889–1914, like those for freight-car output, were secured from Dr. Edmund E. Day's article in the *Review of Economic Statistics,* II (November 1920), 329. (Cf. the section on freight-car production, immediately preceding. The comments there made concerning the available data for freight-car output, 1889–1914, apply to passenger cars as well. Also, our passenger-car data, like those for freight cars, exclude production in railroad repair shops.)

Data covering the years 1890–98 were obtained through correspondence with the *Railway Age;* as for freight-car production, the original data were obtained through questionnaires issued by the *Railroad Gazette,* predecessor of the *Railway Age* (see the discussion for freight-car production, 1888–98, just above).

For the period 1871–89, we estimated production figures, basing our estimate on data for orders of passenger cars. No figures are available for passenger-car production, 1871–79. For the years 1880–87, data for passenger-car production—as well as for freight-car production—based on a small sample of fifteen companies are available in the *Railroad Gazette,* January 6, 1888, page 10. (See section on freight-car production, above.) But, since we considered these sample data for passenger-car production to be inadequate, we based our estimates for the whole period 1871–89 on orders for passenger cars. Figures for passenger cars ordered by railroads were secured from John E. Partington, *Railroad Purchasing and the Business Cycle* (Washington, D.C.: The Brookings Institution, 1929), pages 219–226.

A graphical comparison of orders and production for the years 1890–1914 led to three important conclusions. (1) On the whole, the fluctuations of orders preceded those of production by about one full year. (2) In terms of relative movements, both the trend and the short-run fluctuations of passenger-car orders were similar to those of passenger-car output, properly lagged. (3) The ratio of production in 1890 to orders in 1889 (1.309) was approximately equal to the average ratio of production to orders (production lagged one year) in the entire period 1890–1914. We accordingly estimated passenger-car production, by years, 1871–89, as follows: the figure for orders in each year, 1870–88, was multiplied by the ratio 1.309 to secure an estimate of production for the following year.

Automobiles Produced

Our series for automobile production covers output of passenger cars and motor trucks combined, by years, 1899–1914. For the years 1900–14, the data were taken from *Automobile Facts and Figures,* 1936 edition (New York: Automobile Manufacturers Association, Inc., 1936), page 4. The figures are designated as "factory sales," but presumably closely approximate output. This source did not give a total for our base year, 1899, but such total was filled in from an earlier publication—Leonard P. Ayres, *The Automobile Industry and Its Future* (Cleveland: The Cleveland Trust Company, 1921), page 8.[96]

[96] This publication also gives estimated totals for 1895–98, but we did not use these estimates, since the years 1895–98 antedated the base period of our index and the production of automobiles during this interval was so unimportant a part of the total national product.

Rubber Imported

For the years 1860–68, this series was estimated as described below; the figure for 1869 was taken from the *Monthly Report of the Chief of the Bureau of Statistics,* December 1870;[97] and figures for 1870–1914 were transcribed from Arthur F. Burns, *Production Trends in the United States since 1870* (New York: National Bureau of Economic Research, Inc., 1934), pages 294–295.

The data as transcribed, 1869–1914, pertain to calendar years; for the period 1860–67, we secured calendar-year estimates by straight-line interpolation between fiscal-year data (a detailed description is given below); for 1868, we were obliged to estimate a figure for the calendar year by straight-line interpolation between the estimated calendar-year figure for 1867 and the reported calendar-year figure for 1869. The figures for 1869–1914 are presumably accurate. But because of the irregularity of the fiscal-year series, as well as the degree of approximation involved in many of the fiscal-year estimates themselves, the interpolated calendar-year figures for 1860–68 cannot be assumed to measure year-to-year movements accurately; all that can be claimed for the estimates is that they furnish a fairly reliable indication of the general drift of net imports over this period.

During the entire period, the series consists of net imports of India rubber (general imports minus foreign exports); and for some years, gums other than India rubber are included (cf. Burns, *Production Trends,* page 336). Imports of rubber scrap are excluded throughout.

We turn now to a detailed statement of the process which we followed to obtain a continuous fiscal-year series, 1860–68; in the following discussion, all dates refer to fiscal years ending June 30. Quantity figures for imports were not available for 1860–61 or 1864–67; and quantity figures for re-exports were not available

---

[97] For a detailed description of the source used here, see the introduction to this Appendix.

for 1866–67. Value data for both imports and re-exports were available, however, for every year of the period 1860–68; and, by making use of these value data, we estimated the lacking quantity figures.[98]

Imports. Figures for imports were estimated as follows. First, quarterly prices of Para rubber at New York were averaged, by fiscal years, 1860–70.[99] We then divided the value of imports for each year by the average price in the same year. We thus obtained a "preliminary series" for the quantity figures desired (this series, as will shortly be seen, fluctuated at too low a level). For five years of this period (1862, 1863, 1868, 1869, 1870) actual quantity figures were available, and for each of these years we calculated the ratio of the actual quantity figures to the "preliminary series," just described. These ratios were 1.60, 2.58, 3.16, 2.59, and 2.72, respectively.[100] We omitted the extreme items, 1.60 and 3.16, in this group of ratios, and averaged the three remaining ratios, securing a figure of 2.63. The wide dispersion of the ratios indicated that the average just computed is nontypical and that its use could lead to results yielding only very rough approximations. However, in the absence of any published quantity figures for imports, a rough approximation was preferred to no data at all. We accordingly multiplied the "preliminary series," described above, by the average ratio which we had computed (2.63), and thus obtained estimates of imports, by years, 1860–61 and 1864–67.

Re-exports. Since actual figures for re-exports of rubber in 1866 and 1867 were not available in published sources, we estimated these data as follows:

[98] Both value data and quantity data were obtained from annual issues of *Commerce and Navigation of the United States.* For a detailed description of this source, see the introduction to this Appendix.

[99] Price quotations were taken from 52nd Congress, 2nd Session, Senate Report No. 1394, *Wholesale Prices, Wages, and Transportation,* Report by Mr. Aldrich from the Committee on Finance, March 3, 1893, part II (Washington: Government Printing Office, 1893), p. 291.

[100] The fact that the ratios of the reported figures to the "preliminary series" (for the five years 1862, 1863, 1868, 1869, and 1870) were all well above unity indicated that the actual prices at which rubber imports were valued differed considerably in general level from the prices of Para rubber at New York, used in our computation.

$$\frac{\text{value of re-exports, 1866}}{\text{value of imports, 1866}} \times \left(\begin{array}{c} \text{quantity of imports for 1866,} \\ \text{as estimated above} \end{array} \right)$$

$$= \left(\begin{array}{c} \text{quantity of re-exports} \\ \text{for 1866} \end{array} \right);$$

$$\frac{\text{value of re-exports, 1867}}{\text{value of imports, 1867}} \times \left(\begin{array}{c} \text{quantity of imports for 1867,} \\ \text{as estimated above} \end{array} \right)$$

$$= \left(\begin{array}{c} \text{quantity of re-exports} \\ \text{for 1867} \end{array} \right).$$

Obviously, the estimates thus obtained are crude, but the magnitude of re-exports, compared with imports, in other years for which actual data are available for both series suggests that the effect of any errors in estimating re-exports is not important in the net-imports series.

VESSELS PRODUCED

These data were taken from the United States Department of Commerce, Bureau of Navigation, *Merchant Marine Statistics,* 1930 (Washington: Government Printing Office, 1930), pages 37–39, where production is stated in terms of gross tonnage of vessels built and documented in the United States. The figures pertain to fiscal years ending June 30.[101]

[101] In the computation of the manufacture index, however, this series was adjusted to a calendar-year basis. See Chapter III.

APPENDIX B

MANUFACTURE INDEX—DERIVATION OF WEIGHTS (SUPPLEMENTARY NOTES TO TABLE 3)

Group I—Food and Kindred Products

Cane sugar, cane-sugar refining, and beet sugar. The value-added total shown in Table 3 was obtained by summing the value-added figures for cane sugar and cane-sugar refining ($18,326,000; cf. *1914 Abstract,* page 53) and beet sugar ($2,520,000; cf. *1914 Abstract,* page 697).

Coffee and spice, roasting and grinding. The 1899 Census value-added figure was calculated from data given in United States Department of the Interior, *Twelfth Census of the United States, 1900,* volume VII, *Manufactures,* part 1 (Washington: United States Census Office, 1902), page 161. The process was to deduct cost of materials ($55,112,000) from value of products ($69,-527,000), thus obtaining $14,415,000 as the Census value-added figure. However—since, because of the limited coverage of available physical-quantity series within the food group rather broad imputation was necessary, and the coffee series was presumably somewhat unrepresentative of foods as a whole—it seemed best to depart from the strict imputation principle here and for weighting purposes reduce the value-added figure for coffee. Accordingly, the value-added figure for use in Table 12 has been reduced to one-half of $14,415,000, or to $7,208,000.

Group II—Textiles and Their Products

Sub-group weighting. Deducting from the Census value-added total for Group II ($733,760,000), the Census value-added figure for the sub-group *textile fabrics and materials* ($383,371,000), we obtained the value-added figure for the sub-group *articles from textile fabrics* ($350,389,000)—cf. Columns 2 and 3 of Table 3.

Textile fabrics and materials. The weight for this sub-group was allocated among the four constituent series in proportion to the following 1899 value-added totals (these totals are partly imputed by indirect estimation, as explained in detail below):

Raw cotton consumed	$192,824,000
Raw wool consumed	129,178,000
Raw silk and spun silk imported	45,965,000
Minor fibers imported	13,655,000
	$381,622,000

Raw cotton consumed. Consumption of raw cotton has been used as an indicator of the output of cotton fabrics. The weight applied was based upon value added in 1899 for the industry described in the Census reports as "cotton manufactures," plus an imputed portion of the value added for the "hosiery and knit goods" industry. The *1914 Abstract,* page 59, gives an 1899 figure ($162,648,000) for value added in the "manufacture of 'cotton goods,'" which includes the spinning of cotton and the weaving of piece goods, for 'cotton lace,' and for 'cotton small wares' " (*loc. cit.*). Value-added data are also published for the "hosiery and knit goods" industry as a whole, but not separately for cotton. The lacking figure therefore had to be estimated. First, the ratio of the value of cotton materials used in the "hosiery and knit goods" industry to the total value of cotton, wool, and silk materials used in this industry was obtained, as shown in Table 23. The ratio thus secured (67.6 per cent) was then applied to the value-added figure ($44,639,000) for the entire hosiery and knit goods industry, given on page 637 of the *1914 Abstract,* to obtain the portion imputed to raw cotton consumed ($30,176,000). This amount, plus value added for "manufacture of cotton goods" ($162,648,000; see above), yielded the figure set down in the immediately preceding tabulation for the total value added assigned to raw cotton consumed ($192,824,000).

Raw wool consumed. Consumption of raw wool has been used as an indicator of the production of wool fabrics.[1] The weight attributed to raw wool consumed was based on value added in 1899 for the Census classification "wool manufactures" plus an imputed portion of the value added for the "hosiery and knit goods" in-

TABLE 23

DATA FOR IMPUTING VALUE ADDED BY MANUFACTURE IN THE HOSIERY AND KNIT GOODS INDUSTRY TO COTTON, WOOL, AND SILK*

(*Data pertain to census year 1899*)

Materials	Cost of materials (*unit: one thousand dollars*)		Percentage distribution of cost of materials
Cotton			
Domestic cotton..............	3,562	..	..
Cotton yarn.................	22,205	..	..
		25,767	67.6
Wool			
Domestic wool..............	5,262	..	..
Woolen yarn.................	1,258	..	..
Worsted yarn...............	4,865	..	..
		11,385	29.9
Silk			
Spun silk....................................		947	2.5
Cotton, wool, and silk, combined.................		38,099	100.0

* Source of basic data: United States Department of Commerce, Bureau of the Census, *Abstract of the Census of Manufactures*, 1914 (Washington: Government Printing Office, 1917), pp. 64, 65.

dustry. This imputed figure was derived by the method described in the paragraph on raw cotton consumed (just preceding), from the data presented in Table 23. The imputed item (29.9 per cent of $44,639,000, or $13,347,000), plus the value-added item for "wool manufactures" ($115,831,000) obtained from the *1914 Abstract*, page 71, yielded a total ($129,178,000) for the value added assigned to raw wool consumed.

[1] For statistics on the quantities of wool used in the manufacture of woolen and worsted goods, felt goods, wool-felt hats, carpets and rugs other than rag, and hosiery and knit goods, see the *1914 Abstract*, pp. 65, 71–79.

Raw silk and spun silk imported. The series of imports of raw and spun silk.has been taken to represent the manufacture of silk fabrics.[2] The value added in the manufacture of "silk goods, including throwsters" ($44,849,000) is published on page 688 of the *1914 Abstract;* this amount plus the portion of the value added for the "hosiery and knit goods" industry which has been imputed to silk (2.5 per cent of $44,639,000, or $1,116,000; cf. Table 23 and the discussion for cotton and wool immediately preceding), yielded a figure ($45,965,000) for the value added assigned to the series raw silk and spun silk imported.

Minor fibers imported. The value added attributed to this series ($13,655,000) was obtained by adding the value-added figures for "cordage and twine" ($11,218,000), "jute goods" ($2,369,-000), and "flax and hemp, dressed" ($68,000), published on pages 606, 645, and 621, respectively, of the *1914 Abstract.*

Articles from textile fabrics. No figures were available for making a direct allocation of the weight for this sub-group (9.03; cf. Column 6 of Table 3) among the two constituent series—raw cotton consumed, adjusted for foreign trade in cotton goods; and raw wool consumed, adjusted for foreign trade in wool goods. It was felt, however, that a reasonably satisfactory approximation might be obtained by making the allocation between the series in proportion to the value-added totals ($192,824,000 and $129,178,-000), previously assigned to raw cotton consumed and raw wool consumed, respectively, in the sub-group *textile fabrics and materials,* as set down above.

Group III—Iron and Steel and Their Products

The allocation of the weight for this group (21.09; cf. Column 5 of Table 3) among the five individual production series was made on the basis of the 1899 value-added totals assigned the several series, which were as follows:

Pig iron produced ....$ 52,100,000
Steel ingots and castings produced 34,200,000

[2] For quantities of raw and spun silk used in the manufacture of silk goods and hosiery and knit goods, see *1914 Abstract,* pp. 65, 69.

Rails produced 11,200,000
Structural iron and steel produced 7,600,000
Iron and steel "end products," other than rails and struc-
tural iron and steel 713,400,000

$818,500,000

The derivation of these value-added figures is discussed below.

Pig iron produced. Because of the unusual market conditions of 1899 in iron and steel manufacture, the Census value-added figure for "iron and steel, blast furnaces" is abnormally large and therefore not suited to serve as representative of the relative importance of this industry.[3] Examination of the historical movement of the data for "iron and steel, blast furnaces," as published in the *1914 Abstract*, reveals how much out of line the 1899 value-added figure is (see Table 24).

TABLE 24

UNITED STATES CENSUS DATA ON "IRON AND STEEL, BLAST FURNACES"*

Year	Number of establish- ments	Wage earners (average number)	Primary horsepower	Capital	Wages	Cost of materials	Value of products	Value added by manu- facture
				Expressed in thousands				
1914	160	29,356	1,222,273	462,282	22,781	264,580	317,654	53,074
1909	208	38,429	1,173,422	487,581	24,607	320,638	391,429	70,791
1904	190	35,078	773,278	236,146	18,935	178,942	231,823	52,881
1899	223	39,241	497,272	143,159	18,484	131,504	206,757	75,253
1889	304	33,415	248,928	129,547	14,614	110,099	145,643	35,544
1879	341	41,695	..	89,531	12,655	58,620	89,316	30,696
1869	386	27,554	63,900	56,145	12,475	45,498	69,640	24,142
1859	286	15,927	..	24,673	4,545	12,293	20,870	8,577
1849	404	21,054	..	16,648	5,011	7,538	13,492	5,954

* This table is copied from United States Department of Commerce, Bureau of the Census, *Abstract of the Census of Manufactures*, 1914 (Washington: Government Printing Office, 1917), p. 640.

The 1899 value-added figure for "iron and steel, steel works and rolling mills" is, however, quite in line with such figures for previous and subsequent years. The following method was accord-

[3] For a description of the unusual state of the iron and steel market in 1899, see *Statistics of the American and Foreign Iron Trades for 1899, Annual Statistical Report of the American Iron and Steel Association* (Philadelphia: The American Iron and Steel Association, 1900), pp. 17–26.

ingly used to obtain a modified 1899 value-added figure for "iron and steel, blast furnaces" (basic data from *1914 Abstract,* pages 640–641). The sum of the 1899 value added for "blast furnaces" and "steel works and rolling mills" was multiplied by the ratio of (1) the 1904 value added for "blast furnaces" to (2) the sum of the 1904 values added for "blast furnaces" and "steel works and rolling mills."

	1899	1904
Value added for "iron and steel, blast furnaces"	$ 75,253,000	$ 52,881,000
Value added for "iron and steel, steel works and rolling mills"	206,317,000	232,761,000
Sum	$281,570,000	$285,642,000

Modified 1899 value added for "blast furnaces"
$$= \$281,570,000 \times \frac{\$52,881,000}{\$285,642,000} = \$52,100,000.$$

Steel ingots and castings produced, rails produced, and structural iron and steel produced. The 1899 value-added figures for these three series, as set down at the beginning of this section, were obtained in each case by multiplying (1) value added per ton of product, 1899, by (2) the number of tons produced in 1899. The estimated value-added totals for these three series were derived by Mr. Louis Weiner, and have been furnished to the present writer by Mr. Weiner.

Iron and steel "end products," other than rails and structural iron and steel. The 1899 value-added assigned to this series is a residual figure, secured by deducting from the total value-added of Group III ($818,500,000) the sum of the value-added items for the other four constituent series ($105,100,000); see tabulation at beginning of this section. For discussion of the "end-products" series itself, see Appendix A.

GROUP IV—LUMBER AND ITS REMANUFACTURES

Sub-group weighting. Deducting from the Census value-added total for Group IV ($526,602,000) the Census value-added figure for the sub-group *lumber and timber products and pulp wood* ($312,425,000), we obtained the value-added figure for the sub-group *other products* ($214,177,000)—cf. Columns 2 and 3 of Table 3. Basic data were taken from the *1914 Abstract,* pages 29 and 134.

GROUP VI—PAPER AND PRINTING

Sub-group weighting. Deducting from the Census value-added total for Group VI ($393,341,000) the Census value-added figure for the sub-group *paper and wood pulp* ($56,796,000), we obtained the value-added figure for the sub-group *other products* ($336,-545,000)—cf. Columns 2 and 3 of Table 3. Basic data were taken from the *1914 Abstract,* pages 29 and 666.

GROUP VII—LIQUORS AND BEVERAGES

"The figures [published in the Census reports] for both value of products and value added by manufacture in the case of the brewery and distillery industries include a very large amount of tax paid to the Federal Government, and are therefore misleading as an indication of the relative importance of these industries from a purely manufacturing standpoint." [4] Because of certain technical difficulties, a direct computation of 1899 value-added totals, excluding federal taxes, for Group VII could not be made. We accordingly estimated this figure, as described below.

The ratio of the Census figures for (1) total wages paid in the Liquors and Beverages group to (2) total wages paid for "other groups" [5] was computed for 1899 and for 1909. The two ratios agreed fairly closely—0.0193 for 1899 and 0.0184 for 1909. Next, the ratio of value added, including federal taxes, for the Liquors and Beverages group to the value added for "other groups" was computed for 1899 and also for 1909.[6] The two ratios, like the wages ratios, differed only slightly—0.071 for 1899 and 0.068 for 1909.

---

[4] *1914 Abstract,* p. 28.

[5] Data on wages paid were obtained from the *1914 Abstract,* p. 29. The entity "other groups" here includes all of the fourteen Census groups except Group VII, the Liquors and Beverages group itself; Group XIII, Railroad Repair Shops (omitted as not strictly a manufacturing group); and Group XIV, Miscellaneous Industries (omitted because of its heterogeneity, and the small number of physical-volume series available).

[6] The value-added figures were secured from the *1914 Abstract,* p. 29.

Since for each of the two sets of ratios the difference between 1899 and 1909 was small, we assumed that the ratio of value added, *excluding* federal taxes, for the Liquors and Beverages group to the total value added for "other groups" would be practically the same in the two years. For the year 1909 we were able to obtain an estimate of taxes paid in the Liquors and Beverages group, made by Dr. Warren M. Persons.[7] We deducted this estimate— amounting to $213,000,000—from $488,183,000, the figure for value added by manufacture, including federal taxes, for the Liquors and Beverages group in 1909 (from page 29 of the *1914 Abstract*), thus obtaining $275,183,000 as the estimated value added for the group, excluding federal taxes. We next computed the ratio of this estimated value-added figure to the 1909 value-added total for "other groups," obtaining as result 0.039.[8]

Finally, we applied this ratio to the 1899 value-added total for "other groups," to secure an estimate of the 1899 value added, excluding federal taxes, for Liquors and Beverages ($160,000,-000).[9] This estimate is entered in Column 2 of Table 3. The deduction for federal taxes in the Liquors and Beverages group, 1899, was thus the difference between $289,083,000 (the total value added, as given by the *1914 Abstract*, p. 29) and $160,-000,000—or, in round numbers, $129,000,000.

For the two sub-groups—*liquors, malt* and *liquors, distilled*— we estimated 1899 value-added figures, excluding federal taxes, as explained below.

[7] See Edmund E. Day, *An Index of the Physical Volume of Production* (Cambridge, Mass.: Harvard University Committee on Economic Research, 1921), p. 33; or Edmund E. Day and Warren M. Persons, "An Index of the Physical Volume of Production," *Review of Economic Statistics*, II (November 1920), 314.

[8] Value added, excluding federal taxes, for Liquors and Beverages, 1909 = $275,-183,000 (as above).

Value added for "other groups," 1909 = $8,529,261,000 — ($488,183,000 + $222,982,000 + $681,163,000) = $8,529,261,000 — $1,392,328,000 = $7,136,933,000. Data taken from *1914 Abstract*, p. 29.

The ratio of $275,183,000 to $7,136,933,000 = 0.039.

[9] Value added, 1899, for "other groups" = $4,831,076,000 — ($289,083,000 + $113,676,000 + $345,046,000) = $4,831,076,000 — $747,805,000 = $4,083,271,000. Data taken from *1914 Abstract*, p. 29.

Then, $4,083,271,000 × 0.039 = $159,248,000—or, in round numbers, $160,-000,000.

The 1899 value-added figures for these two industries, including federal taxes in each case, are $185,317,000 and $81,649,000, respectively (*1914 Abstract*, pp. 649, 650); the sum of these is $266,966,000. Deducting from this sum the estimated federal taxes (set down just above) of $129,000,000, we obtained, in round numbers, $138,000,000 as the 1899 value added, excluding federal taxes, for the two industries combined.

To secure an estimated allocation of this "value-added, excluding federal taxes" between the two sub-groups, we divided the total of $138,000,000 in proportion to wages paid in 1899 (*1914 Abstract*, pages 649, 650). On this basis, 93.7 per cent—or, in round numbers, $129,000,000—went to *liquors, malt;* and 6.3 per cent—or, in round numbers, $9,000,000—to *liquors, distilled.*[10]

GROUP VIII—CHEMICALS AND ALLIED PRODUCTS

Coke. The 1899 value-added figure of $15,919,000 given under the Census heading "coke, not including gas-house coke" was deemed adequate, inasmuch as the production of by-product coke in 1899 was relatively small.

Paint and varnish. The weight for this sub-group (2.18; cf. Column 6 of Table 3) was allocated between the two available series—white lead produced, and flaxseed consumed—on a "cost of materials" basis; that is, the sub-group weight was divided between the two series in the proportion which the cost of pig lead used by the "paint and varnish" industry in 1899 ($8,585,688) bore to the cost of linseed oil used ($7,495,196)[11]—in the proportion 53.4 per cent and 46.6 per cent, respectively.

Oils, cottonseed, and cake. In allocating the weight for this sub-group (1.19; cf. Column 6 of Table 3) between the two available series—cottonseed oil produced, and cottonseed cake and meal produced—there was, of course, no possibility of using the value-added criterion, or such "standard criteria" as cost of materials, wages, capital. Indeed, this is the classic case of joint cost! The

---

[10] The wages-paid figures were $25,776,000 and $1,733,000, respectively. Allocation on the basis of capital (*loc. cit.*) would give very similar results, the percentages being 92.7 and 7.3, respectively.

[11] These cost figures are taken from the *1914 Abstract*, p. 192.

sub-group weight was divided between the two series in proportion to estimated value of product.

The value of cottonseed oil and that of cottonseed cake and meal produced in 1899 were estimated by use of production figures obtained from the *1914 Abstract,* page 190, and price data secured from United States Department of Commerce and Labor, *Bulletin of the Bureau of Labor,* No. 87, March 1910 (Washington: Government Printing Office, 1910), pages 544 and 545. The amount of cottonseed oil produced in 1899 was 93,325,729 gallons and the average price was $0.2663 per gallon. Thus the value of the output was estimated as $24,853,000. For cottonseed cake and meal, 884,391 tons were produced, and the average price was $20.-7958 per ton, yielding an estimate of $18,392,000 for the value of product.

The total of the two value figures just derived—$24,853,000 and $18,392,000—was $43,245,000: of this total, the value of cottonseed oil constituted 57.5 per cent; and the value of cottonseed cake and meal, 42.5 per cent.

Group X—Metals and Metal Products, Other than Iron and Steel

The individual physical-quantity series attaching to this group are copper consumed, lead consumed, zinc consumed, and tin imported. No statistical data are available from which one could readily make an allocation of value added among these four series. In view of this, the weight for the group (5.63; cf. Column 5 of Table 3) was allocated by a method based upon use of data for value consumed of the several materials—copper, lead, zinc, tin—in 1899.

In the *1914 Abstract* (page 211) it is stated that "some of the industries included in the group extract these metals from ores, or refine them or alloy them, while other industries use the metals in the manufacture of more highly elaborated commodities." The Census thus divides the group into two sub-groups: *metals* and *metal products.* In Table 131 on page 211 of the *1914 Abstract* a list of the individual industries included in the *metals* sub-group is presented; and in Table 223, on page 568 and following pages, figures are given for the 1899 value added in individual industries. By use of these data, an 1899 value-added total for the *metals* sub-group—$111,753,000—was computed (see Table 25). Subtraction of this figure from $218,459,000, the 1899 value added for the major Census group Metals and Metal Products, Other than Iron and Steel (page 29 of the *1914 Abstract*), yielded $106,706,000 as the 1899 value added for the other sub-group, *metal products*. Allocation of the weight for the whole Census group (5.63; cf. Column 5 of Table 3) between the two sub-groups

TABLE 25

VALUE ADDED BY MANUFACTURE, 1899, FOR INDUSTRIES
OF THE METALS SUB-GROUP*

(*Unit: one thousand dollars*)

Industry	Value added by manufacture, 1899
Babbitt metal and solder...	1,193
Brass, bronze, and copper products..............................	27,465
Gold and silver, reducing and refining, not from the ore...........	880
Lead, bar, pipe, and sheet..	1,199
Smelting and refining, copper....................................	42,958
Smelting and refining, lead......................................	31,271
Smelting and refining, zinc......................................	4,902
Smelting and refining, not from the ore.........................	1,885
Total...	111,753

* For source, see accompanying text.

in proportion to the value-added totals just obtained—$111,753,-000 for *metals*, and $106,706,000 for *metal products*—yielded sub-group weights of 2.88 and 2.75, respectively.

As a preliminary step to the allocation of weight within the sub-groups, there was computed for each of the four metals—copper, lead, zinc, and tin—an estimate of the value of the 1899 consumption. Such estimate was obtained, in each case, by taking the product of (1) the average price in 1899—as given in United States Department of Labor, *Bulletin of the Department of Labor*, No. 39, March 1902 (Washington: Government Printing Office, 1902), pages 397, 401, 407, 409—by (2) the 1899 consumption figures, as given in our Table 1 (for tin, imports have been taken to represent consumption). These estimates of the value of the 1899 consumption are shown in Column 2 of Table 26.

We now turn to the allocation of weight within the two sub-groups, taking each in turn.

TABLE 26

DERIVATION OF WEIGHTS FOR CONSTITUENT SERIES OF GROUP X*

Series	Estimated value, 1899	A. Metals		B. Metal products		Total weight
	(unit: one million dollars)	Percentage distribution of 1899 value	Sub-group weight	Percentage distribution of 1899 value	Sub-group weight	
(1)	(2)	(3)	(4)	(5)	(6)	(7)
Copper consumed.....	69.3	66.4	1.91	56.1	1.54	3.45
Lead consumed.......	20.3	19.5	0.56	16.5	0.45	1.01
Zinc consumed........	14.7	14.1	0.41	11.9	0.33	0.74
Tin imported.........	19.1	..	..	15.5	0.43	0.43
Totals..............	123.4	100.0	2.88	100.0	2.75	5.63

* For explanation, see accompanying text.

Metals. The allocation of the weight for this sub-group (2.88, set down in an earlier paragraph) among the individual series was in proportion to the estimated value of 1899 consumption, as just derived. This allocation was confined to the three metals copper, lead, and zinc—excluding tin, which is imported. The percentage distribution of value of 1899 consumption is shown in Column 3 of Table 26, and the allocation of the total sub-group weight (2.88) in proportion to these percentages is shown in Column 4.

Metal products. The procedure in allocating the weight for this sub-group (2.75, set down in an earlier paragraph) is similar to that just described, but here tin, which is a raw material in numerous metal products, is included in the allocation. The results are shown in Column 6 of Table 26.

The total weight assigned each of the four series is obtained by adding Columns 4 and 6 of Table 26. The results of this addition

(Column 7 of the same table) have been entered as the series weights in Column 7 of Table 3.

GROUP XI—TOBACCO MANUFACTURES

In setting up the 1899 value-added figures for this group, a deduction was made for federal taxes paid. The value-added items entered in Columns 2 and 3 of Table 3 were obtained in each case by subtracting, from 1899 value added as given by the Census— *1914 Abstract*, pages 29, 700—the amount of taxes paid in the fiscal year ending June 30, 1899 as reported by the Commissioner of Internal Revenue—cf. *Annual Report of the Commissioner of Internal Revenue*, 1900 (Washington: Government Printing Office, 1900), page 32. The computations are shown in the accompanying tabulation.

	Value added, including federal taxes	Federal taxes	Value added, excluding federal taxes
Tobacco, cigars and cigarettes............	$102,131,000	$21,068,000	$81,063,000
Tobacco, chewing and smoking, and snuff..	68,716,000	30,206,000	38,510,000
Group total.........................	$170,847,000	$51,274,000	$119,573,000

Tobacco, cigars and cigarettes. Prior to 1909 the Census did not give separate data for cigars and cigarettes in the standard tables showing value added, value of products, etc. We have divided the weight for the sub-group *tobacco, cigars and cigarettes* (2.09; cf. Column 6 of Table 3) between the two constituent series —cigars produced and cigarettes produced—in proportion to the number of pounds of tobacco consumed, as given in United States Department of the Interior, *Twelfth Census of the United States*, 1900, volume IX, *Manufactures*, part III, *Special Reports on Selected Industries* (Washington: United States Census Office, 1902), page 639. The total amount of tobacco used in the output of the two products in 1899 was 108,163,625 pounds; of this total 86.7 per cent was used for cigars and 13.3 per cent for cigarettes. (For the series weights, correspondingly allocated, see Column 7 of Table 3.)

GROUP XII—VEHICLES FOR LAND TRANSPORTATION

Cars, steam railroad, not including operations of railroad companies. Value-added data are not available to serve as a basis for allocating the weight for this sub-group (3.04; cf. Column 6 of Table 3) between the two constituent series—railroad freight cars produced and railroad passenger cars produced. The allocation was made in proportion to Census data on value of product in 1899; the figures were $62,161,013 and $7,368,299, respectively (*1914 Abstract*, page 232). This procedure gives 89.4 per cent and 10.6 per cent, respectively, for the two series (cf. Column 7 of Table 3).

Automobiles, including bodies and parts. The Census gives as the 1899 value added for this industry $2,944,000 (*1914 Abstract*, page 225). It seemed quite clear, however, that for purposes of weighting this figure ought to be reduced materially. Automobile production did not begin to have any significant influence on our general index of manufacturing production until the closing years of our period (i.e., during a few years prior to and including 1914) —an era when "mass production" was truly getting under way. The weighting year 1899 lies in an interval when production of automobiles, in most decided contrast, was on a small-scale basis. Correspondingly, the *value added per automobile* was on a much higher level in 1899 than in 1914. The Census data on *factory* production in the two years—taken in conjunction with the consideration that part of the 1899 production did not occur in automobile establishments, but rather in plants producing carriages, wagons, or bicycles—indicate that value added per automobile in 1899 must have been decidedly higher than that of 1914—perhaps almost double. But for manufacturing production in general, the available evidence suggests that "value added per unit of product" was somewhat *lower* in 1899 than in 1914.[12] We have therefore reduced the 1899 Census value-added total for the automobile industry ($2,944,000, as above) by one-half, thus arrriving at a

[12] Cf. Frederick C. Mills, *Economic Tendencies in the United States* (New York: National Bureau of Economic Research, Inc., in Coöperation with Committee on Recent Economic Changes, 1932), p. 41.

figure of $1,472,000 to serve as basis for weighting (cf. Column 3 of Table 3).

GROUP XIV—MISCELLANEOUS INDUSTRIES

As is explained in Chapter II, it seemed best—having in mind the heterogeneity of the constituent industries of this group—to confine the value-added total to the sum of the value-added figures for the two industries represented in the physical-quantity statistics—rubber industries; and shipbuilding, including boat building (new construction). Compare the entries for Miscellaneous Industries in Columns 2 and 3 of Table 3.

Rubber industries. The 1899 value-added figure shown in the table was obtained by adding the value-added items for "belting and hose, rubber," "boots and shoes, rubber," and "rubber and elastic goods." These items were $2,093,000, $18,407,000, and $19,141,000, respectively.[13]

Shipbuilding, including boat building (new construction). The Census does not segregate new construction from repair work in the 1899 value-added tabulation. The 1899 *value* figure for new construction is almost precisely one-half the corresponding figure for new construction plus repair work ($37,729,000 out of $74,-578,000). Accordingly, we have taken one-half of the Census 1899 value-added figure for new construction and repairs combined, $41,057,000 (*1914 Abstract*, page 259), to obtain, as estimated 1899 value-added figure for new construction only, $20,528,000 (cf. Column 3 of Table 3).[14]

---

[13] For the first two items, see *1914 Abstract*, pp. 575, 580. The third was derived by subtracting the cost of materials ($33,486,000) from the value of the produce ($52,627,000). These latter figures are published in United States Department of the Interior, *Twelfth Census of the United States*, 1900, vol. VII, *Manufactures*, part I, *United States by Industries* (Washington: United States Census Office, 1902), p. 53.

[14] The value figure for new construction was secured by going to United States Department of the Interior, *Twelfth Census of the United States*, 1900, vol. X, *Manufactures*, part IV (Washington: United States Census Office, 1902), p. 215, and summing the value-of-product items for "iron and steel vessels" ($25,454,943), "wooden vessels" ($10,300,971), and "small boats, wooden" ($1,972,825). The value figure for new construction plus repairs ($74,578,000) was taken from the same publication, p. 212 (the *1914 Abstract*, p. 259, gives a slightly different figure —$74,532,000).

APPENDIX C

TRANSPORTATION AND COMMUNICATION INDEX— CONSTITUENT SERIES (OTHER THAN STEAM-RAILROAD)

Figures for the majority of the series (other than steam-railroad) included in the index of transportation and communication were obtained directly from governmental sources, either federal or state; details concerning the exact sources used are set forth in the descriptions of the various series, presented below. For material covering two of the series—the number of telephone conversations completed and the number of telegrams transmitted—we are indebted to officials of the American Telephone and Telegraph Company and the Western Union Telegraph Company. Data measuring the volume of street-railway transportation and the volume of transportation services rendered by automobiles during the period covered by our study were not obtainable from any published sources; therefore, we estimated figures by methods which are described fully in the following pages. In the selection of sources for certain of the governmental series, we were aided by information secured from Arthur F. Burns, *Production Trends in the United States since 1870* (New York: National Bureau of Economic Research, Inc., 1934).

Street Railways: Revenue Passengers Carried

The measurement of the volume of street-railway transportation in the United States during the period 1860–1914 has been based upon a series showing the actual or estimated number of revenue passengers carried on such railways (animal traction, cable, electric, etc.). In the various sources available, the year 1890 is the earliest for which the number of passengers carried on street railways in the country as a whole has been compiled. The Data for the fiscal year ending June 30, 1890 were published in United States Department of the Interior, Census Office, *Report on Transportation Business in the United States at the Eleventh Census: 1890*, part 1, *Transportation by Land* (Washington: Government Printing Office, 1895), page 682. Twelve years later a similar compilation was made for the fiscal year ending June 30, 1902; and, beginning with 1907, reports for the years ending December 31 were issued every five years.

In view of our inability to obtain a direct measurement of the number of passengers carried on street railways in the United States as a whole for years prior to 1890, resort was had to a method of estimation, based upon mileage data. The mileage figures were the only physical-volume data, appropriate for the purposes of this estimate, which we were able to discover for years earlier than 1890. A chart of mileage figures—covering the years 1860, 1870, 1880, 1885, and annually thereafter—was published in Martin G. Glaeser, *Outlines of Public Utility Economics* (New York: The Macmillan Company, 1927), page 69; and an annual mileage series for the period 1880–89 was published in *Report on Transportation Business in the United States at the Eleventh Census: 1890*, part 1, *Transportation by Land*, page 692. From these data, we estimated the mileage of street-railway lines in the United States for certain years within the period 1860–89, as follows. For the years 1860, 1870, and 1880, mileage figures were read from the chart in *Outlines of Public Utility Economics*, and those figures were taken to be as of July 1 of each year given. for the period 1881–89, July 1 estimates were secured by averaging adjacent December 31 figures, obtained from the 1890 Census report. The July 1 estimates were employed as presumably good approximations to calendar-year averages.

Estimates of the number of revenue passengers carried on street railways of the United States in the years 1860, 1870, 1880, and 1881–89 were obtained by assuming that relative changes in number of passengers carried, measuring back from 1890, were proportional to our mileage figures (secured by the methods just described).[1] The passenger data thus estimated are, of course, only rough approximations. Nevertheless, the method followed in estimating the data (as well as the assumption concerning the dating of the figures) is given support by a graphical comparison of Census figures for street railways, covering 1890 and subsequent years, for several series; length of line, in miles, of street railways; the number of miles of single track; the number of employees; the number of passengers carried. All of these series showed a rapid upward long-run growth from 1890 through 1907, and a continued secular increase, though much less swift, through 1917; and the extent of the increase shown from one census year to another was roughly similar for all the series.

As stated above, the Census figures for the number of passengers carried, 1890 and 1902, cover years ending June 30; and beginning with 1907, calendar years. For 1890 and 1902, we estimated calendar-year figures from census-year figures by making an adjustment based upon the average percentage change over the twelve-year interval.[2] For inter-censal years of the period 1890–1917, estimates of the number of passengers carried annually were derived by use of figures for the number employed on street railways, by years, 1889–1917, published in Paul H. Douglas, *Real Wages in the United States, 1890–1926* (Boston and New York:

---

[1] Details of the procedure adopted to secure the estimates are as follows. The Census reports for 1890 and subsequent years include figures on the length of line—in miles—of street railways, the number of miles of single track, and the number of employees, as well as the number of passengers carried. From these Census data we computed, for the fiscal year ending June 30, 1890, the ratio of number of passengers carried to mileage. This ratio was then applied to the annual mileage data previously estimated for years prior to 1890, to secure an approximation to the number of revenue passengers carried in 1860, 1870, 1880, and 1881–89.

[2] The actual procedure was as follows. The first step was to determine the (geometric) average ratio of increase between the fiscal year 1890 and the fiscal year 1902; this ratio was calculated by taking the difference between the logarithm of the figure for the year ending June 30, 1902 and that of the figure for the year ending June 30, 1890. The difference was then divided by 24 (the number of half-yearly periods in the twelve-year interval), and the antilogarithm of this quotient was found. The antilogarithm, which represented the average ratio of increase of a calendar year over the corresponding fiscal year, was multiplied by the fiscal-year figure for 1890 to obtain an estimate for the calendar year 1890. The same general procedure was followed to secure a figure for the calendar year 1902; the estimate of the average ratio of increase was based upon figures for the fiscal year 1902 and the calendar year 1907 (an interval of eleven half-yearly periods).

Houghton Mifflin Company, 1930), pages 434–440. For these employment data, annual percentage changes were computed. Then, using as a starting figure the estimate for passenger traffic in the calendar year 1890 (described above), the percentage changes of the employment series were applied year by year, to obtain preliminary annual estimates of the number of passengers carried. The passenger figure thus calculated for each census year was then compared with the actual Census figure for that year. (For 1902, the estimate for the calendar year, derived as described above, was used for the comparison.) If a discrepancy between the actual figure and the preliminary estimated figure was found, this discrepancy was distributed evenly (on a geometric basis) over the period between the two adjacent census years, to obtain our final estimated figure.[3]

AUTOMOBILES IN USE

In the absence of data directly indicative of the volume of transportation services rendered by automobiles, we have employed figures for the number of automobiles in use on June 30 of each year, 1899–1914. We have estimated these figures from data for automobiles in use as of December 31 each year, 1898–1914, published in Leonard P. Ayres, *The Automobile Industry and Its Future* (Cleveland: The Cleveland Trust Company, 1921), page 8. The series includes both passenger cars and trucks. Our estimates were secured by logarithmic interpolation; thus, the percentage increase shown between adjacent December 31 dates was assumed to have been distributed evenly (on a geometric basis) over the intervening twelve-month period.

SAULT STE. MARIE CANALS TRAFFIC

Figures covering the total tonnage of freight moved through the canals at Sault Ste. Marie, Michigan and Ontario, by years, 1860–1914, were secured from *Statistical Report of Lake Commerce Passing Through Canals at Sault Ste. Marie, Michigan and Ontario, During Season of 1929* (Washington: Government Printing

---

[3] That is to say, the "post method" of estimation was used here. For a description of the method, see the opening pages of Chapter IV.

Office, 1930),[4] page 19. The period covered each year is the season for which the canals were open, usually the months May through November. The data represent the total tonnage of freight moved through both American and Canadian canals at Sault Ste. Marie, of which less than 10 per cent ordinarily is carried by Canadian and other foreign vessels.

New York Canals Traffic

The series indicative of traffic through New York canals, by years, 1860–1914, was obtained from State of New York, Department of Public Works, *Annual Report of the Superintendent for the Year 1930* (Albany: J. B. Lyon Company, Printers, 1931), pages 34–35. The data cover the total tonnage moved each season on all canals in the state, the season generally running from May 1 through November 30.

Coastal Trade: Gross Tonnage of Vessels Documented

In the absence of data for the amount of tonnage carried in the coastal trade of the United States, we have employed figures for the gross tonnage of vessels licensed for domestic commerce and outstanding as of June 30, 1860–1914. The series was secured from United States Department of Commerce, Bureau of Marine Inspection and Navigation, *Merchant Marine Statistics,* 1936 (Washington: Government Printing Office, 1937), pages 29–31.

Foreign Trade: Tonnage of American Vessels Entered

Figures for the tonnage of American vessels entered in the foreign trade of the United States, by fiscal years ending June 30, 1860–1914, were transcribed from United States Department of Commerce, Bureau of Navigation, *Merchant Marine Statistics,* 1930 (Washington: Government Printing Office, 1930), pages 79–80. This series was taken as an approximate indicator of relative changes in the volume of shipping services rendered by American vessels in foreign trade.

[4] Prepared under direction of Major D. McCoach, Jr., Corps of Engineers, United States Army.

FOREIGN TRADE: TONNAGE OF FOREIGN VESSELS ENTERED

Figures for the tonnage of foreign vessels entered in the foreign trade of the United States, by fiscal years ending June 30, 1860–1914, were transcribed from United States Department of Commerce, Bureau of Navigation, *Merchant Marine Statistics,* 1930 (Washington: Government Printing Office, 1930), pages 79–80. This series has been included in the index, not in connection with its *direct* implications—with reference to which it would indeed have to be considered as indicative of ocean-transportation services rendered by foreign vessels, and hence no part of the domestic "production" of transportation services—but as an *indirect* measurement of harborage services (such as towing) rendered in American ports.[5]

TELEPHONE CONVERSATIONS COMPLETED

Data representing the number of completed telephone conversations—not the number of originating calls—by calendar years, 1880–1914, were obtained through correspondence with the American Telephone and Telegraph Company.

TELEGRAPH MESSAGES TRANSMITTED

The calendar year 1866 is apparently the earliest year for which a report on the number of telegraph messages transmitted in the United States is available; the figure was published on page 40 of the Annual Report of the Western Union Telegraph Company, issued in the year 1869.[6] For the calendar years 1880, 1900, 1902, 1905, 1907, 1909, 1910, 1912, 1913, 1914, figures were obtained by correspondence with the American Telephone and Telegraph Company. Data for three of the years—1902, 1907, 1912—were reported by the United States Department of Commerce in its Census of Telegraphs; the remaining figures were estimated by the

---

[5] As explained in Appendix D, which deals with the weights assigned to the components of the index of transportation and communication, this series has been given a weight that reflects the importance of these harborage services relative to total transportation and communication services in the United States.

[6] The author is indebted to Mr. J. M. McKenna, Statistician, The Western Union Telegraph Company, for information concerning the source of this early figure.

American Telephone and Telegraph Company. The data relate to commercial land lines, and do not include any ocean cable messages.

POSTAGE STAMPS: REVENUE

The series for postage stamps used in our study covers the value of postage stamps issued, plain stamped envelopes, stamped envelopes bearing printed cards and requests, and newspaper wrappers, by fiscal years ending June 30, 1860–69; and the revenue derived from the sale of postage stamps, postal cards, and stamped envelopes, and from first-, second-, third-, and fourth-class mail matter dispatched under permit without stamps, by fiscal years ending June 30, 1870–1914. Revenue from second-class postage paid in money (which covers postage paid at pound rates on copies of publications entered as second-class matter) is not included. All data were secured from the *Annual Report of the Postmaster-General of the United States*[7] (Washington: Government Printing Office) for 1864 and subsequent years. In the compilation of these data, we have been aided by information secured from Arthur F. Burns, *Production Trends in the United States since 1870* (New York: National Bureau of Economic Research, Inc., 1934), pages 302–303, 342.

In a production index for postal services rendered, a physical-quantity series, rather than a revenue series, naturally would be preferable; but, in the absence of a suitable physical-quantity series extending over our period of analysis, we have included the revenue series as the best obtainable indicator, rather than allow this significant branch of communications activity to be omitted entirely from our combined index of transportation and communication. There is some evidence that the revenue series may be considered representative, at least for certain purposes.[8]

[7] Over the period studied, slight variations in the title occur as follows: *Report of the Postmaster-General of the United States; Annual Report of the Post-Office Department; Post-Office Department Annual Report.*

[8] For a discussion of the relation between postal revenues and general business-cycle fluctuations in the United States, see C. J. Bullock, B. Fox, and A. R. Eckler, "Postal Revenues and the Business Cycle," *Review of Economic Statistics*, XIII (May 1931), 47–58.

Postal Money Orders Issued

The number of postal money orders issued in the United States, by fiscal years ending June 30, 1866–1914, were transcribed from the *Annual Report of the Postmaster-General for the Fiscal Year Ended June 30, 1930* (Washington: Government Printing Office, 1930), page 149. For 1866–71, the series includes only domestic money orders; beginning 1872, international money orders are added; and for the years 1884–94, postal notes also are included.

APPENDIX D

TRANSPORTATION AND COMMUNICATION INDEX— WEIGHTS

STEAM RAILROADS: (A) FREIGHT TONNAGE CARRIED, AND (B) PASSENGERS CARRIED

The Interstate Commerce Commission in its *Twelfth Annual Report on the Statistics of Railways in the United States,* Year Ending June 30, 1899 (Washington: Government Printing Office, 1900), presents data on gross earnings from operation of the railroads of the United States. On page 75, the gross earnings from operation for the fiscal year ending June 30, 1899 are given as 1,313.6 million dollars. This figure was used for weighting steam railroad traffic in the aggregate (cf. Column 2 of Table 16).

On page 80 of the *Report,* this lump sum is broken down into several major classifications. For weighting of (A) freight tonnage carried, the two items "freight revenue" and "other earnings, freight service" were added; these gave a total of 918.0 million dollars. For weighting (B) passengers carried, the two items "passenger revenue" and "other earnings, passenger service" were added; these gave a total of 298.8 million dollars. The total weight of steam railroads was divided between (A) freight tonnage carried and (B) passengers carried, in proportion to the earnings ascribed to each of these two services, as just set down.

The details of this procedure are as follows:

(Unit: one million dollars)

Earnings, freight service	918.0
Earnings, passenger service	298.8
Total earnings, freight and passenger service	1216.8

Of the total weight assigned to steam-railroad traffic, $\dfrac{918.0}{1216.8}$, or

75.4 per cent, was allocated to freight tonnage carried, and $\dfrac{298.8}{1216.8}$,

or 24.6 per cent, was allocated to passengers carried (cf. Columns 3, 4, and 5 of Table 16).

STREET RAILWAYS: REVENUE PASSENGERS CARRIED

The weight for this series was based on an estimate of the gross income, from all sources, of street-railway companies in 1899. Gross-income figures of 91.7 million dollars for 1890 and 250.5 million dollars for 1902 were published in United States Department of Commerce and Labor, Bureau of the Census, Special Reports, *Street and Electric Railways*, 1902 (Washington: Government Printing Office, 1905), page 11. From these figures we estimated, by straight-line logarithmic interpolation, gross income for 1899; the estimate obtained was 194.8 million dollars[1] (cf. Column 2 of Table 16).

Straight-line logarithmic interpolation was used as being a simple method which would give a sufficiently good approximation —especially as the general statistical evidence suggests that the *secular-trend* movements in the street-railway industry over these years were relatively smooth on charts with logarithmic vertical scale; so far as *cyclical* fluctuations are concerned, 1890 and 1902 (each taken as a whole) were years of fairly good business, while 1899 was a year of considerable activity, and, therefore, the danger that cyclical fluctuations—as among the three years 1890,

---

[1] The method of logarithmic interpolation was as follows:

(1) Revenue for 1890................ 91.7 million dollars—cf. text above
Revenue for 1902................ 250.5 million dollars—cf. text above

(2) Log revenue for 1890........................... 1.9624
Log revenue for 1902........................... 2.3988

(3) $\dfrac{\text{(Log revenue for 1902)} - \text{(Log revenue for 1890)}}{12} = 0.03637$

(4) Log of estimated revenue for 1899
= Log revenue for 1890 + 9 × 0.03637 = 2.2897

(5) Estimated revenue for 1899 = antilog of (4) = 194.8 (million dollars)

1899, 1902—might invalidate the use of straight-line logarithmic interpolation was minimized.

Automobiles in Use

We have, as is explained in Appendix C, taken the number of automobiles in use as an indicator of the volume of automobile traffic, by years, 1899–1914.

Automobile traffic presented peculiar difficulties in assignment of weight for index-number computation. For the other series included in the transportation and communication index, published figures could be found from which it was possible to determine gross income of the industry in 1899, or at least to make a tolerable approximation thereto. This was not true for automobile traffic; a substitute method had to be found. The procedure finally settled upon was based on the principle that for industries in general "cost of operation" may be used to yield at least a rough approximation to gross income. The application of this principle to the present case necessitated an estimate of operating cost.

Our estimate of operating cost involved the various elements set forth below.

(1) *The average number of automobiles in use in 1899.* Here we used 6,298 cars—obtained by taking the figures given in Leonard P. Ayres, *The Automobile Industry and Its Future* (Cleveland: The Cleveland Trust Company, 1921), page 8—and adjusting to the middle of the year (see the discussion for "automobiles in use," in our Appendix C).

(2) *The dollar cost of transportation per car*, subdivided as indicated below:

(a) *Depreciation.* For the amount per car, we used the Automobile Manufacturers Association total value of cars produced in 1914, divided by their figure for the total number of cars produced in the same year $\left(\dfrac{\$458,957,843}{569,054} = \$807 \text{ per car} \right)$.[2] The value per car

---

[2] *Automobile Facts and Figures*, 1936 edition (New York: Automobile Manufacturers Association, Inc., 1936), p. 4.

was based on 1914 data rather than on 1899 data because automobile transport became important in the
index of transportation and communication only during the later years of the period 1899–1914. To have
used the 1899 figure would have been to overstate the
significance of automobile traffic during our period of
study. In 1899 the automobile industry was just
emerging from the experimental stage and the technological background was unsettled; consequently prices
were high and not representative of the situation even
a few years later.

We assumed the depreciation to be distributed
evenly over five and one-half years, neglecting as relatively unimportant any residual value at the end of the
period of service. In Ayres, *The Automobile Industry
and Its Future,* page 13, the author (writing in 1921)
concludes:

"Now it is true that some cars are destroyed almost
as soon as they are put into service, while others that
were first registered 10 years ago or more are still
running, but the outstanding fact about the registra-
tion figures is that they have been for the past nine
years about equal each year to the sum of the cars
produced in that year and the five previous years.
This means that the average length of life of the cars
has been about six registrations, for if it had been only
five registrations or as much as seven registrations,
the figures for all cars registered each year would have
been about equal to the new cars put into service over
a five-year period, or a seven-year period, as the case
might be. The fact that some individual cars have
much longer or shorter terms of use does not alter the
inference about the average term of use. There is
available some additional evidence tending to substantiate the proposition that the average length of
service of automobiles is about six registrations, which

is equal to something more than five full years. For example, the report of the Postmaster General for 1916 indicates that the depreciation of cars in the postal service has been at the average rate of 22.9 per cent per year. The annual reports of the statistics of express companies, published by the Interstate Commerce Commission, show substantially the same depreciation. These cars receive exceptionally hard usage."

We have accordingly taken five and one-half years as a reasonably good estimate of average length of service. Dividing the average value of car, obtained above as $807, by 5½, we obtained $147—or, in round numbers, $150—as our measure of annual depreciation per car.

(b) *Other operating costs*. We assumed that five cents per mile would cover all costs other than depreciation. These would include gasoline and oil, maintenance, storage, taxes, etc. We further assumed that on the average the cars traveled 5,000 miles per year. We thus obtained a total of 5,000 × $0.05 = $250, as an estimate of "other operating costs" per car per year.

The estimate of total operating costs per car per year was thus the sum of the depreciation and other operating costs, or $150 + $250 = $400. Multiplying this amount by the number of cars, 6,298 as set down above, we reached $400 × 6,298, or $2,519,200, as the figure approximating the required "total cost of operation" for automobile traffic.

However, if this figure had been used as the basis for weighting in the construction of the index, there would have been some distortion of the measurement of changes in the volume of transportation, 1899–1914, for a considerable part of the increasing traffic by automobile was a substitute for carriage by horse-drawn vehicles. Since this latter is not represented in our index, to assign automobile traffic its full weight (as just determined) would mean overstatement of the increase in the volume of transportation. On this ground, it was clearly desirable materially to reduce the weight assigned to automobile traffic. Accordingly, to effect an approximate correction, we reduced the "total cost of operation" figure secured just above—$2,519,200—by one-half, obtaining $1,259,600 as the basic figure for the determination of the weight for automobile traffic (cf. Column 2 of Table 16). The correction thus applied is admittedly only a rough approximation, but in view of the fact that the weight of automobile traffic in the combined index of transportation and communication is, in any event, quite small,[3] it appears that the correction is adequate for purposes of computing this combined index.

We may now turn to the presentation of some evidence as to the validity of certain estimates—of depreciation and other costs of operation per car per year—set forth above.

(1) *Depreciation.* In an article by C. E. Griffin, "The Life History of Automobiles," *Michigan Business Studies,* I, No. 1 (February 1926), 1, about seven years (with some qualifications) is given as the average life of an automobile. It is further stated that "the average length of life of automobiles has shown a definite though not a steady increase." In Robley Winfrey, *Automobile Operating Cost and Mileage Studies* (Iowa State College of Agriculture and Mechanic Arts, Official Production Bulletin 106, July 22, 1931), page 35, a partial count of Iowa cars retired from service, 1920–29, reveals the average life per car as varying from 5.90 years in 1920 to 7.81 years in 1927, and to 7.56 years in 1929. The estimate of five and one-half years, for our period of study, seems reasonably consistent with these independent estimates, since the life of cars produced in the earlier years of the present century was presumably shorter than the life of those produced when the

---

[3] Using $1,259,600 as basis, the automobile-traffic weight is 0.07 per cent; if the unreduced amount, $2,519,200, had been used, the weight would have been 0.13 per cent (cf. Table 16).

manufacture of automobiles became a mature industry. This assumption is supported by the consideration that the Iowa study shows an average life per car of 5.90 years in 1920, and it was not until 1925 that the average life reached seven years. On the other hand, Ayres in *The Automobile Industry and Its Future* (above referred to) was writing in 1921, and his data were based on an earlier period in the development of the automobile.[4]

(2) *Average annual mileage per car.* The assumption of an average annual mileage per car of 5,000 was based on an estimate made in the Iowa study (referred to above). It was there estimated from gas-tax receipts (page 29) that the average annual mileage was 5,947 miles in 1925, 6,084 miles in 1926, and 7,416 miles in 1930. These estimates were closely approximated by a second study based on mileage information submitted by Iowa owners.

These figures seem consistent with our estimate of 5,000 miles. It appears reasonable to suppose that average annual mileage during the earlier years of the automobile was less than during its maturity. Furthermore, the Iowa study reveals that average annual mileage was increasing from 1925 through 1930. The probability is that average annual mileage was less than 5,947 in years preceding 1925.

(3) *Operating costs.* The Iowa study makes a detailed study of operating costs for different types of automobiles and for varying yearly mileages. This study also furnishes an analysis for a composite car (page 18) based on these individual estimates. The pertinent data for the composite Iowa automobile for an annual mileage of 5,000 are as indicated in detail in the tabulation which is shown at the top of the following page.

---

[4] It is true that Ayres says (*The Automobile Industry and Its Future*, p. 15) that "the average length of service of the cars appears to have stayed nearly constant toward the end of the period covered," but this conclusion is stated with reference to *his* period of study (1912–20).

(cents per mile)

Gasoline, 20 cents per gallon 1.27
Oil, 25 cents per quart 0.25
Tires and tubes 0.43
Maintenance 1.22
Garage, four dollars per month 0.96
Interest, six per cent 0.74

Total 4.87

The above total of 4.87 cents agrees fairly closely with our estimate of five cents.

Most of the data used in our cost calculations were derived from figures pertaining to conditions many years after 1899. It is therefore illuminating to turn to an estimate made contemporaneously with the early development of the automobile. Ray Stannard Baker, in an article entitled "The Automobile in Common Use," *McClure's Magazine,* XIII (July 1899), 205, writes:

Mr. A. S. Winslow, of the National Motor Carriage Company, has made some interesting comparisons, based on an average daily run of twenty-five miles for five years—more than the maximum endurance of a first-class horse. His estimates represent ordinary city conditions, and rate the cost of the gasoline used at one-half cent a mile:

GASOLINE MOTOR VEHICLE

Original cost of vehicle $1000.00
Cost of operation, 1 cent per mile, twenty-five miles
   per day 456.50
New sets of tires, during five years 100.00
Repairs on motor and vehicle 150.00
Painting vehicle four times 100.00
Storing and care of vehicle, $100.00 per year 500.00

$2306.50

"At the end of five years," said Mr. Winslow, "the motor vehicle should be in reasonably good condition, while the value of the horse and carriage would be doubtful."

We may compare Mr. Winslow's figures with our own estimates, as follows:

(1) Taking Mr. Winslow's original cost of $1,000, and spreading depreciation over his period of five years, we obtain $200 per year as average annual depreciation (this might perhaps be lowered moderately if we take into consideration Mr. Winslow's remark, above quoted, that "at the end of five years, the motor vehicle should be in reasonably good condition," and assign a "residual value" to the car).

(2) Following Mr. Winslow in assuming that the five-year "cost of operation"—in the narrow sense; that is, presumably including only the allowance for gasoline and oil —was $456.50, we get $91 per year.

(3) Mr. Winslow's allowance over five years for tires, repairs, painting, and storage is $850, or $170 per year.

(4) Adding the various costs per year as determined in (1), (2), and (3) above, we arrive at a total cost per year of $461.

This total of $461 is appreciably above our figure of $400, arrived at as previously described. The fact that the Winslow estimate is appreciably higher than ours, is, however, an indication of consistency, rather than of inconsistency, between the two estimates; that is to say, we should *expect* his estimate to be higher, in view of the consideration (set forth on an earlier page) that conditions in 1899, when the automobile industry was still in the experimental stage and the technological background was unsettled, could not be taken as representative of the situation in later years of our period of study.

The several factors entering into our estimate of "total cost of operation" for automobile traffic are no doubt in each case open to a considerable margin of possible error; but—taking into account the various pieces of supporting evidence—it would seem that the estimate for the *total* is a reasonably good approximation.

SAULT STE. MARIE CANALS TRAFFIC

Figures for the total tonnage of freight moved through the canals at Sault Ste. Marie (cf. Appendix C) have been taken as an indicator of fluctuations over time in a much broader entity— the volume of traffic on the Great Lakes and St. Lawrence River system.

To secure a weight for the series, we estimated gross income in 1899 by use of income data for 1906 and data on the tonnage of freight moved in 1899 and 1906. In this connection, we employed gross income in 1906 of vessels engaged in transportation on the Great Lakes and St. Lawrence River. A figure of 65.3 million dollars in 1906, the earliest year for which such data have been published, was obtained from United States Department of Commerce and Labor, Bureau of the Census, Special Reports, *Transportation by Water,* 1906 (Washington: Government Printing Office, 1908), page 30.

As a first step in estimating gross income for 1899, we assumed that between the two years—1899 and 1906—gross income was proportional to the amount of tonnage carried on the Sault Ste. Marie canals. The ratio of tonnage of freight moved through canals at Sault Ste. Marie in 1899 to tonnage moved in 1906 was found to be 0.49.[5] This ratio, when applied to the gross income of 65.3 million dollars for 1906, given above, yielded an estimate of 32.0 million dollars for gross income in 1899 (cf. Column 2 of Table 16).

Even though the interval from 1899 to 1906 is comparatively short, the assumption that over such period gross income is proportional to the amount of freight traffic can, of course, be expected to yield only an approximation to the fact; but, as is indicated in Chapter VII, for the series of the transportation and communication index which have relatively small weight—as

---

[5] $\dfrac{\text{Tonnage of freight moved through Sault Ste. Marie canals, 1899}}{\text{Tonnage of freight moved through Sault Ste. Marie canals, 1906}}$

$= \dfrac{25,256 \text{ thousand short tons}}{51,751 \text{ thousand short tons}} = 0.49.$

(For a description of the source from which the data were obtained, see Appendix C.)

Sault Ste. Marie canals traffic (weight, 1.68 out of 100)—a reasonable approximation to the proper weight is quite adequate from
the point of view of the accuracy of the combined index.

It will be noted that here—in contrast with New York canals
traffic, next discussed—we do not concern ourselves with the question of an additional allowance for interest, maintenance, etc., on
the "investment" in the canals. Even if in the present case the tolls
did not pay in full for these elements, the amount justly addible
to total gross revenue would be only a small fraction of such gross
revenue. This is true because the canals constitute but a short link
in the Great Lakes system, and practically all of the mileage is
traversed on natural waterways. As is suggested above, Sault Ste.
Marie canals traffic is important as an index of this larger traffic,
rather than for its own direct contribution.

New York Canals Traffic

The earliest year for which we could obtain a published figure
for the gross income of vessels engaged in transportation on the
canals and other inland waters of New York State was 1906. A
gross-income figure of 2.8 million dollars was published in United
States Department of Commerce and Labor, Bureau of the Census, Special Reports, *Transportation by Water*, 1906 (Washington: Government Printing Office, 1908), page 30. In the absence
of an actual gross-income figure for 1899, we made an estimate by
a method somewhat similar to that employed for Sault Ste. Marie
canals traffic, described just above.[6]

We assumed that gross income, as between 1899 and 1906,
changed in proportion to amount of traffic carried. We first computed the ratio of the tonnage moved on New York canals in 1899
to the tonnage moved in 1906.[7] This ratio (1.04) we then applied

[6] For comment on the accuracy of this general procedure, and the usability of
the results, cf. the corresponding discussion for Sault Ste. Marie canals, in the
immediately preceding section.

[7] Details of the computation of the ratio are as follows:

$$\frac{\text{Tonnage moved on New York canals, 1899}}{\text{Tonnage moved on New York canals, 1906}} = \frac{3,686 \text{ thousand short tons}}{3,541 \text{ thousand short tons}} = 1.04.$$

(For a description of the source of the tonnage data, see Appendix C.)

to the 1906 gross-income figure (2.8 million dollars, as above) to obtain an estimate of 2.9 million dollars for gross income in 1899. This estimate, however, was for our purposes too small; certain important elements were omitted.

The money paid into the state treasury by the superintendent of public works during the fiscal year ending September 30, 1899 was but $5,045.96. Only a small portion of this amount was from lock collections, etc., since at this time the canal was toll free. The outgo for ordinary repairs and operating expenses on these canals for the same period was $844,582.22.[8] Expenditures such as these, ascribable to "plant," would for a private organization be reflected in the gross income in the long run. The figure of 2.9 million dollars, given in the preceding paragraph, also omits such elements as "interest on investment" (which is undoubtedly large).

To allow for these various elements which did not enter into the stated gross income of the carriers, the figure of 2.9 million dollars, obtained above, was doubled. We thus arrived at a rough final estimate of a proper weighting figure; this doubling does not seem greatly out of line, in view of the elements just discussed and especially bearing in mind that maintenance alone on the canals amounted to nearly one million dollars in 1899. The weighting figure, then, comes out as 2 × 2.9 million dollars, or 5.8 million dollars (cf. Column 2 of Table 16).

COASTAL TRADE: GROSS TONNAGE OF VESSELS DOCUMENTED

As is elsewhere indicated (cf. Appendix C), we have, in the absence of data for the amount of tonnage carried in the coastal trade of the United States, employed figures for the gross tonnage of vessels licensed for domestic commerce. The weight assigned to this series has been derived by use of data from several sources.

In United States Department of Commerce and Labor, Bureau of the Census, Special Reports, *Transportation by Water*, 1906 (Washington: Government Printing Office, 1908), page 30, data are presented on the gross income of all vessels and craft, by di-

---

[8] See *Annual Report of the Superintendent of Public Works on the Canals of the State* [of New York], Year Ended September 30, 1899 (Albany: James B. Lyon, State Printer, 1900), pp. 37 and 28.

visions and occupations, for 1906. No similar data are available
for any earlier year. For 1906, the total revenue from all sources
of vessels from the Atlantic Coast and Gulf of Mexico, and from
the Pacific Coast (including Alaska) was 208.3 million dollars.
Gross income for 1899 was therefore estimated from that of 1906
in an indirect fashion. We assumed that the change in gross income, between 1899 and 1906, was proportional to that in gross
tonnage of vessels documented. We computed the ratio of gross
tonnage of vessels licensed for coastal trade, June 30, 1899, to the
corresponding figure for June 30, 1906,[9] and applied this ratio
(0.70) to the gross-income figure for 1906 (208.3 million dollars,
as above). We thus obtained an estimate of 145.8 million dollars
for gross income in 1899. This procedure could not, of course, be
expected to yield anything more than a rough approximation—an
approximation, however, probably sufficiently accurate for our
purposes.[10]

FOREIGN TRADE: TONNAGE OF AMERICAN VESSELS ENTERED

As is indicated in Appendix C, we have taken the series for
tonnage of American vessels entered in the foreign trade of the
United States as an approximate indicator of relative changes in
the volume of shipping services rendered by American vessels in
foreign trade.

In arriving at a weighting figure for this series, reference was
made to an article by Charles J. Bullock, John H. Williams, and
Rufus S. Tucker, "The Balance of Trade of the United States,"
Review of Economic Statistics, 1 (July 1919). On page 231 of this
article, in connection with a discussion of the period 1896–1914,
the authors use 5 per cent as the approximate ratio of freight to
value of trade, and support this figure by some supplementary
evidence.

---

[9] Details of the computation are as follows:

$$\frac{\text{Gross tonnage of vessels licensed for coastal trade, June 30, 1899}}{\text{Gross tonnage of vessels licensed for coastal trade, June 30, 1906}} = \frac{3{,}965 \text{ thousand gross tons}}{5{,}674 \text{ thousand gross tons}} = 0.70.$$

(Sources of the coastal trade data are described in Appendix C.)

[10] Cf. the corresponding discussion for Sault Ste. Marie canals, above.

In United States Department of Commerce and Labor, *Statistical Abstract of the United States,* 1906 (Washington: Government Printing Office, 1907), page 620, the value of the foreign trade of the United States carried in American vessels, fiscal year ending June 30, 1899, is given as 161 million dollars. We took 5 per cent of this amount, or 8.0 million dollars, as the figure to serve as basis for weighting our series of tonnage of American vessels entered in the foreign trade of the United States (cf. Column 2 of Table 16).

FOREIGN TRADE: TONNAGE OF FOREIGN VESSELS ENTERED

As is indicated in Appendix C, the series for tonnage of foreign vessels entered in the foreign trade of the United States has been included in the index, not in connection with its *direct* implications —with reference to which it would indeed have to be considered as indicative of ocean-transportation services rendered by foreign vessels, and hence no part of the domestic "production" of transportation services—but as an *indirect* measurement of harborage services (such as towing) rendered in American ports—cf. the statement on page 221.

To arrive at a weighting figure for this series, we have taken 5 per cent as the approximate ratio of freight to value of trade (cf. the discussion, just above, in connection with tonnage of American vessels entered in foreign trade); and we have taken one-fifth of this, or 1 per cent, as the approximate ratio of harborage charges to value of trade.[11]

In United States Department of Commerce and Labor, *Statistical Abstract of the United States,* 1906 (Washington: Government Printing Office, 1907), page 620, the value of the foreign trade of the United States carried in foreign vessels, fiscal year ending June 30, 1899, is given as 1,646 million dollars. We took 1 per cent of this amount, or 16.5 million dollars, as the figure to serve as basis for weighting our series of tonnage of foreign vessels entered in the foreign trade of the United States (cf. Column 2 of Table 16).

---

[11] Cf. the article by Bullock, Williams, and Tucker referred to in the preceding section, *loc. cit.*

Telephone Conversations Completed

The weight used for this series was based on an estimate of total revenue of all telephone systems in 1899. Figures for total revenue of all telephone systems in 1890 and 1902 were published in United States Department of Commerce and Labor, Bureau of the Census, Special Reports, *Telephones and Telegraphs,* 1902 (Washington: Government Printing Office, 1906), page 5. The published data were: for 1890, 16.4 million dollars; for 1902, 86.8 million dollars. By straight-line logarithmic interpolation between the figures for 1890 and 1902, we estimated total revenue for 1899; the estimate thus obtained was 57.2 million dollars[12] (cf. Column 2 of Table 16).

Telegraph Messages Transmitted

We derived a weight for this series by making an estimate of total revenue of commercial telegraph systems in 1899. Figures for total revenue from all sources of all commercial[13] telegraph systems in 1880 and 1902 were published in United States Department of Commerce and Labor, Bureau of the Census, Special Reports, *Telephones and Telegraphs,* 1902 (Washington: Government Printing Office, 1906), page 99. No similar data were given for intervening years.

The figures for 1880 and 1902 are not quite comparable, since the total for 1902 contains revenue from cable messages, amounting to 1.3 million dollars, while the total for 1880 does not include such revenue. However, in view of the fact that revenue from cable messages in 1902 was small in relation to total revenue, we made no attempt to adjust for this inconsistency between the 1880 and 1902 totals.

The total-revenue figures, published by the Census, were 16.7 million dollars for 1880 and 40.9 million dollars for 1902. By straight-line logarithmic interpolation between these figures, we

---

[12] For detailed description of the general procedure, and also discussion of its probable validity, see the section in this Appendix dealing with revenue passengers carried on street railways, above.

[13] Railroad telegraph statistics were not included.

estimated revenue for 1899 as 36.2 million dollars[14] (cf. Column 2 of Table 16).

(A) Postage Stamps: Revenue, and (B) Postal Money Orders Issued

In *Annual Report of the Postmaster-General of the United States for the Fiscal Year Ending June 30, 1899* (Washington: Government Printing Office, 1899), page 3, postal revenue from all sources in the fiscal year ending June 30, 1899 was stated as 95.0 million dollars. Of this, 1.3 million dollars was assigned to postal money orders, and the remainder—93.7 million dollars—to postage stamps (cf. Column 2 of Table 16). Practically all of this latter amount was revenue from the sale of postage stamps, stamped envelopes, newspaper wrappers, postal cards, and second-class postage.

[14] For detailed description of the general procedure, and also discussion of its probable validity, see the section in this Appendix dealing with revenue passengers carried on street railways, above. The terminal years for the interpolation are further apart here than in the street-railway case; but, on the other hand, the weight for telegraph messages in the combined index of transportation and communication is materially less than that for street-railway traffic, and consequently a less close approach to precision in the interpolation process presumably will suffice.

APPENDIX E

SUNDRY TECHNICAL DETAILS

PART ONE

THE MANUFACTURE INDEX:
INTERPOLATIONS AND EXTRAPOLATIONS TO FILL GAPS IN ORIGINAL ITEMS OF CONSTITUENT SERIES

The interpolations and extrapolations which are described and discussed below were made to fill certain gaps in the array of original items for constituent series shown in Tables 1 and 2. We also make below certain statements regarding the probable effects of these interpolations and extrapolations upon the various group indexes involved, and also upon combined indexes of manufacturing production—(a) the preliminary combined annual index, described in Chapter III; (b) the combined census-year index, described in Chapter IV; and (c) the final combined index, also described in Chapter IV.[1]

We shall throughout, in our discussions of errors of interpolation and extrapolation, distinguish between the periods 1866–1914 and 1860–65, respectively. As is set forth at the beginning of Chapter I, in developing the new indexes of manufacturing production our primary interest was in the years 1866–1914; we were concerned only secondarily and incidentally with the years 1860–65.

The discussion which follows is divided into three parts, relating respectively to (a) the preliminary combined annual index, (b) the combined census-year index, and (c) the final combined annual index.

---

[1] In this connection, note carefully the statements in pp. 44–46 of Chapter III, and pp. 56, 58 of Chapter IV (especially fn. 12 on p. 46).

(A) THE PRELIMINARY COMBINED ANNUAL INDEX

We turn now to a detailed consideration of the individual cases, by groups, to be followed by a summary statement.

Group II

Raw cotton consumed, adjusted for foreign trade in cotton goods. The gap for 1860–63 was filled in by taking as a starting point the actual 1864 figure for this series and applying to it, going backward over the interval 1860–63, the year-to-year percentage changes shown by raw cotton consumed. The year-to-year percentage movements of the two series are very closely similar over the entire interval 1864–1914—even in the war years 1864 and 1865 and the period immediately following. Nevertheless, in view of the disturbed conditions of the cotton and cotton-goods markets in the Civil-War years, it seems wise to allow for the possibility of at least a moderate extrapolation error in the years 1860–63.

Raw wool consumed. In the absence of any clear basis for extrapolation, the missing item for 1860 was filled in by assuming a horizontal movement between 1860 and 1861. It is, of course, quite possible that an appreciable error of extrapolation is here involved.[2]

Raw wool consumed, adjusted for foreign trade in wool goods. For the years *1861–66*, the missing items were filled in by taking as a starting point the actual figure for 1867 and applying to it, going backward over the interval 1861–66, the year-to-year percentage changes shown by raw wool consumed. The year-to-year percentage movements of the two series over the interval 1867–1914 exhibit quite high correlation. Nevertheless, it seems wise to allow for the possibility of at least a moderate extrapolation error during 1861–66. For the year *1860*, the missing item was filled in by assuming a horizontal movement between 1860 and 1861 (cf. the comments just above, in the paragraph on raw wool consumed).

---

[2] Note, however, that the method of derivation of the series is such that most of the statistical data involved in the computation of the 1861 item pertain to time periods antedating the outbreak of the Civil War (cf. the section for this series in Appendix A).

Minor fibers imported. In the absence of any clear basis for extrapolation, the missing item for 1860 was filled in by assuming a horizontal movement between 1860 and 1861. It is quite possible, especially in view of the large year-to-year fluctuations which the series exhibits in later years, that a considerable error of extrapolation is here involved for the *series itself;* but, bearing in mind the comparatively small weight of the series—0.36, as compared with 9.88 for the sub-group index of textile fabrics and materials and 18.91 for the textile group as a whole—it seems certain that the effect of the 1860 extrapolation error upon those indexes must in any case be unimportant.

Effect on the group and sub-group indexes. In considering the effect of the several extrapolations upon the index for Group II and upon the indexes for its two sub-groups, we shall (following a plan announced in an earlier paragraph) consider separately the periods 1866–1914 and 1860–65. (1) *The period 1866–1914:* here only one extrapolated figure is involved—that for raw wool consumed, adjusted for foreign trade in wool goods, in 1866, extrapolating backward from 1867; and—in view of the facts that but a single year is involved in the extrapolation interval and that the correlation is quite high over the long period 1867–1914 between the year-to-year movements of the series itself and the series which constitutes the extrapolation basis—it seems unlikely that any significant error of extrapolation has been introduced into either the 1866 index for the textile group itself or the 1866 index for the sub-group textile fabrics and materials. (2) *The period 1860–65:* here the extrapolations are more numerous and more serious, and it is quite possible that appreciable errors of extrapolation are present, especially in the year 1860.

Group III

Steel ingots and castings produced. The gap for 1861–62 was filled simply by straight-line interpolation between the actual reported figures for 1860 and 1863. In view of the slight importance of steel making in the nation's ferrous industries over these earlier years, we may feel sure that so far as the group index for iron and steel is concerned, any error of interpolation here involved can be safely neglected.

Structural iron and steel produced. The gaps for the years *1880–88 and 1890–91* were filled by interpolation, using the "post method" (for a description of this method, see the opening pages of Chapter IV). In this interpolation, we used as "posts" the reported data for the years 1879, 1889, and 1892: and we used the annual fluctuations of pig-iron production as a guide in estimating the short-run movements for structural iron and steel; this seemed justifiable in view of the very close similarity in short-run movement between the two series in later years. *Prior to 1879,* no statistical data were available for output of structural iron and steel, and the item was entered as zero on our calculation sheets for the group index; this seemed a sufficiently good approximation for the purposes of computing the group index, taking into account the fact that the 1879 figure was only 87 thousand long tons, as compared to 3,432 thousand long tons for pig iron consumed and 994 thousand long tons for rails produced.

Effect on the group index. In view of the statements just above, and the fact that cyclical fluctuations in the iron and steel industry over our period of analysis (as well as subsequently) have very high amplitude, we may feel safe in concluding that the interpolations and extrapolations involved in the computation of our index for Group III could not have produced any appreciable modification of the contour of its short-run movement.

Group X

Tin imported. The missing figures for *1860–61* were filled in by taking as a starting point the actual 1862 item for this series and applying to it, going backward from 1861, the percentage changes shown by the weighted average index computed for the remaining series of Group X; the missing figure for *1864* was filled in similarly, taking as starting point the actual 1865 item for tin imported.

Effect on the group index. In view of the comparatively low weight of tin imported in the index for Group X (0.43 out of 5.63), it seems improbable that any errors of extrapolation or interpolation for this series in the years 1860, 1861, and 1864 should have any significant effect on the group index; in this connection, we should also bear in mind that the index for the non-ferrous metals has quite high amplitude of cyclical fluctuation, and consequently a very large error in tin imported would be required to effect any noticeable alteration in the contour of short-run movement for the group index.

Groups VII and XI

For Group VII, Liquors and Beverages, and Group XI, Tobacco Manufactures, no reliable indexes could be computed over the years 1860–69. (To be sure, fundamental data of a sort were available for 1863–69, but these clearly were untrustworthy, and were rejected—cf. the sections of Appendix A relating to these two groups.) When we came to the calculation of the preliminary combined index for manufacture, the question arose as to the extrapolation basis for Groups VII and XI over the years 1860–69.[3] There did not appear to be available any clear and direct basis for such extrapolations. Perhaps the best obtainable guide was that furnished by the movements of the index for the most nearly related of our major groups—that for Group I, Food and Kindred Products. Accordingly, in each of the two cases (Group VII and Group XI), the gap for 1860–69 was filled in on the computation sheet for the preliminary combined manufacture index by taking as starting point the actual 1870 index for the group and applying to it, going backward over the interval 1860–69, the successive year-to-year percentage changes shown by the index for Group I.

Effect of Interpolations and Extrapolations on the Preliminary Combined Annual Index

What now can be said as to the effect of the above interpolations and extrapolations, taken as a whole, upon the preliminary com-

---

[3] It should be definitely borne in mind, of course, that the extrapolations worked out for Groups VII and XI, 1860–69, were developed *for the purposes of computation of combined manufacture indexes;* there was no thought of presenting these extrapolations as necessarily being approximations to the *group indexes themselves* (cf. the pertinent discussion at the top of p. 45).

bined annual index of manufacturing production described in Chapter III? As previously, we distinguish between the periods 1866–1914 and 1860–65.

(1) *The period 1866–1914.* Within this period there were involved, in interpolations and extrapolations, two individual series and also the indexes for Groups VII and XI. The two individual series were raw wool consumption, adjusted for foreign trade in wool goods, in the year 1866 only; and structural iron and steel produced, in the years 1866–78, 1880–88, and 1890–91. On the basis of the statements made above about the two individual series, we may safely dismiss them from consideration, so far as any significant error in the combined index is concerned. This leaves still the extrapolations for Groups VII and XI over the four years 1866–69. Let us consider, in turn, (i) year-to-year movements and (ii) long-run drift.[4] (i) With regard to *year-to-year movements:* in view of the relatively slight intensity of short-run fluctuation (compared, for example, with the indexes for ferrous and non-ferrous metals) shown by the indexes for liquors and beverages and tobacco manufactures over the period 1870–1914—as well as by the index for food and kindred products (the extrapolation basis)—we may feel confident that the extrapolation for Groups VII and XI, 1866–69, could not have produced any appreciable alteration in the contour of short-run movement for the preliminary combined manufacture index (which itself has cyclical fluctuations of quite high amplitude). (ii) With regard to *long-run drift:* taking into account that the aggregate weight of Groups VII and XI in the preliminary combined manufacture index is relatively so small (7.20 [4.12 plus 3.08], compared with 65.11 over the years 1860–69 for the preliminary combined manufacture index), we may feel confident that any error in long-run drift which might accumulate through the extrapolations for

[4] It is here convenient to use the expression "long-run drift" somewhat broadly to denote general tendencies which continue over several business cycles. The expression does not need to be any more definite for our present purposes. In particular, there is no necessity to go into the question whether such general tendencies constitute "secular trends" in the strict connotation of this latter term. With reference to the connotation of "secular trend," cf. Edwin Frickey, *Economic Fluctuations in the United States* (Cambridge, Mass.: Harvard University Press, 1942), *passim.*

Groups VII and XI *within the brief four-year period 1866–69* could hardly have any appreciable effect on the preliminary combined manufacture index.

(2) *The period 1860–65.* For this interval—as contrasted with 1866–1914—the interpolations and extrapolations for individual series are more numerous; and, as before, we have to take into account the extrapolations for Groups VII and XI. What is the probable net effect of these gap-filling operations upon the preliminary combined manufacture index? (i) With regard to *year-to-year movements:* it is quite possible that through the various interpolations and extrapolations some errors in year-to-year movement have been introduced into the preliminary combined manufacture index, 1860–65, but—taking into account all of the considerations which have been adduced on preceding pages in connection with the discussion of the several elements involved in the interpolations and extrapolations, and also with respect to the amplitude of short-run fluctuation for the combined index—it does not seem likely that such errors could have produced any very noteworthy alteration in the picture of short-run fluctuation presented by the preliminary combined annual index over those years. (ii) With regard to *long-run drift:* here the main probable source of error in the preliminary combined index is that related to the extrapolations for the two group indexes—VII and XI.[5] Now

[5] So far as the seven *individual series* involved in interpolations and extrapolations, 1860–65, are concerned, we may analyze the situation as follows (the date after the series name represents, in each instance, the interval *within the period 1860–65* covered by the interpolation or extrapolation; the figure in parenthesis represents, in each instance, the weight of the series, which may be compared with 65.11—the total weight for the preliminary combined annual index). Four series— minor fibers imported, 1860 (0.36); steel ingots produced, 1861–62 (0.88); structural iron and steel produced, 1860–65 (0.20); and tin imported, 1860–61 and 1864 (0.43)—clearly are, in any event, of negligible importance in the present connection (cf. the discussion of these series, above). Two others—raw cotton consumed, adjusted for foreign trade in cotton goods, 1860–63 (5.41); and raw wool consumed, 1860 (3.34)—are of somewhat greater importance, but the extrapolation interval is, in each case, so short that the *long-run* drift of the preliminary combined annual index can hardly have been seriously altered. This leaves only the series raw wool consumed, adjusted for foreign grade in wool goods, 1860–65 (3.62): the extrapolation interval here is long enough so that some "pull" due to error of extrapolation might indeed be exerted upon the long-run drift of the preliminary combined index; but, taking into account the low weight of the series as compared with that for the preliminary combined manufacture index (3.62 out of 65.11), it seems highly

over the interval 1860–65 (as contrasted with the interval 1866–69, previously considered) there is admittedly more opportunity, going backward from the starting point of the extrapolation (1870), for extrapolation error in long-run drift to *accumulate:* it is quite possible that the preliminary combined annual index over the years 1860–65 has on this account suffered some deflection in long-run drift; but—once more taking into account that the aggregate weight of Groups VII and XI in the preliminary combined annual manufacture index is relatively so small (7.20 out of 65.11)—it seems unlikely that such deflection can be very significant.[6]

(B) THE COMBINED CENSUS-YEAR INDEX

Several gap-filling operations—in addition to certain of those listed above—affect the census-year index of manufacturing activity described in Chapter IV. These additional operations are set forth below.

Group VIII

Coke produced. For the purposes of the census-year index for Group VIII, the coke-production figures for the years 1859, 1869, and 1879 were roughly interpolated or extrapolated. As a starting point in securing the desired interpolations and extrapolations we used statements concerning output in 1865 and 1874 which were made by Mr. William B. Phillips in an article entitled "Coal and Coke," published in *The Mineral Industry*, 1892.[7] Mr. Phillips wrote: "In 1865 it is not likely that the production of coke amounted to 100,000 [short] tons per annum; but in 1874 the production of coke and bituminous pig-iron had increased to 813,-137 tons, which would imply that the production of coke in that year was not less that 1,000,000 tons. It is therefore probable

---

improbable that this "pull" can be quantitatively sufficient appreciably to affect the long-run drift of the preliminary combined annual index.

[6] A brief summary statement of the above conclusions regarding the preliminary combined annual index is set forth on pp. 45–46 of Chapter III.

[7] Richard P. Rothwell, Editor, *The Mineral Industry, Its Statistics, Technology and Trade in the United States and Other Countries from the Earliest Times to the End of 1892,* I (New York: The Scientific Publishing Company, 1893), 73–106.

that within the ten years ending with 1875 the production of coke rose from 100,000 to more than 1,000,000 tons . . ." [8] On the basis of this statement we took 100,000 short tons and 1,000,000 short tons as approximations to production in 1865 and 1874, respectively. Using a logarithmic vertical scale, we plotted these approximations for 1865 and 1874, and also the figure for 1880 which we had secured from the United States Department of Commerce's *Mineral Resources* (cf. the section on "coke produced" in our Appendix A). We extrapolated backward the line connecting the points for 1865 and 1874, and from the extrapolated line we read an estimate of production in 1859. Interpolations for 1869 and 1879 were read from straight lines connecting the points for 1865 and 1874, and for 1874 and 1880, respectively. These graphic readings are in each case open to a considerable margin of error, but they appeared adequate for our purposes in computing the census-year index for Group VIII.

Flaxseed consumed. In the computation of the census-year index for Group VIII, 1859 and 1869, the missing relative (to base 1899) for flaxseed consumption was in each case filled in by inserting on the computation sheet the corresponding relative for white lead produced. The two series of relatives traced out quite similar general tendencies over those years of our pre-war period of analysis for which both were available (1884–1914), but there was very little resemblance between their short–run movements. Each, however, seemed in general the "most probable" interpolation basis readily available for the other—though, judging by the 1884–1914 experience, an error of (say) 5 to 10 per cent is reasonably to be anticipated in any one year.

Superphosphate produced. In the derivation of the census-year index for Group VIII, the item for superphosphate produced was missing for 1859. In the absence of any clear basis for extrapolation, this missing item was filled in on the computation sheet by assuming the same percentage movement, measuring backward from the census year 1869, as was shown by the weighted average

---

[8] *The Mineral Industry*, 1892, p. 85. On p. 84 Mr. Phillips had written: "Reliable statistics of the manufacture of coke prior to 1880 are not available. The industry had indeed gained a foothold as early as 1850 . . ."

computed for those four constituent series of the group for which actual or previously extrapolated figures were available for both 1859 and 1869—petroleum produced, white lead produced, flaxseed consumed, coke produced.

Cottonseed oil produced and *cottonseed cake and meal produced*. In the computation of the *1869* census-year index for Group VIII, the missing items for these two series were filled in by inserting their respective values for 1872—the first year for which data were available; for *1859*, in the absence of any clear basis for extrapolation, the missing item for each of these series was filled in on the computation sheet by the method just described for superphosphate production—i.e., on the basis of the average movement shown, 1869 to 1859, by petroleum, white lead, flaxseed, coke.

Effect on the group index. In considering the effect of the several extrapolations upon the index for Group VIII, we need devote attention only to the three years 1859, 1869, and 1879, since there were no gaps in fundamental data for subsequent census years. For convenience, let us take up the years 1859, 1869, and 1879 in reverse order. *The year 1879:* the only gap in basic data is that for coke produced; now—since the interpolated figure would seem a fairly good one (the interpolation interval is short, and the interpolated 1879 figure bears a reasonable relationship to the actual reported 1880 figure, taking into account the cyclical movements of 1879–80 in industrial production generally, and in the ferrous industries in particular) and the series has only a moderate weight compared to that for the whole group (1.39 out of 7.99)—we may have confidence that no important error has been transmitted to the group index. *The year 1869:* the effect upon the group index of any extrapolation error in the two cottonseed series is almost certainly negligible,[9] and the interpolated

[9] The use of the seed of cotton for industrial purposes was on such a low level during this epoch that any error of extrapolation which is reasonably conceivable could not have affected the group index more than a fraction of a point. Since the cottonseed industries were here in a developmental stage, it is likely that such error as may be involved in taking the 1872 figures to stand for those of 1869 is in the direction of overstatement; and if we go all the way and put production for each of the series at *zero* in 1869 (rather than as equal to the 1872 production), the alteration in the Group VIII index is only one-third of a point (from 12.3 to 12.0).

figures for coke produced and flaxseed consumed are probably reasonably good (cf. earlier discussion); on the whole, we would not expect that anything more than a moderate error has been transmitted to the group index. *The year 1859:* here the 1859 extrapolations for the cottonseed industries and for coke produced may be safely neglected, for these series stood at very low levels in this epoch and any error transmitted to the final index must be small; the effect of the other extrapolations involved is, however, not so clear, and it seems best to regard the 1859 index for Group VIII as only a rough estimate. The utilization of even such a rough estimate, taken with a liberal allowance for error of extrapolation, is nevertheless decidedly to be preferred, in the derivation of the 1859 combined manufacture index, to the device of simply leaving Group VIII out of the calculation, and thereby (by implication) assuming the 1859 Group VIII index to be equal to weighted average of the group indexes available in that year[10]— for, since most of these other indexes were in 1859 on a distinctly higher level than Group VIII, the "estimate" for Group VIII implied in this latter procedure would have to be regarded as quite unreasonable.

The Extrapolation of the 1859 Item for the Preliminary Combined Annual Index

The preliminary combined annual index based upon nine groups (described in Chapter III) goes back only as far as 1860; further backward extension is impossible, owing to lack of adequate data for constituent series. For the purposes of computing the 1859 census-year index, an extrapolated figure for the preliminary annual index was needed for entry upon the calculation sheet.

The question thus arose as to the most reasonable assumption regarding the relation of the unknown 1859 item for the preliminary combined annual index to the 1860 item previously computed. Now it is true that nearly all published "indexes of economic activity" (or "business barometers") which extend back beyond the Civil War indicate that activity in 1859 was several per cent lower

---

[10] The various indexes, it will be remembered, are expressed as relative to the base 1899 = 100.

than that of 1860.[11] But these indexes, or barometers, are largely made up of components which are *outside* the field of manufacture. For the problem at hand, we should fix our attention on manufacturing production—or, rather, still more specifically, upon manufacturing production in those major groups included in our preliminary combined annual index. Now for the nine groups embraced by this index, the available statistical evidence as to the $\frac{1859}{1860}$ relationship seems about as strong one way as the other: the series for which figures are obtainable for both years are about equally divided between those which show 1859 higher than 1860 and those which show a contrary movement; and if we take weighted averages (using the weights of Table 3) for the available series in the two years, the plus and minus differences in the "weighted products" more or less offset one another. For the particular entity at hand—the preliminary combined annual index based upon nine groups—we get the impression from the obtainable data of a "stand off" as between 1860 and 1859.

Accordingly, on the calculation sheet for the combined census-year index we filled the gap in 1859 for the preliminary combined annual index by taking the 1859 item as equal to the 1860 item. While this seems the most reasonable extrapolation upon the basis of available statistical information, we must recognize that our material is incomplete (and otherwise somewhat unsatisfactory); we must, therefore, allow for the effect of a possible error of extrapolation in the combined census-year index for 1859, though it does not seem probable that such error is very large.

(It is strongly to be emphasized that we made the extrapolation *only for the purpose of deriving the 1859 "post" for the computation of the final combined annual index;* we do not, at any stage of our procedure, put forward any 1859 manufacturing production index as such. This distinction should be kept carefully in mind; its force will become more apparent as we proceed.)

---

[11] This statement refers to the implications of these indexes, or barometers, with respect to changes in the *unadjusted* figure (that is, *before* adjustment for secular trend)—and, of course, the change pertinent to our present discussion is that in the figure before trend adjustment.

Effect of Interpolations and Extrapolations
on the Combined Census-Year Index

The combined census-year index is affected by many of the interpolations and extrapolations described on preceding pages. In considering the effect of the various pertinent interpolations and extrapolations, taken as a whole, upon the combined census-year index, we need give serious attention only to the census year 1859.[12]

Turning now to the consideration of the census-year index for 1859 and its possible error due to extrapolation of components, we first note that the possible elements of error mentioned in the final summarizing paragraphs of the earlier division entitled "(a) The Preliminary Combined Annual Index" may be brought forward and repeated here. Our earlier general conclusion was that over the Civil-War and immediately preceding years, the preliminary combined annual index was through the various interpolations and extrapolations subject to some error, but it did seem likely that such error was very noteworthy or significant. However, in extending this conclusion to apply to the 1859 census-year combined index, we must modify it somewhat. The possibility of error due to gap-filling operations is here increased by the presence of one important additional element[13]—the extrapolation of the 1859

[12] No interpolations or extrapolations occur in the census-year computations subsequent to 1879. For *1879* itself, there is involved only the interpolation for coke produced; in view of our preceding discussion of this interpolation and the fact that the weight of the series in the combined census-year index is so comparatively small (1.39 out of 100.00), we quite clearly may treat as negligible any effect on the combined index. For *1869*, we may, from the point of view of the combined index, safely ignore the five gap-filling operations involved for individual series (cf. the pertinent detailed discussion on earlier pages, bearing in mind also that no one of these series has a weight of as much as 1½ per cent and their aggregate weight is less than 5 per cent); so far as the extrapolations for Groups VII and XI are concerned, no appreciable error is to be expected in the combined index (cf. the discussion of these extrapolations on earlier pages, bearing in mind that the extrapolation interval is here only one year, that the year-to-year movements of both the actual and the extrapolated indexes for the two groups may be taken as comparatively smooth, and that the aggregate weight for the two groups is only a little more than 7 per cent).

[13] The only other new element introduced in connection with the combined census-year index is that relating to the extrapolations involved in the computation of the 1859 index for Group VIII. In view of the weight of this group (7.99 out of 100.00) and the fact that the group index stood at a comparatively low level (on

item for the preliminary combined annual index as equal to the 1860 item (cf. the discussion of this point, just above). If we join this new important element to those which had been discussed previously, it would seem that we should allow for the possibility of a moderate extrapolation error in the 1859 census-year index.

To be sure, as we have already said, the 1859 census-year index was not, so to speak, computed for its own sake, and we nowhere present any combined index for 1859. The 1859 census-year index —since it constitutes a "post" in the computation process—does, however, play a part in the derivation of the 1860–68 final combined annual index, as is more fully set forth below.

(c) THE FINAL COMBINED ANNUAL INDEX

The final combined index is, of course, affected by all of the interpolations and extrapolations described in the two earlier divisions, headed "(a) The Preliminary Combined Annual Index," and "(b) The Combined Census-Year Index," respectively. There is here involved only one (relatively minor) additional gap-filling operation, described just below.

Group VIII

White lead produced. The gap for 1880–83 was filled in by inserting on the computation sheet in each year the relative (to base 1899) for flaxseed consumed. This is probably a reasonably good interpolation (cf. the discussion of the converse case, on an earlier page).

Effect on the group index. Taking into account the weight of white lead in the Group VIII index (1.16 out of 7.99) and the nature of the interpolation, it seems unlikely that any appreciable error has been transmitted to the group index.

Effect of Interpolations and Extrapolations on the Final Combined Annual Index

What now can be said as to the effect of the various interpolations and extrapolations described up to this point, taken as a

---

1899 base), it seems unlikely that any important extrapolation error could have been transmitted to the combined index from this source.

whole, upon the final combined annual index of manufacturing activity described in Chapter IV? In general, our statement of conclusions here can follow closely the pattern of the statement presented on pages 244–247 above, in answer to a corresponding question asked with reference to the preliminary combined annual index. Some modification, however, is required: one additional significant element has entered the situation. This additional element is the possibility, set forth just above, of an extrapolation error in the 1859 census-year combined index.[14] Now, since the 1859 census-year index is one of the "posts" for the estimation of the inter-censal indexes for 1860–68, this new element intensifies the possibility—alluded to in the earlier discussion pertaining to the preliminary combined annual index—of a deflection in long-run drift, 1860–68. Therefore, in bringing forward the conclusions of the earlier division, "(a) The Preliminary Combined Annual Index," and applying them to the present case, certain modification of language is called for: the conclusions regarding "long-run drift" must be stated in slightly more conservative form.[15]

PART TWO

THE 1871 ESTIMATES FOR STEAM-RAILROAD SERIES

As indicated in the early pages of Chapter VI, the basic data for our 1871 "cross-section" estimates of the steam-railroad series consisted of figures on mileage and volume of traffic for individual roads, taken from the summary tables of *Poor's Manual of Railroads*.[16]

TONS

From the point of view of availability of data for individual roads, the railroads of 1871 may be divided into three groups: (1)

---

[14] The various interpolations and extrapolations for Group VIII may safely be ignored in the present connection (cf. the discussions of these interpolations and extrapolations on preceding pages).

[15] Compare the brief summary statement of the conclusions regarding the final combined index, as set forth on pp. 56, 58 of Chapter IV, with the corresponding statement regarding the preliminary combined annual index, on pp. 44–46 of Chapter III.

[16] For explanatory statement on designation of source, see fn. 3 of Chapter V.

those for which both mileage operated and tonnage are tabulated; (2) those for which mileage operated is tabulated, but not tonnage; (3) those for which neither mileage operated nor tonnage is tabulated. We now consider each of these groups in turn.

(1) The first group of roads, with an aggregate mileage operated of 32,801, were found to have moved a total of 112.1 million tons of freight.

(2) The second group of roads (mainly made up of smaller companies) showed an aggregate mileage operated of 19,989, but no tonnage data were tabulated. It did not seem appropriate to impute, to the roads of this second group, the average tonnage per mile (nearly 3½ thousand) shown by the first group, which included many of the larger railroads of the country. Such a "blanket" estimate did not appear justified, considering the difference between the two groups as to size of road. We instead adopted the more tedious procedure of dealing with the roads of the second group individually.

For each of the constituent roads of the second group, an estimate was made of the ratio of tonnage moved to miles of road operated. Each of these estimates was based upon the corresponding ratio for other roads in the contiguous geographical area. However, not all of the other roads in such area were used, but only those which were of comparable size—of the same order of magnitude as indicated by the criterion of mileage operated. In a few instances, the estimate had to be made on the basis of the ratio for only one other road. Usually, however, it was possible to bring two or more other roads into the picture, thus establishing a range of tonnage-per-mile ratios, and an average ratio was computed and used as a guide.

Next, for each road of the second group the estimated tonnage-per-mile ratio (derived as just derived) was multiplied by the number of miles operated, to obtain the estimated tonnage moved. And, finally, these estimates of tonnage moved were summed. The result was to show for the roads of the second group, which had a total mileage operated of 19,989, an estimated aggregate tonnage moved of 41.4 million.

The procedure here employed is doubtless open to a considerable margin of error for each individual road, but for the group taken as a whole it would seem superior to the device of setting up a "blanket" assumption as to tonnage per mile and then multiplying this figure by the total mileage operated.[17]

(1 and 2 combined) The totals for the first and second groups combined were 52,790 miles operated and 153.5 million tons moved —indicating an average ratio of almost 3,000 tons per mile of road.

(3) There still remained to be considered the third group of roads, with total mileage operated of 8,062,[18] for which neither mileage nor tonnage data were tabulated for individual roads. Here some sort of "blanket" estimate indeed seemed necessary. But it did not appear suitable to use, as the basis for such estimate, the ratio of approximately 3,000 tons per mile developed in the preceding paragraph. For this ratio—while, to be sure, embracing numerous small roads—included many large and well established systems, as contrasted with the third group made up mainly of roads smaller and less well developed. For the third group, then, a more conservative ratio of 2,000 tons per mile was adopted. We thus obtained for this group, having an aggregate mileage of 8,062, an estimated tonnage moved of 16.1 million. It is recognized that even this estimate is open to an appreciable margin of percentage error, but fortunately this group had comparatively small mileage compared with the grand total for the whole United States.

Summing the tonnages for the three groups, as set forth above, we obtained a grand total of 169.6 million. This figure—rounded off to 170 million, to avoid undue implication of approach to precision—was adopted as our 1871 "cross-section" estimate.

[17] For about three-quarters of the roads of the second group, data are available for freight earnings. Ratios computed for these give confirmation to the above results.

[18] This figure was obtained by subtracting, from the 1871 total mileage of all railroads in the United States (60,852—cf. *Poor's Manual of Railroads* for 1872–73, p. xxxiii), the combined total for our first two groups (52,790).

PASSENGERS

Since the reasoning and procedure employed in obtaining the 1871 "cross-section" estimate for passengers carried was entirely analogous to that for freight moved, only a brief statement need be presented in the present connection.

(1) Here the first group of roads, with an aggregate mileage operated of 35,614,[19] were found to have carried a total of 107.3 million passengers.

(2) The second group of roads here showed an aggregate mileage of 17,176, with no report on passengers carried. By methods quite comparable to those earlier employed in the tonnage case, the aggregate of passengers carried for the group was estimated at 37.0 million.

(1 and 2 combined) The totals for the first and second groups combined were thus 52,790 for miles operated and 144.3 million for passengers carried—indicating an average ratio falling not far short of 3,000 passengers per mile of road.

(3) For the third group of roads, with total mileage operated of 8,062, we here—on the basis of reasoning comparable to that of the tonnage case—set up an estimated ratio of passengers carried to mileage operated which was somewhat more conservative than the ratio of nearly 3,000 developed in the preceding paragraph. Specifically, we adopted a ratio of 2,000 passengers per mile, thus obtaining for the third group estimated passengers carried of 16.1 million.

Summing the passengers-carried aggregates for the three groups, as set forth individually above, we obtained a grand total of 160.4 million. This figure, rounded off to 160 million, was adopted as our 1871 "cross-section" estimate.

[19] The tabulated data for passengers carried were slightly more extensive than those for freight moved.

INDEX

INDEX

(The notation "ch. 36" below refers to the insert chart opposite page 36.)

Articles from textile fabrics, 20, 33, 38–40, 204

Automobiles, 22, 32, 37, 41–43, 44, 214
in use, 106, 108-109, 112, 216, 219, 226–232
produced, 14–15, 22, 197

Ayres, Leonard P., 197, 219, 226–228, 230

Baker, Ray Stannard, 231–232
Bank clearings, 35n
Base period, choice of, 18–19, 107
Bullock, C. J., 222n, 236–237
Burns, Arthur F., 18n, 62n, 135, 143, 154, 156, 182, 189, 198, 216, 222

Calendar year basis, *see* Time-reference adjustment
Canals traffic, *see* Sault Ste. Marie canals traffic, New York canals traffic
Cane sugar, cane-sugar refining, and beet sugar, 20, 25, 201
Cars, steam railroad, *see* Steam-railroad cars
Census groups
manufacture (*see also* individual groups), 19, 24
transportation, *see* Steam railroads, geographical grouping
Census of Manufactures, 5, 19
Chemicals and allied products, 17, 21, ch. 36, 41–43, 52–53, 55, 209–210
Chocolate and cocoa products, 20, 25
Cigarettes produced, 14–15, 22, 192, 213
Cigars produced, 14–15, 22, 189–191, 213
Clark, W. A. Graham, 145
Coastal trade: gross tonnage of vessels documented, 106, 108–109, 112, 220, 235
Cocoa imported, 8–9, 20, 144
Coffee
and spice, roasting and grinding, 20, 25, 201

imported, 8–9, 20, 143–144
Coke, 21, 209
produced, 12–13, 16, 21, 180, 247–248, 249, 252n
Cole, Arthur H., 70–71, 114n, 116, 119n, 152
Compound-interest curve, 60
Compromise base, 18–19
Compromise weights, 16–19
"Consumption-of-materials" series, 4
Copper consumed, 12–13, 22, 183–187, 210–212
Cotton consumed, *see* Raw cotton consumed
Cottonseed cake and meal produced, 12–13, 16, 22, 183, 209–210, 249
Cottonseed oil produced, 12–13, 16, 22, 182–183, 209–210, 249
Crandall, Ruth, 71n
Cyclical fluctuations, value added, 26-28

Day, Edmund E., 17, 30, 48n, 126, 193, 208n
Day-Persons manufacture index, 17
Depew, Chauncey M., 181n
Distilled liquors produced, 12–13, 21, 179–180
Douglas, Paul H., 218

Earned weighting, 30, 113
Eckler, A. R., 222n
Encyclopedia Americana, 139n, 140n
Encyclopaedia Britannica, 139n
Extrapolation, *see* Manufacture index, extension of basic series, *and* Steam railroads, extension of basic series

Fabricant, Solomon, 4n, 26–30
Fermented liquors produced, 10–11, 21, 178–179
Fertilizers, 21
Fiscal-year data, adjustment to calendar-

year basis, *see* Time-reference adjustment

Fisher, Russell T., 145n

Flaxseed consumed, 12–13, 16, 22, 182, 248

Flour produced, *see* Wheat flour produced

Flour-mill and gristmill products, 20, 25

Food and kindred products, 19, 20, 25, 31, ch. 36, 38–40, 201

Ford, Worthington C., 147, 152n

Foreign trade
tonnage of American vessels entered, 106, 108–109, 112, 220, 236–237
tonnage of foreign vessels entered, 106, 108–109, 112, 221, 237

Foss, C. N., 193

Fox, B., 222n

Frickey, Edwin, 3n, 18n, 28n, 35n, 36n, 59n, 62n, 66n, 102n, 119n, 125n, 168n, 245n

General business conditions, index, 36n

Glaeser, Martin G., 217

Gries, Caroline G., 147

Griffin, C. E., 229

Gross-income weights, 111–112

Growth rate, 30, 60, 63, 118, 127–128

Humphreys, Walter, 153n

Imputed weighting, 25, 30, 113, 233–234, 237

Index numbers
formula, 18, 31, 107–111, 126–127
"hierarchy principle," 32, 52–53
"post method," 47–51, 55, 66, 97n, 219n, 243
sampling, *see* Steam railroads, sampling
specific, *see* Day-Persons manufacture index, General business conditions, index, Manufacture index, Production index, Railroad earnings, index, Stewart transportation index, Transportation and communication index
technical bias, 18, 61
weighting, 18, 30, 111–112, 126

Indirect measurement, 3–4, 106–107

Industrial and commercial production, index, *see* Production index

Ingalls, Walter Renton, 187–188

Interpolation, *see* Manufacture index,

extension of basic series, Steam railroads, extension of basic series

Iron and steel
and their products, 19, 21, 28, 32, ch. 36, 38–40, 204–206
"end products," other than rails and structural iron and steel, 10–11, 21, 158–177, 205–206

Iron produced, *see* Pig iron produced, Structural iron and steel produced

Jacob, K. D., 180

Jacobstein, Meyer, 190n

Lead consumed, 12–13, 22, 187–188, 210–212

Leather and its finished products, 19, 24

Liquors
and beverages, 19, 21, 24, 32, 34–35, ch. 36, 41–43, 207–209, 244
distilled, 21, 208–209
malt, 21, 208–209
produced, *see* Fermented liquors produced, Distilled liquors produced

Logarithmic parabola, 35, 59–61, 118, 128

Lumber
and its remanufactures, 19, 21, ch. 36, 38–40, 52, 55, 206–207
and timber products and pulpwood, 21, 206
consumed, 10–11, 16, 21, 177–178
produced, 10–11, 16, 21, 177

McCoach, D., Jr., 220n

McKenna, J. M., 221n

Manufacture index, ch. 36, 57, 61, 125
basic data, 4–17, 133–200
combined census year index, 53–55
comparison with Day-Persons index, 17
continuity, 4–5, 46, 58, 67
coverage, 17
Day-Persons, 17
durable and non-durable commodities, 63–67
extension of basic series, 6, 33n, 44–46, 53n, 56–58, 135–200, 240–254
final index, 54, 56, 60
growth bias, 61–63
long-run drift, 45, 58, 245–247, 254
new series, 4, 44
"post method," *see* Index numbers, "post method"

short-run fluctuations, 45, 58, 63n, 245–246
time interval for basic series, 4
weights, 18–30, 201–215
Manufactured tobacco and snuff produced, 14–15, 22, 193–194
Marsh, R. E., 178
Maxwell, W. Floyd, 3n
Metals and metal products, other than iron and steel, 22, 24, 32, ch. 36, 41–43, 210–212
Mills, Frederick C., 214n
Minor fibers imported, 8–9, 20, 155–156, 204, 242, 246n
Miscellaneous industries (Census group XIV), 23, 24, 32, 34–36, 215

National real income, 126
Net value added, 26
ratio to census value added, 26–30
New York canals traffic, 106, 108–109, 112, 220, 234–235
Non-ferrous metals, *see* Metals and metal products, other than iron and steel
North, S. N. D., 152n

Oils, cottonseed, and cake, 22, 209–210
Olmstead, Frank L., 190

Paint and varnish, 22, 209
Paper
and printing, 19, 21, ch. 36, 38–40, 52–53, 207
and wood pulp, 21, 207
consumed, 10–11, 16, 21, 178
produced, 10–11, 16, 21, 178
Partington, John E., 195
Persons, Warren M., 17, 18n, 208
Petroleum
produced, 12-13, 16, 21, 180
refining, 21
Phillips, William B., 247–248
Pig iron produced, 10–11, 21, 28, 157, 204–206
Poor, Henry V., 69n
Poor's Manual of Railroads, 69–70, 71–72, 90n, 94–95, 98, 103, 115n
"Post method," *see* Index numbers, "post method"
Postage stamps, revenue, 106, 110–112, 222, 239
Postal money orders issued, 106, 110–112, 223, 239

Production index, 57, 61, 125–129
weights, 126

Railroad earnings, index, 71n, 116, 121
Railroad freight cars produced, 14–15, 22, 193–196, 214
Railroad passenger cars produced, 14–15, 22, 196–197, 214
Railroad repair shops, 24
Railroads, *see* Steam railroads
Rails produced, 10–11, 21, 157–158, 205–206, 243
Raw cotton consumed, 8–9, 20, 144–145, 202
adjusted for foreign trade in cotton goods, 8–9, 20, 145–147, 204, 241, 246n
Raw silk and spun silk imported, 8–9, 20, 153–155, 202–204
Raw wool consumed, 8–9, 20, 147–151, 202–203, 241, 246n
adjusted for foreign trade in wool goods, 8–9, 20, 151–153, 204, 241, 246n
Refined sugar produced, 8–9, 20, 139–143
Retardation rate, 59, 118, 127–129
Richards, Preston, 148n
Rothwell, Richard P., 183, 247n
Rubber imported, 14–15, 23, 198–200
Rubber industries, 23, 24, 215

Sault Ste. Marie canals traffic, 106, 108–109, 112, 219–220, 233–234
Scrap, consumption of, 163–167
Secular trend, 35, 59–61, 66, 101–105, 118–119, 127–129, 245n
Shelton, W. Arthur, 180
Shipbuilding, including boat building (new construction), 23, 24, 215
Silk imported, *see* Raw silk and spun silk imported
"Standard list," Census, 26
"Standard pattern," 28n, 34–36
Steam-railroad cars, 22, 32, ch. 36, 41–43, 44, 214
Steam railroads
cross-section totals, *1855,* 98
1871, 95, 254–257
1890, 94
extension of basic series, 72, 90–91
geographical grouping, 72–90
gross earnings
1855–71, 90–93
1866–90, 72–90

mileage operated, *1866–90*, 72–90
passenger-miles
  1855–71, 90–93
  1855–1914, 98–99
  1866–90, 72–90, 95
  1890–1914, 69
passengers, 112, 224–225, 257
  1855–71, 90–93, 98–99
  1855–1914, 100
  1860–1914, 113
  1866–90, 72–90, 95, 97–98, 101–105
  1890–1914, 69
rectification, 92–100
sample list,
  1855–71, 90–93, 116n
  1866–90, 72–90
sampling, 70–72, 93, 94, 101–105
short-run fluctuations, 99–105
tests, 101–105
ton-miles
  1855–71, 90–93
  1855–1914, 98–99
  1866–90, 72–90, 95
  1890–1914, 69
tonnage, 112, 224–225, 254–256
  1855–71, 90–93, 98–99
  1855–1914, 100
  1860–1914, 113
  1866–90, 72–90, 95–97, 101–105
  1890–1914, 69
weights, 112
Steel, *see also* Iron and steel and their
  products
Steel ingots and castings produced, 10–
  11, 21, 157, 204–206, 242, 246n
Stewart transportation index, 68n
Stewart, Walter W., 68n
Stone, clay, and glass products, 19, 24
Stoughton, Bradley, 106
Street railways, revenue passengers
  carried, 107–109, 112, 216–219, 225–
  226
Structural iron and steel produced, 10–11,
  21, 158, 205–206, 243, 246n
Sugar produced, *see* Refined sugar pro-
  duced
Superphosphate produced, 12–13, 16, 21,
  180–181, 248–249
Swank, James M., 161n

Taussig, F. W., 149, 153
"Taussig-volume principle," 62–63
Technical bias, *see* Index numbers, tech-
  nical bias

Telegraph messages transmitted, 106,
  110–112, 216, 221–222, 238
Telephone conversations completed, 106,
  110–112, 216, 221, 238
Textile fabrics, *see also* Articles from
  textile fabrics
Textile fabrics and materials, 20, 33, 38–
  40, 201–204
Textiles and their products, 19, 20, 32–33,
  ch. 36, 38–41, 201–204
Thompson, W. P., 181
Time-reference adjustment, 7, 17, 34–36,
  63n, 69, 114–116, 143, 154, 175, 187,
  188, 191, 192, 195, 198, 219
Tin imported, 14–15, 22, 189, 210–212,
  243, 246n
Tobacco
  chewing and smoking, and snuff, 22,
    213
  cigars and cigarettes, 22, 213
  manufactures, 22, 24, 32, ch. 36, 41–43,
    213, 244
Transportation and communication index (*see also* Steam railroads), 57,
  61, 106–124, 125
  basic data, 106–111, 216–223
  continuity, 111, 116–118
  extension of basic series, 114n, 117,
    216–219
  monthly estimates, 119–124
  short-run fluctuations, 121–124
  weights, 111–112, 224–239
Transportation index, Stewart, 68n
Tucker, Rufus S., 236–237
Type bias, *see* Index numbers, technical
  bias

Value added
  cyclical fluctuations, 26–28
  ratio to net value added, 26–30
Value-added weights, 18, 26–30, 111,
  201–215
  adjustment, 28, 30, 205–206, 207–209,
    214
Vehicles for land transportation (*see
  also* Automobiles, Steam-railroad
  cars), 22, 24, 32, 41–43, 214
Vessels produced, 14–15, 23, 34–36, 200

Wanders, H. H., 184n
Weight bias, *see* Index numbers, techni-
  cal bias
Weiner, Louis, 206
Wheat flour produced, 8–9, 20, 135–139

White lead produced, 12–13, 16, 22, 181–182, 209, 248–249, 253
Willett and Gray, 139, 141n
Williams, John H., 236–237
Winfrey, Robley, 229–231

Winslow, A. S., 231–232
Wool consumed, *see* Raw wool consumed

Zimmerman, Harvey J., 144n
Zinc consumed, 14–15, 22, 188, 210–212